C-2014   CAREER EXAMINATION SERIES

This is your
PASSBOOK for...

Administrative Clerk

Test Preparation Study Guide
Questions & Answers

COPYRIGHT NOTICE

This book is SOLELY intended for, is sold ONLY to, and its use is RESTRICTED to individual, bona fide applicants or candidates who qualify by virtue of having seriously filed applications for appropriate license, certificate, professional and/or promotional advancement, higher school matriculation, scholarship, or other legitimate requirements of education and/or governmental authorities.

This book is NOT intended for use, class instruction, tutoring, training, duplication, copying, reprinting, excerption, or adaptation, etc., by:

1) Other publishers
2) Proprietors and/or Instructors of "Coaching" and/or Preparatory Courses
3) Personnel and/or Training Divisions of commercial, industrial, and governmental organizations
4) Schools, colleges, or universities and/or their departments and staffs, including teachers and other personnel
5) Testing Agencies or Bureaus
6) Study groups which seek by the purchase of a single volume to copy and/or duplicate and/or adapt this material for use by the group as a whole without having purchased individual volumes for each of the members of the group
7) Et al.

Such persons would be in violation of appropriate Federal and State statutes.

PROVISION OF LICENSING AGREEMENTS – Recognized educational, commercial, industrial, and governmental institutions and organizations, and others legitimately engaged in educational pursuits, including training, testing, and measurement activities, may address request for a licensing agreement to the copyright owners, who will determine whether, and under what conditions, including fees and charges, the materials in this book may be used them. In other words, a licensing facility exists for the legitimate use of the material in this book on other than an individual basis. However, it is asseverated and affirmed here that the material in this book CANNOT be used without the receipt of the express permission of such a licensing agreement from the Publishers. Inquiries re licensing should be addressed to the company, attention rights and permissions department.

All rights reserved, including the right of reproduction in whole or in part, in any form or by any means, electronic or mechanical, including photocopying, recording, or by any information storage and retrieval system, without permission in writing from the Publisher.

Copyright © 2024 by
National Learning Corporation

212 Michael Drive, Syosset, NY 11791
(516) 921-8888 • www.passbooks.com
E-mail: info@passbooks.com

PUBLISHED IN THE UNITED STATES OF AMERICA

PASSBOOK® SERIES

THE *PASSBOOK® SERIES* has been created to prepare applicants and candidates for the ultimate academic battlefield – the examination room.

At some time in our lives, each and every one of us may be required to take an examination – for validation, matriculation, admission, qualification, registration, certification, or licensure.

Based on the assumption that every applicant or candidate has met the basic formal educational standards, has taken the required number of courses, and read the necessary texts, the *PASSBOOK® SERIES* furnishes the one special preparation which may assure passing with confidence, instead of failing with insecurity. Examination questions – together with answers – are furnished as the basic vehicle for study so that the mysteries of the examination and its compounding difficulties may be eliminated or diminished by a sure method.

This book is meant to help you pass your examination provided that you qualify and are serious in your objective.

The entire field is reviewed through the huge store of content information which is succinctly presented through a provocative and challenging approach – the question-and-answer method.

A climate of success is established by furnishing the correct answers at the end of each test.

You soon learn to recognize types of questions, forms of questions, and patterns of questioning. You may even begin to anticipate expected outcomes.

You perceive that many questions are repeated or adapted so that you can gain acute insights, which may enable you to score many sure points.

You learn how to confront new questions, or types of questions, and to attack them confidently and work out the correct answers.

You note objectives and emphases, and recognize pitfalls and dangers, so that you may make positive educational adjustments.

Moreover, you are kept fully informed in relation to new concepts, methods, practices, and directions in the field.

You discover that you are actually taking the examination all the time: you are preparing for the examination by "taking" an examination, not by reading extraneous and/or supererogatory textbooks.

In short, this PASSBOOK®, used directedly, should be an important factor in helping you to pass your test.

ADMINISTRATIVE CLERK

DUTIES
In charge of clerks in a bureau or office. Performs highly difficult, complex, and responsible clerical functions which may involve supervision over a large number of subordinate personnel. Performs related work as required.

SCOPE OF THE WRITTEN TEST
The written test will be designed to cover knowledges, skills, and/or abilities in the following areas:
 1. Office and secretarial practices;
 2. Public and interpersonal relations;
 3. Preparation of written material;
 4. Reading comprehension;
 5. Arithmetic reasoning;
 6. Supervision; and
 7. Administration.

HOW TO TAKE A TEST

I. YOU MUST PASS AN EXAMINATION

A. WHAT EVERY CANDIDATE SHOULD KNOW

Examination applicants often ask us for help in preparing for the written test. What can I study in advance? What kinds of questions will be asked? How will the test be given? How will the papers be graded?

As an applicant for a civil service examination, you may be wondering about some of these things. Our purpose here is to suggest effective methods of advance study and to describe civil service examinations.

Your chances for success on this examination can be increased if you know how to prepare. Those "pre-examination jitters" can be reduced if you know what to expect. You can even experience an adventure in good citizenship if you know why civil service exams are given.

B. WHY ARE CIVIL SERVICE EXAMINATIONS GIVEN?

Civil service examinations are important to you in two ways. As a citizen, you want public jobs filled by employees who know how to do their work. As a job seeker, you want a fair chance to compete for that job on an equal footing with other candidates. The best-known means of accomplishing this two-fold goal is the competitive examination.

Exams are widely publicized throughout the nation. They may be administered for jobs in federal, state, city, municipal, town or village governments or agencies.

Any citizen may apply, with some limitations, such as the age or residence of applicants. Your experience and education may be reviewed to see whether you meet the requirements for the particular examination. When these requirements exist, they are reasonable and applied consistently to all applicants. Thus, a competitive examination may cause you some uneasiness now, but it is your privilege and safeguard.

C. HOW ARE CIVIL SERVICE EXAMS DEVELOPED?

Examinations are carefully written by trained technicians who are specialists in the field known as "psychological measurement," in consultation with recognized authorities in the field of work that the test will cover. These experts recommend the subject matter areas or skills to be tested; only those knowledges or skills important to your success on the job are included. The most reliable books and source materials available are used as references. Together, the experts and technicians judge the difficulty level of the questions.

Test technicians know how to phrase questions so that the problem is clearly stated. Their ethics do not permit "trick" or "catch" questions. Questions may have been tried out on sample groups, or subjected to statistical analysis, to determine their usefulness.

Written tests are often used in combination with performance tests, ratings of training and experience, and oral interviews. All of these measures combine to form the best-known means of finding the right person for the right job.

II. HOW TO PASS THE WRITTEN TEST

A. NATURE OF THE EXAMINATION

To prepare intelligently for civil service examinations, you should know how they differ from school examinations you have taken. In school you were assigned certain definite pages to read or subjects to cover. The examination questions were quite detailed and usually emphasized memory. Civil service exams, on the other hand, try to discover your present ability to perform the duties of a position, plus your potentiality to learn these duties. In other words, a civil service exam attempts to predict how successful you will be. Questions cover such a broad area that they cannot be as minute and detailed as school exam questions.

In the public service similar kinds of work, or positions, are grouped together in one "class." This process is known as *position-classification*. All the positions in a class are paid according to the salary range for that class. One class title covers all of these positions, and they are all tested by the same examination.

B. FOUR BASIC STEPS

1) Study the announcement

How, then, can you know what subjects to study? Our best answer is: "Learn as much as possible about the class of positions for which you've applied." The exam will test the knowledge, skills and abilities needed to do the work.

Your most valuable source of information about the position you want is the official exam announcement. This announcement lists the training and experience qualifications. Check these standards and apply only if you come reasonably close to meeting them.

The brief description of the position in the examination announcement offers some clues to the subjects which will be tested. Think about the job itself. Review the duties in your mind. Can you perform them, or are there some in which you are rusty? Fill in the blank spots in your preparation.

Many jurisdictions preview the written test in the exam announcement by including a section called "Knowledge and Abilities Required," "Scope of the Examination," or some similar heading. Here you will find out specifically what fields will be tested.

2) Review your own background

Once you learn in general what the position is all about, and what you need to know to do the work, ask yourself which subjects you already know fairly well and which need improvement. You may wonder whether to concentrate on improving your strong areas or on building some background in your fields of weakness. When the announcement has specified "some knowledge" or "considerable knowledge," or has used adjectives like "beginning principles of…" or "advanced … methods," you can get a clue as to the number and difficulty of questions to be asked in any given field. More questions, and hence broader coverage, would be included for those subjects which are more important in the work. Now weigh your strengths and weaknesses against the job requirements and prepare accordingly.

3) Determine the level of the position

Another way to tell how intensively you should prepare is to understand the level of the job for which you are applying. Is it the entering level? In other words, is this the position in which beginners in a field of work are hired? Or is it an intermediate or advanced level? Sometimes this is indicated by such words as "Junior" or "Senior" in the class title. Other jurisdictions use Roman numerals to designate the level – Clerk I, Clerk II, for example. The word "Supervisor" sometimes appears in the title. If the level is not indicated by the title, check the description of duties. Will you be working under very close supervision, or will you have responsibility for independent decisions in this work?

4) Choose appropriate study materials

Now that you know the subjects to be examined and the relative amount of each subject to be covered, you can choose suitable study materials. For beginning level jobs, or even advanced ones, if you have a pronounced weakness in some aspect of your training, read a modern, standard textbook in that field. Be sure it is up to date and has general coverage. Such books are normally available at your library, and the librarian will be glad to help you locate one. For entry-level positions, questions of appropriate difficulty are chosen – neither highly advanced questions, nor those too simple. Such questions require careful thought but not advanced training.

If the position for which you are applying is technical or advanced, you will read more advanced, specialized material. If you are already familiar with the basic principles of your field, elementary textbooks would waste your time. Concentrate on advanced textbooks and technical periodicals. Think through the concepts and review difficult problems in your field.

These are all general sources. You can get more ideas on your own initiative, following these leads. For example, training manuals and publications of the government agency which employs workers in your field can be useful, particularly for technical and professional positions. A letter or visit to the government department involved may result in more specific study suggestions, and certainly will provide you with a more definite idea of the exact nature of the position you are seeking.

III. KINDS OF TESTS

Tests are used for purposes other than measuring knowledge and ability to perform specified duties. For some positions, it is equally important to test ability to make adjustments to new situations or to profit from training. In others, basic mental abilities not dependent on information are essential. Questions which test these things may not appear as pertinent to the duties of the position as those which test for knowledge and information. Yet they are often highly important parts of a fair examination. For very general questions, it is almost impossible to help you direct your study efforts. What we can do is to point out some of the more common of these general abilities needed in public service positions and describe some typical questions.

1) General information

Broad, general information has been found useful for predicting job success in some kinds of work. This is tested in a variety of ways, from vocabulary lists to questions about current events. Basic background in some field of work, such as sociology or economics, may be sampled in a group of questions. Often these are principles which have become familiar to most persons through exposure rather than through formal training. It is difficult to advise you how to study for these questions; being alert to the world around you is our best suggestion.

2) Verbal ability

An example of an ability needed in many positions is verbal or language ability. Verbal ability is, in brief, the ability to use and understand words. Vocabulary and grammar tests are typical measures of this ability. Reading comprehension or paragraph interpretation questions are common in many kinds of civil service tests. You are given a paragraph of written material and asked to find its central meaning.

3) Numerical ability

Number skills can be tested by the familiar arithmetic problem, by checking paired lists of numbers to see which are alike and which are different, or by interpreting charts and graphs. In the latter test, a graph may be printed in the test booklet which you are asked to use as the basis for answering questions.

4) Observation

A popular test for law-enforcement positions is the observation test. A picture is shown to you for several minutes, then taken away. Questions about the picture test your ability to observe both details and larger elements.

5) Following directions

In many positions in the public service, the employee must be able to carry out written instructions dependably and accurately. You may be given a chart with several columns, each column listing a variety of information. The questions require you to carry out directions involving the information given in the chart.

6) Skills and aptitudes

Performance tests effectively measure some manual skills and aptitudes. When the skill is one in which you are trained, such as typing or shorthand, you can practice. These tests are often very much like those given in business school or high school courses. For many of the other skills and aptitudes, however, no short-time preparation can be made. Skills and abilities natural to you or that you have developed throughout your lifetime are being tested.

Many of the general questions just described provide all the data needed to answer the questions and ask you to use your reasoning ability to find the answers. Your best preparation for these tests, as well as for tests of facts and ideas, is to be at your physical and mental best. You, no doubt, have your own methods of getting into an exam-taking mood and keeping "in shape." The next section lists some ideas on this subject.

IV. KINDS OF QUESTIONS

Only rarely is the "essay" question, which you answer in narrative form, used in civil service tests. Civil service tests are usually of the short-answer type. Full instructions for answering these questions will be given to you at the examination. But in case this is your first experience with short-answer questions and separate answer sheets, here is what you need to know:

1) Multiple-choice Questions

Most popular of the short-answer questions is the "multiple choice" or "best answer" question. It can be used, for example, to test for factual knowledge, ability to solve problems or judgment in meeting situations found at work.

A multiple-choice question is normally one of three types—
- It can begin with an incomplete statement followed by several possible endings. You are to find the one ending which *best* completes the statement, although some of the others may not be entirely wrong.
- It can also be a complete statement in the form of a question which is answered by choosing one of the statements listed.

- It can be in the form of a problem – again you select the best answer.

Here is an example of a multiple-choice question with a discussion which should give you some clues as to the method for choosing the right answer:

When an employee has a complaint about his assignment, the action which will *best* help him overcome his difficulty is to
- A. discuss his difficulty with his coworkers
- B. take the problem to the head of the organization
- C. take the problem to the person who gave him the assignment
- D. say nothing to anyone about his complaint

In answering this question, you should study each of the choices to find which is best. Consider choice "A" – Certainly an employee may discuss his complaint with fellow employees, but no change or improvement can result, and the complaint remains unresolved. Choice "B" is a poor choice since the head of the organization probably does not know what assignment you have been given, and taking your problem to him is known as "going over the head" of the supervisor. The supervisor, or person who made the assignment, is the person who can clarify it or correct any injustice. Choice "C" is, therefore, correct. To say nothing, as in choice "D," is unwise. Supervisors have and interest in knowing the problems employees are facing, and the employee is seeking a solution to his problem.

2) True/False Questions

The "true/false" or "right/wrong" form of question is sometimes used. Here a complete statement is given. Your job is to decide whether the statement is right or wrong.

SAMPLE: A roaming cell-phone call to a nearby city costs less than a non-roaming call to a distant city.

This statement is wrong, or false, since roaming calls are more expensive.

This is not a complete list of all possible question forms, although most of the others are variations of these common types. You will always get complete directions for answering questions. Be sure you understand *how* to mark your answers – ask questions until you do.

V. RECORDING YOUR ANSWERS

Computer terminals are used more and more today for many different kinds of exams.

For an examination with very few applicants, you may be told to record your answers in the test booklet itself. Separate answer sheets are much more common. If this separate answer sheet is to be scored by machine – and this is often the case – it is highly important that you mark your answers correctly in order to get credit.

An electronic scoring machine is often used in civil service offices because of the speed with which papers can be scored. Machine-scored answer sheets must be marked with a pencil, which will be given to you. This pencil has a high graphite content which responds to the electronic scoring machine. As a matter of fact, stray dots may register as answers, so do not let your pencil rest on the answer sheet while you are pondering the correct answer. Also, if your pencil lead breaks or is otherwise defective, ask for another.

Since the answer sheet will be dropped in a slot in the scoring machine, be careful not to bend the corners or get the paper crumpled.

The answer sheet normally has five vertical columns of numbers, with 30 numbers to a column. These numbers correspond to the question numbers in your test booklet. After each number, going across the page are four or five pairs of dotted lines. These short dotted lines have small letters or numbers above them. The first two pairs may also have a "T" or "F" above the letters. This indicates that the first two pairs only are to be used if the questions are of the true-false type. If the questions are multiple choice, disregard the "T" and "F" and pay attention only to the small letters or numbers.

Answer your questions in the manner of the sample that follows:

32. The largest city in the United States is
    A. Washington, D.C.
    B. New York City
    C. Chicago
    D. Detroit
    E. San Francisco

1) Choose the answer you think is best. (New York City is the largest, so "B" is correct.)
2) Find the row of dotted lines numbered the same as the question you are answering. (Find row number 32)
3) Find the pair of dotted lines corresponding to the answer. (Find the pair of lines under the mark "B.")
4) Make a solid black mark between the dotted lines.

VI. BEFORE THE TEST

Common sense will help you find procedures to follow to get ready for an examination. Too many of us, however, overlook these sensible measures. Indeed, nervousness and fatigue have been found to be the most serious reasons why applicants fail to do their best on civil service tests. Here is a list of reminders:

- Begin your preparation early – Don't wait until the last minute to go scurrying around for books and materials or to find out what the position is all about.
- Prepare continuously – An hour a night for a week is better than an all-night cram session. This has been definitely established. What is more, a night a week for a month will return better dividends than crowding your study into a shorter period of time.
- Locate the place of the exam – You have been sent a notice telling you when and where to report for the examination. If the location is in a different town or otherwise unfamiliar to you, it would be well to inquire the best route and learn something about the building.
- Relax the night before the test – Allow your mind to rest. Do not study at all that night. Plan some mild recreation or diversion; then go to bed early and get a good night's sleep.
- Get up early enough to make a leisurely trip to the place for the test – This way unforeseen events, traffic snarls, unfamiliar buildings, etc. will not upset you.
- Dress comfortably – A written test is not a fashion show. You will be known by number and not by name, so wear something comfortable.

- Leave excess paraphernalia at home – Shopping bags and odd bundles will get in your way. You need bring only the items mentioned in the official notice you received; usually everything you need is provided. Do not bring reference books to the exam. They will only confuse those last minutes and be taken away from you when in the test room.
- Arrive somewhat ahead of time – If because of transportation schedules you must get there very early, bring a newspaper or magazine to take your mind off yourself while waiting.
- Locate the examination room – When you have found the proper room, you will be directed to the seat or part of the room where you will sit. Sometimes you are given a sheet of instructions to read while you are waiting. Do not fill out any forms until you are told to do so; just read them and be prepared.
- Relax and prepare to listen to the instructions
- If you have any physical problem that may keep you from doing your best, be sure to tell the test administrator. If you are sick or in poor health, you really cannot do your best on the exam. You can come back and take the test some other time.

VII. AT THE TEST

The day of the test is here and you have the test booklet in your hand. The temptation to get going is very strong. Caution! There is more to success than knowing the right answers. You must know how to identify your papers and understand variations in the type of short-answer question used in this particular examination. Follow these suggestions for maximum results from your efforts:

1) Cooperate with the monitor

The test administrator has a duty to create a situation in which you can be as much at ease as possible. He will give instructions, tell you when to begin, check to see that you are marking your answer sheet correctly, and so on. He is not there to guard you, although he will see that your competitors do not take unfair advantage. He wants to help you do your best.

2) Listen to all instructions

Don't jump the gun! Wait until you understand all directions. In most civil service tests you get more time than you need to answer the questions. So don't be in a hurry. Read each word of instructions until you clearly understand the meaning. Study the examples, listen to all announcements and follow directions. Ask questions if you do not understand what to do.

3) Identify your papers

Civil service exams are usually identified by number only. You will be assigned a number; you must not put your name on your test papers. Be sure to copy your number correctly. Since more than one exam may be given, copy your exact examination title.

4) Plan your time

Unless you are told that a test is a "speed" or "rate of work" test, speed itself is usually not important. Time enough to answer all the questions will be provided, but this does not mean that you have all day. An overall time limit has been set. Divide the total time (in minutes) by the number of questions to determine the approximate time you have for each question.

5) Do not linger over difficult questions

If you come across a difficult question, mark it with a paper clip (useful to have along) and come back to it when you have been through the booklet. One caution if you do this – be sure to skip a number on your answer sheet as well. Check often to be sure that you have not lost your place and that you are marking in the row numbered the same as the question you are answering.

6) Read the questions

Be sure you know what the question asks! Many capable people are unsuccessful because they failed to *read* the questions correctly.

7) Answer all questions

Unless you have been instructed that a penalty will be deducted for incorrect answers, it is better to guess than to omit a question.

8) Speed tests

It is often better NOT to guess on speed tests. It has been found that on timed tests people are tempted to spend the last few seconds before time is called in marking answers at random – without even reading them – in the hope of picking up a few extra points. To discourage this practice, the instructions may warn you that your score will be "corrected" for guessing. That is, a penalty will be applied. The incorrect answers will be deducted from the correct ones, or some other penalty formula will be used.

9) Review your answers

If you finish before time is called, go back to the questions you guessed or omitted to give them further thought. Review other answers if you have time.

10) Return your test materials

If you are ready to leave before others have finished or time is called, take ALL your materials to the monitor and leave quietly. Never take any test material with you. The monitor can discover whose papers are not complete, and taking a test booklet may be grounds for disqualification.

VIII. EXAMINATION TECHNIQUES

1) Read the general instructions carefully. These are usually printed on the first page of the exam booklet. As a rule, these instructions refer to the timing of the examination; the fact that you should not start work until the signal and must stop work at a signal, etc. If there are any *special* instructions, such as a choice of questions to be answered, make sure that you note this instruction carefully.

2) When you are ready to start work on the examination, that is as soon as the signal has been given, read the instructions to each question booklet, underline any key words or phrases, such as *least, best, outline, describe* and the like. In this way you will tend to answer as requested rather than discover on reviewing your paper that you *listed without describing*, that you selected the *worst* choice rather than the *best* choice, etc.

3) If the examination is of the objective or multiple-choice type – that is, each question will also give a series of possible answers: A, B, C or D, and you are called upon to select the best answer and write the letter next to that answer on your answer paper – it is advisable to start answering each question in turn. There may be anywhere from 50 to 100 such questions in the three or four hours allotted and you can see how much time would be taken if you read through all the questions before beginning to answer any. Furthermore, if you come across a question or group of questions which you know would be difficult to answer, it would undoubtedly affect your handling of all the other questions.

4) If the examination is of the essay type and contains but a few questions, it is a moot point as to whether you should read all the questions before starting to answer any one. Of course, if you are given a choice – say five out of seven and the like – then it is essential to read all the questions so you can eliminate the two that are most difficult. If, however, you are asked to answer all the questions, there may be danger in trying to answer the easiest one first because you may find that you will spend too much time on it. The best technique is to answer the first question, then proceed to the second, etc.

5) Time your answers. Before the exam begins, write down the time it started, then add the time allowed for the examination and write down the time it must be completed, then divide the time available somewhat as follows:
    - If 3-1/2 hours are allowed, that would be 210 minutes. If you have 80 objective-type questions, that would be an average of 2-1/2 minutes per question. Allow yourself no more than 2 minutes per question, or a total of 160 minutes, which will permit about 50 minutes to review.
    - If for the time allotment of 210 minutes there are 7 essay questions to answer, that would average about 30 minutes a question. Give yourself only 25 minutes per question so that you have about 35 minutes to review.

6) The most important instruction is to *read each question* and make sure you know what is wanted. The second most important instruction is to *time yourself properly* so that you answer every question. The third most important instruction is to *answer every question*. Guess if you have to but include something for each question. Remember that you will receive no credit for a blank and will probably receive some credit if you write something in answer to an essay question. If you guess a letter – say "B" for a multiple-choice question – you may have guessed right. If you leave a blank as an answer to a multiple-choice question, the examiners may respect your feelings but it will not add a point to your score. Some exams may penalize you for wrong answers, so in such cases *only*, you may not want to guess unless you have some basis for your answer.

7) Suggestions
    a. Objective-type questions
        1. Examine the question booklet for proper sequence of pages and questions
        2. Read all instructions carefully
        3. Skip any question which seems too difficult; return to it after all other questions have been answered
        4. Apportion your time properly; do not spend too much time on any single question or group of questions

5. Note and underline key words – *all, most, fewest, least, best, worst, same, opposite,* etc.
6. Pay particular attention to negatives
7. Note unusual option, e.g., unduly long, short, complex, different or similar in content to the body of the question
8. Observe the use of "hedging" words – *probably, may, most likely,* etc.
9. Make sure that your answer is put next to the same number as the question
10. Do not second-guess unless you have good reason to believe the second answer is definitely more correct
11. Cross out original answer if you decide another answer is more accurate; do not erase until you are ready to hand your paper in
12. Answer all questions; guess unless instructed otherwise
13. Leave time for review

   b. Essay questions
1. Read each question carefully
2. Determine exactly what is wanted. Underline key words or phrases.
3. Decide on outline or paragraph answer
4. Include many different points and elements unless asked to develop any one or two points or elements
5. Show impartiality by giving pros and cons unless directed to select one side only
6. Make and write down any assumptions you find necessary to answer the questions
7. Watch your English, grammar, punctuation and choice of words
8. Time your answers; don't crowd material

8) Answering the essay question

Most essay questions can be answered by framing the specific response around several key words or ideas. Here are a few such key words or ideas:

M's: manpower, materials, methods, money, management
P's: purpose, program, policy, plan, procedure, practice, problems, pitfalls, personnel, public relations

   a. Six basic steps in handling problems:
1. Preliminary plan and background development
2. Collect information, data and facts
3. Analyze and interpret information, data and facts
4. Analyze and develop solutions as well as make recommendations
5. Prepare report and sell recommendations
6. Install recommendations and follow up effectiveness

   b. Pitfalls to avoid
1. *Taking things for granted* – A statement of the situation does not necessarily imply that each of the elements is necessarily true; for example, a complaint may be invalid and biased so that all that can be taken for granted is that a complaint has been registered

2. *Considering only one side of a situation* – Wherever possible, indicate several alternatives and then point out the reasons you selected the best one
3. *Failing to indicate follow up* – Whenever your answer indicates action on your part, make certain that you will take proper follow-up action to see how successful your recommendations, procedures or actions turn out to be
4. *Taking too long in answering any single question* – Remember to time your answers properly

IX. AFTER THE TEST

Scoring procedures differ in detail among civil service jurisdictions although the general principles are the same. Whether the papers are hand-scored or graded by machine we have described, they are nearly always graded by number. That is, the person who marks the paper knows only the number – never the name – of the applicant. Not until all the papers have been graded will they be matched with names. If other tests, such as training and experience or oral interview ratings have been given, scores will be combined. Different parts of the examination usually have different weights. For example, the written test might count 60 percent of the final grade, and a rating of training and experience 40 percent. In many jurisdictions, veterans will have a certain number of points added to their grades.

After the final grade has been determined, the names are placed in grade order and an eligible list is established. There are various methods for resolving ties between those who get the same final grade – probably the most common is to place first the name of the person whose application was received first. Job offers are made from the eligible list in the order the names appear on it. You will be notified of your grade and your rank as soon as all these computations have been made. This will be done as rapidly as possible.

People who are found to meet the requirements in the announcement are called "eligibles." Their names are put on a list of eligible candidates. An eligible's chances of getting a job depend on how high he stands on this list and how fast agencies are filling jobs from the list.

When a job is to be filled from a list of eligibles, the agency asks for the names of people on the list of eligibles for that job. When the civil service commission receives this request, it sends to the agency the names of the three people highest on this list. Or, if the job to be filled has specialized requirements, the office sends the agency the names of the top three persons who meet these requirements from the general list.

The appointing officer makes a choice from among the three people whose names were sent to him. If the selected person accepts the appointment, the names of the others are put back on the list to be considered for future openings.

That is the rule in hiring from all kinds of eligible lists, whether they are for typist, carpenter, chemist, or something else. For every vacancy, the appointing officer has his choice of any one of the top three eligibles on the list. This explains why the person whose name is on top of the list sometimes does not get an appointment when some of the persons lower on the list do. If the appointing officer chooses the second or third eligible, the No. 1 eligible does not get a job at once, but stays on the list until he is appointed or the list is terminated.

X. HOW TO PASS THE INTERVIEW TEST

The examination for which you applied requires an oral interview test. You have already taken the written test and you are now being called for the interview test – the final part of the formal examination.

You may think that it is not possible to prepare for an interview test and that there are no procedures to follow during an interview. Our purpose is to point out some things you can do in advance that will help you and some good rules to follow and pitfalls to avoid while you are being interviewed.

What is an interview supposed to test?

The written examination is designed to test the technical knowledge and competence of the candidate; the oral is designed to evaluate intangible qualities, not readily measured otherwise, and to establish a list showing the relative fitness of each candidate – as measured against his competitors – for the position sought. Scoring is not on the basis of "right" and "wrong," but on a sliding scale of values ranging from "not passable" to "outstanding." As a matter of fact, it is possible to achieve a relatively low score without a single "incorrect" answer because of evident weakness in the qualities being measured.

Occasionally, an examination may consist entirely of an oral test – either an individual or a group oral. In such cases, information is sought concerning the technical knowledges and abilities of the candidate, since there has been no written examination for this purpose. More commonly, however, an oral test is used to supplement a written examination.

Who conducts interviews?

The composition of oral boards varies among different jurisdictions. In nearly all, a representative of the personnel department serves as chairman. One of the members of the board may be a representative of the department in which the candidate would work. In some cases, "outside experts" are used, and, frequently, a businessman or some other representative of the general public is asked to serve. Labor and management or other special groups may be represented. The aim is to secure the services of experts in the appropriate field.

However the board is composed, it is a good idea (and not at all improper or unethical) to ascertain in advance of the interview who the members are and what groups they represent. When you are introduced to them, you will have some idea of their backgrounds and interests, and at least you will not stutter and stammer over their names.

What should be done before the interview?

While knowledge about the board members is useful and takes some of the surprise element out of the interview, there is other preparation which is more substantive. It *is* possible to prepare for an oral interview – in several ways:

1) Keep a copy of your application and review it carefully before the interview

This may be the only document before the oral board, and the starting point of the interview. Know what education and experience you have listed there, and the sequence and dates of all of it. Sometimes the board will ask you to review the highlights of your experience for them; you should not have to hem and haw doing it.

2) Study the class specification and the examination announcement

Usually, the oral board has one or both of these to guide them. The qualities, characteristics or knowledges required by the position sought are stated in these documents. They offer valuable clues as to the nature of the oral interview. For example, if the job involves supervisory responsibilities, the announcement will usually indicate that knowledge of modern supervisory methods and the qualifications of the candidate as a supervisor will be tested. If so, you can expect such questions, frequently in the form of a hypothetical situation which you are expected to solve. NEVER go into an oral without knowledge of the duties and responsibilities of the job you seek.

3) Think through each qualification required

Try to visualize the kind of questions you would ask if you were a board member. How well could you answer them? Try especially to appraise your own knowledge and background in each area, *measured against the job sought*, and identify any areas in which you are weak. Be critical and realistic – do not flatter yourself.

4) Do some general reading in areas in which you feel you may be weak

For example, if the job involves supervision and your past experience has NOT, some general reading in supervisory methods and practices, particularly in the field of human relations, might be useful. Do NOT study agency procedures or detailed manuals. The oral board will be testing your understanding and capacity, not your memory.

5) Get a good night's sleep and watch your general health and mental attitude

You will want a clear head at the interview. Take care of a cold or any other minor ailment, and of course, no hangovers.

What should be done on the day of the interview?

Now comes the day of the interview itself. Give yourself plenty of time to get there. Plan to arrive somewhat ahead of the scheduled time, particularly if your appointment is in the fore part of the day. If a previous candidate fails to appear, the board might be ready for you a bit early. By early afternoon an oral board is almost invariably behind schedule if there are many candidates, and you may have to wait. Take along a book or magazine to read, or your application to review, but leave any extraneous material in the waiting room when you go in for your interview. In any event, relax and compose yourself.

The matter of dress is important. The board is forming impressions about you – from your experience, your manners, your attitude, and your appearance. Give your personal appearance careful attention. Dress your best, but not your flashiest. Choose conservative, appropriate clothing, and be sure it is immaculate. This is a business interview, and your appearance should indicate that you regard it as such. Besides, being well groomed and properly dressed will help boost your confidence.

Sooner or later, someone will call your name and escort you into the interview room. *This is it.* From here on you are on your own. It is too late for any more preparation. But remember, you asked for this opportunity to prove your fitness, and you are here because your request was granted.

What happens when you go in?

The usual sequence of events will be as follows: The clerk (who is often the board stenographer) will introduce you to the chairman of the oral board, who will introduce you to the other members of the board. Acknowledge the introductions before you sit down. Do not be surprised if you find a microphone facing you or a stenotypist sitting by. Oral interviews are usually recorded in the event of an appeal or other review.

Usually the chairman of the board will open the interview by reviewing the highlights of your education and work experience from your application – primarily for the benefit of the other members of the board, as well as to get the material into the record. Do not interrupt or comment unless there is an error or significant misinterpretation; if that is the case, do not hesitate. But do not quibble about insignificant matters. Also, he will usually ask you some question about your education, experience or your present job – partly to get you to start talking and to establish the interviewing "rapport." He may start the actual questioning, or turn it over to one of the other members. Frequently, each member undertakes the questioning on a particular area, one in which he is perhaps most competent, so you can expect each member to participate in the examination. Because time is limited, you may also expect some rather abrupt switches in the direction the questioning takes, so do not be upset by it. Normally, a board member will not pursue a single line of questioning unless he discovers a particular strength or weakness.

After each member has participated, the chairman will usually ask whether any member has any further questions, then will ask you if you have anything you wish to add. Unless you are expecting this question, it may floor you. Worse, it may start you off on an extended, extemporaneous speech. The board is not usually seeking more information. The question is principally to offer you a last opportunity to present further qualifications or to indicate that you have nothing to add. So, if you feel that a significant qualification or characteristic has been overlooked, it is proper to point it out in a sentence or so. Do not compliment the board on the thoroughness of their examination – they have been sketchy, and you know it. If you wish, merely say, "No thank you, I have nothing further to add." This is a point where you can "talk yourself out" of a good impression or fail to present an important bit of information. Remember, *you close the interview yourself.*

The chairman will then say, "That is all, Mr. _____, thank you." Do not be startled; the interview is over, and quicker than you think. Thank him, gather your belongings and take your leave. Save your sigh of relief for the other side of the door.

How to put your best foot forward

Throughout this entire process, you may feel that the board individually and collectively is trying to pierce your defenses, seek out your hidden weaknesses and embarrass and confuse you. Actually, this is not true. They are obliged to make an appraisal of your qualifications for the job you are seeking, and they want to see you in your best light. Remember, they must interview all candidates and a non-cooperative candidate may become a failure in spite of their best efforts to bring out his qualifications. Here are 15 suggestions that will help you:

1) Be natural – Keep your attitude confident, not cocky

If you are not confident that you can do the job, do not expect the board to be. Do not apologize for your weaknesses, try to bring out your strong points. The board is interested in a positive, not negative, presentation. Cockiness will antagonize any board member and make him wonder if you are covering up a weakness by a false show of strength.

2) Get comfortable, but don't lounge or sprawl

Sit erectly but not stiffly. A careless posture may lead the board to conclude that you are careless in other things, or at least that you are not impressed by the importance of the occasion. Either conclusion is natural, even if incorrect. Do not fuss with your clothing, a pencil or an ashtray. Your hands may occasionally be useful to emphasize a point; do not let them become a point of distraction.

3) Do not wisecrack or make small talk

This is a serious situation, and your attitude should show that you consider it as such. Further, the time of the board is limited – they do not want to waste it, and neither should you.

4) Do not exaggerate your experience or abilities

In the first place, from information in the application or other interviews and sources, the board may know more about you than you think. Secondly, you probably will not get away with it. An experienced board is rather adept at spotting such a situation, so do not take the chance.

5) If you know a board member, do not make a point of it, yet do not hide it

Certainly you are not fooling him, and probably not the other members of the board. Do not try to take advantage of your acquaintanceship – it will probably do you little good.

6) Do not dominate the interview

Let the board do that. They will give you the clues – do not assume that you have to do all the talking. Realize that the board has a number of questions to ask you, and do not try to take up all the interview time by showing off your extensive knowledge of the answer to the first one.

7) Be attentive

You only have 20 minutes or so, and you should keep your attention at its sharpest throughout. When a member is addressing a problem or question to you, give him your undivided attention. Address your reply principally to him, but do not exclude the other board members.

8) Do not interrupt

A board member may be stating a problem for you to analyze. He will ask you a question when the time comes. Let him state the problem, and wait for the question.

9) Make sure you understand the question

Do not try to answer until you are sure what the question is. If it is not clear, restate it in your own words or ask the board member to clarify it for you. However, do not haggle about minor elements.

10) Reply promptly but not hastily

A common entry on oral board rating sheets is "candidate responded readily," or "candidate hesitated in replies." Respond as promptly and quickly as you can, but do not jump to a hasty, ill-considered answer.

11) Do not be peremptory in your answers

A brief answer is proper – but do not fire your answer back. That is a losing game from your point of view. The board member can probably ask questions much faster than you can answer them.

12) Do not try to create the answer you think the board member wants

He is interested in what kind of mind you have and how it works – not in playing games. Furthermore, he can usually spot this practice and will actually grade you down on it.

13) Do not switch sides in your reply merely to agree with a board member

Frequently, a member will take a contrary position merely to draw you out and to see if you are willing and able to defend your point of view. Do not start a debate, yet do not surrender a good position. If a position is worth taking, it is worth defending.

14) Do not be afraid to admit an error in judgment if you are shown to be wrong

The board knows that you are forced to reply without any opportunity for careful consideration. Your answer may be demonstrably wrong. If so, admit it and get on with the interview.

15) Do not dwell at length on your present job

The opening question may relate to your present assignment. Answer the question but do not go into an extended discussion. You are being examined for a *new* job, not your present one. As a matter of fact, try to phrase ALL your answers in terms of the job for which you are being examined.

Basis of Rating

Probably you will forget most of these "do's" and "don'ts" when you walk into the oral interview room. Even remembering them all will not ensure you a passing grade. Perhaps you did not have the qualifications in the first place. But remembering them will help you to put your best foot forward, without treading on the toes of the board members.

Rumor and popular opinion to the contrary notwithstanding, an oral board wants you to make the best appearance possible. They know you are under pressure – but they also want to see how you respond to it as a guide to what your reaction would be under the pressures of the job you seek. They will be influenced by the degree of poise you display, the personal traits you show and the manner in which you respond.

ABOUT THIS BOOK

This book contains tests divided into Examination Sections. Go through each test, answering every question in the margin. We have also attached a sample answer sheet at the back of the book that can be removed and used. At the end of each test look at the answer key and check your answers. On the ones you got wrong, look at the right answer choice and learn. Do not fill in the answers first. Do not memorize the questions and answers, but understand the answer and principles involved. On your test, the questions will likely be different from the samples. Questions are changed and new ones added. If you understand these past questions you should have success with any changes that arise. Tests may consist of several types of questions. We have additional books on each subject should more study be advisable or necessary for you. Finally, the more you study, the better prepared you will be. This book is intended to be the last thing you study before you walk into the examination room. Prior study of relevant texts is also recommended. NLC publishes some of these in our Fundamental Series. Knowledge and good sense are important factors in passing your exam. Good luck also helps. So now study this Passbook, absorb the material contained within and take that knowledge into the examination. Then do your best to pass that exam.

EXAMINATION SECTION

SUPERVISION, ADMINISTRATION, MANAGEMENT AND ORGANIZATION
EXAMINATION SECTION
TEST 1

DIRECTIONS: Each question or incomplete statement is followed by several suggested answers or completions. Select the one that BEST answers the question or completes the statement. *PRINT THE LETTER OF THE CORRECT ANSWER IN THE SPACE AT THE RIGHT.*

1. The one of the following situations in which you as a supervisor of a group of clerks would probably be able to function MOST effectively from the viewpoint of departmental efficiency is where you are responsible DIRECTLY to
    A. a single supervisor having sole jurisdiction over you
    B. two or three supervisors having coordinate jurisdiction over you
    C. four or five supervisors having coordinate jurisdiction over you
    D. all individuals of higher rank than you in the department

1.____

2. Suppose that it is necessary to order one of the clerks under your supervision to stay overtime a few hours one evening. The work to be done is not especially difficult. It is the custom in your office to make such assignments by rotation. The particular clerk whose turn it is to work overtime requests to be excused that evening, but offers to work the next time that overtime is necessary. Hitherto, this clerk has always been very cooperative.
Of the following, the BEST action for you to take is to
    A. grant the clerk's request, but require her to work overtime two additional nights to compensate for this concession
    B. inform the clerk that you are compelled to refuse any request for special consideration
    C. grant the clerk's request if another clerk is willing to substitute for her
    D. refuse the clerk's request outright because granting her request may encourage her to evade other responsibilities

2.____

3. When asked to comment upon the efficiency of Miss Jones, a clerk, her supervisor said, "Since she rarely makes an error, I consider her very efficient."
Of the following, the MOST valid assumption underlying this supervisor's comment is that
    A. speed and accuracy should be considered separately in evaluating a clerk's efficiency
    B. the most accurate clerks are not necessarily the most efficient
    C. accuracy and competency are directly related
    D. accuracy is largely dependent upon the intelligence of a clerk

3.____

4. The one of the following which is the MOST accurate statement of one of the functions of a supervisor is to
   A. select scientifically the person best fitted for the specific job to be done
   B. train the clerks assigned to you in the best methods of doing the work of your office
   C. fit the job to be done to the clerks who are available
   D. assign a clerk only to those tasks for which she has the necessary experience

5. Assume that you, an experienced supervisor, are given a newly appointed clerk to assist you in performing a certain task. The new clerk presents a method of doing the task which is different from your method but which is obviously better and easy to adopt.
   Of the following you, the supervisor, should
   A. take the suggestion and try it out, even though it was offered by someone less experienced
   B. reject the idea, even though it appears an improvement, as it very likely would not work out
   C. send the new clerk away and get someone else to assist who will be more in accord with your ideas
   D. report him to the head of the office and ask that the new clerk be instructed to do things your way

6. As a supervisor, you should realize that the one of the following general abilities of a junior clerk which is probably LEAST susceptible to improvement by practice and training is
   A. intelligence
   B. speed of typing
   C. knowledge of office procedures
   D. accuracy of filing

7. As a supervisor, when training an employee, you should NOT
   A. correct errors as he makes them
   B. give him too much material to absorb at one time
   C. have him try the operation until he can do it perfectly
   D. treat any foolish question seriously

8. If a supervisor cannot check readily all the work in her unit, she should
   A. hold up the work until she can personally check it
   B. refuse to take additional work
   C. work overtime until she can personally finish it
   D. delegate part of the work to a qualified subordinate

9. The one of the following over which a unit supervisor has the LEAST control is
   A. the quality of the work done in his unit
   B. the nature of the work handled in his unit
   C. the morale of workers in his unit
   D. increasing efficiency of his unit

10. Suppose that you have received a note from an important official in your department commending the work of a unit of clerks under your supervision. Of the following, the BEST action for you to take is to
    A. withhold the note for possible use at a time when the morale of the unit appears to be declining
    B. show the note only to the better members of your staff as a reward for their good work
    C. show the note only to the poorer members of your staff as a stimulus for better work
    D. post the note conspicuously so that it can be seen by all members of your staff

10.____

11. If you find that one of your subordinates is becoming apathetic towards his work, you should
    A. prefer charges against him
    B. change the type of work
    C. request his transfer
    D. advise him to take a medical examination to check his health

11.____

12. Suppose that a new clerk has been assigned to the unit which you supervise. To give this clerk a brief picture of the functioning of your unit in the entire department would be
    A. *commendable*, because she will probably be able to perform her work with more understanding
    B. *undesirable*, because such action will probably serve only to confuse her
    C. *commendable*, because, if transferred, she would probably be able to work efficiently without additional training
    D. *undesirable*, because in-service training has been demonstrated to be less efficient than on-the-job training

12.____

13. Written instructions to a subordinate are of value because they
    A. can be kept up-to-date   B. encourage initiative
    C. make a job seem easier   D. are an aid in training

13.____

14. Suppose that you have assigned a task to a clerk under your supervision and have given appropriate instructions. After a reasonable period, you check her work and find that one specific aspect of her work is consistently incorrect. Of the following, the BEST action for you to take is to
    A. determine whether the clerk has correctly understood instructions concerning the aspect of the work not being done correctly
    B. assign the task to a more competent clerk
    C. wait for the clerk to commit a more flagrant error before taking up the matter with her
    D. indicate to the clerk that you are dissatisfied with her work and wait to see whether she is sufficiently intelligent to correct her own mistakes

14.____

15. If you wanted to check on the accuracy of the filing in your unit, you would
    A. check all the files thoroughly at regular intervals
    B. watch the clerks while they are filing
    C. glance through filed papers at random
    D. inspect thoroughly a small section of the files selected at random

16. In making job assignments to his subordinates, a supervisor should follow the principle that each individual generally is capable of
    A. performing one type of work well and less capable of performing other types well
    B. learning to perform a wide variety of different types of work
    C. performing best the type of work in which he has had least experience
    D. learning to perform any type of work in which he is given training

17. Of the following, the information that is generally considered MOST essential in a departmental organization survey chart is the
    A. detailed operations of the department
    B. lines of authority
    C. relations of the department to other departments
    D. names of the employees of the department

18. Suppose you are the supervisor in charge of a large unit in which all of the clerical staff perform similar tasks.
    In evaluating the relative accuracy of the clerks, the clerk who should be considered to be the LEAST accurate is the one
    A. whose errors result in the greatest financial loss
    B. whose errors cost the most to locate
    C. who makes the greatest percentage of errors in his work
    D. who makes the greatest number of errors in the unit

19. Aside from requirements imposed by authority, the frequency with which reports are submitted or the length of the interval which they cover should depend PRINCIPALLY on the
    A. availability of the data to be included in the reports
    B. amount of time required to prepare the reports
    C. extent of the variations in the data with the passage of time
    D. degree of comprehensiveness required in the reports

20. A serious error has been discovered by a critical superior in work carried on under your supervision.
    It is BEST to explain the situation and prevent its recurrence by
    A. claiming that you are not responsible because you do not check the work personally
    B. accepting the complaint and reporting the name of the employee responsible for the error
    C. assuring him that you hope it will not occur again
    D. assuring him that you will find out how it occurred, so that you can have the work checked with greater care in the future

21. A serious procedural problem develops in your office.
In your solution of this problem, the very FIRST step to take is to
   A. select the personnel to help you
   B. analyze your problem
   C. devise the one best method of research
   D. develop an outline of your report

22. Your office staff consists of eight clerks, stenographers, and typists, cramped in a long narrow room. The room is very difficult to ventilate properly, and, as in so many other offices, the disagreement over the method of ventilation is marked. Two cliques are developing and the friction is carrying over into the work of the office.
Of the following, the BEST way to proceed is to
   A. call your staff together, have the matter fully discussed giving each person an opportunity to be heard, and put the matter to a vote; then enforce the method of ventilation which has the most votes
   B. call your staff together and have the matter fully discussed. If a compromise arrangement is agreed upon, put it into effect. Otherwise, on the basis of all the facts at your disposal, make a decision as to how best to ventilate the room and enforce your decision
   C. speak to the employees individually, make a decision as to how to ventilate the room, and then enforce your decision
   D. study the layout of the office, make a decision as to how best to ventilate the room, and then enforce your decision

23. An organization consisting of six levels of authority, where eight persons are assigned to each supervisor on each level, would consist of APPROXIMATELY _____ persons.
   A. 50   B. 500   C. 5,000   D. 50,000

24. The one of the following which is considered by political scientists to be a GOOD principle of municipal government is
   A. concentration of authority and responsibility
   B. the long ballot
   C. low salaries and a narrow range in salaries
   D. short terms for elected city officials

25. Of the following, the statement concerning the organization of a department which is TRUE is:
   A. In general, no one employee should have active and constant supervision over more than ten persons.
   B. It is basically unwise to have a supervisor with only three subordinates.
   C. It is desirable that there be no personal contact between the rank and file employee and the supervisor once removed from him.
   D. There should be no more than four levels of authority between the top administrative office in a department and the rank and file employees.

26. Assuming that Dictaphones are not available, of the following, the situation in which it would be MOST desirable to establish a central stenographic unit is one in which the unit would serve
    A. ten correspondence clerks assigned to full-time positions answering correspondence of a large government department
    B. seven members of a government commission heading a large department
    C. seven heads of bureaus in a government department consisting of 250 employees
    D. fifty investigators in a large department

27. You are assigned to review the procedures in an office in order to recommend improvements to the commissioner directly. You go into an office performing seen routine operations in the processing of one type of office form.
    The question you should FIRST ask yourself in your study of any one of these operations is:
    A. Can it be simplified?
    B. Is it necessary?
    C. Is it performed in proper order or should its position in the procedure be changed?
    D. Is the equipment for doing it satisfactory?

28. You are assigned in charge of a clerical bureau performing a single operation. All five of your subordinates do exactly the same work. A fine spirit of cooperation has developed and the employees help each other and pool their completed work so that the work of any one employee is indistinguishable. Your office is very busy and all five clerks are doing a full day's work. However, reports come back to you from other offices that they are finding as much as 1% error in the work of your bureau. This is too high a percentage of error.
    Of the following, the BEST procedure for you to follow is to
    A. check all the work yourself
    B. have a sample of the work of each clerk checked by another clerk
    C. have all work done in your office checked by one of your clerks
    D. identify the work of each clerk in some way

29. You are put in charge of a small office. In order to cover the office during the lunch hour, you assign Employee A to remain in the office between the hours of 12 and 1 P.M. On your return to the office at 12:25 P.M., you note that no one is in the office and that the phone is ringing. You are forced to postpone your 12:30 P.M. luncheon appointment, and to remain in the office until 12:50 P.M. when Employee A returns to the office.
    The BEST of the following actions is:
    A. Ask Employee why he left the office
    B. Bring charges against Employee A for insubordination and neglect of duty
    C. Ignore the matter in your conversation with Employee A so as not to embarrass him
    D. Make a note to rate Employee A low on his service rating

30. You are assigned in charge of a large division. It had been the practice in that division for the employees to slip out for breakfast about 10:00 A.M. You had been successful in stopping this practice and for one week no one had gone out for breakfast. One day a stenographer comes over to you at 10:30 A.M. appearing to be ill. She states that she doesn't feel well and that she would like to go out for a cup of tea. She asks your permission to leave the office for a few minutes.
    You should
    A. telephone and have a cup of tea delivered to her
    B. permit her to go out
    C. refuse her permission to go out inasmuch as this would be setting a bad example
    D. tell her she can leave for an early lunch hour

31. The following four remarks from a supervisor to a subordinate deal with different situations. One remark, however, implies a basically POOR supervisory practice.
    Select this remark as your answer.
    A. "I've called the staff together primarily because I am displeased with the work which one of you is doing. John, don't you think you should be ashamed that you are spoiling the good work of the office?"
    B. "James, you have been with us for six months now. In general, I'm satisfied with your work. However, don't you think you could be more neat in your appearance? I also want you to try to be more accurate in your work."
    C. "Joe, when I assigned this job to you, I did it because it requires special care and I think you're one of our best men in this type of work, but here is a slip-up you've made that we should be especially careful to watch out for in the future."
    D. "Tim, first I'd like to tell you that, effective tomorrow, you are to be my assistant and will receive an increase in salary. Although I recommended you for this position because I felt that you are the best man for the job, there are some things about your work which could stand a bit of improvement. For instance, your manner with regard to visitors is not so polite as it could be."

32. Of the following, the BEST type of floor surface for an office is
    A. concrete   B. hardwood   C. linoleum   D. parquet

33. The GENERALLY accepted unit for the measurement of illumination at a desk or work bench is the
    A. ampere   B. foot-candle   C. volt   D. watt

34. The one of the following who is MOST closely allied with "scientific management" is
    A. Mosher   B. Probst   C. Taylor   D. White

35. Eliminating slack in work assignments is
    A. speed-up
    B. time study
    C. motion study
    D. efficient management

36. "Time studies" examine and measure
    A. past performance
    B. present performance
    C. long-run effect
    D. influence of change

37. The maximum number of subordinates who can be effectively supervised by one supervisor is BEST considered as
    A. determined by the law of "span of control"
    B. determined by the law of "span of attention"
    C. determined by the type of work supervised
    D. fixed at not more than six

38. In the theory and practice of public administration, the one of the following which is LEAST generally regarded as a staff function is
    A. budgeting
    B. firefighting
    C. purchasing
    D. research and information

39. Suppose you are part of an administrative structure in which the executive head has regularly reporting directly to him seventeen subordinates. To some of the subordinates there regularly report directly three employees, to others four employees, and to the remaining subordinates five employees.
    Called upon to make a suggestion concerning this organization, you would question FIRST the desirability of
    A. so large a variation among the number of employees regularly reporting directly to subordinates
    B. having so large a number of subordinates regularly reporting directly to the administrative head
    C. so small a variation among the number of employees regularly reporting directly to subordinates
    D. the hierarchical arrangement

40. Administration is the center but not necessarily the source of all ideas for procedural improvement.
    The MOST significant implication that this principle bears for the administrative officer is that
    A. before procedural improvements are introduced, they should be approved by a majority of the staff
    B. it is the unique function of the administrative officer to derive and introduce procedural improvements
    C. the administrative office should derive ideas and suggestions for procedural improvement from all possible sources, introducing any that promise to be effective
    D. the administrative officer should view employee grievances as the chief source of procedural improvements

9 (#1)

41. The merit system should not end with the appointment of a candidate. In any worthy public service system there should be no dead-end jobs. If the best citizen is to be attracted to public service, there must be provided encouragement and incentive to enable such a career employee to progress in the service.
The one of the following which is the MOST accurate statement on the basis of the above statement is that
   A. merit system selection has replaced political appointment in many governmental units
   B. lack of opportunities for advancement in government employment will discourage the better qualified from applying
   C. employees who want to progress in the public service should avoid simple assignments
   D. most dead-end jobs have been eliminated from the public service

41.____

42. Frequently the importance of keeping office records is not appreciated until information which is badly needed cannot be found. Office records must be kept in convenient and legible form, and must be filed where they may be found quickly. Many clerks are required for this work in large offices and fixed standards of accomplishment often can and must be utilized to get the desired results without loss of time.
The one of the following which is the MOST accurate statement on the basis of the above statement is:
   A. In setting up a filing system, the system to be used is secondary to the purpose it is to serve.
   B. Office records to be valuable must be kept in duplicate.
   C. The application of work standards to certain clerical functions frequently leads to greater efficiency.
   D. The keeping of office records becomes increasingly important as the business transacted by an office grows.

42.____

43. The difference between the average worker and the expert in any occupation is to a large degree a matter of training, yet the difference in their output is enormous. Despite this fact, there are many offices which do not have any organized system of training.
The MOST accurate of the following statements on the basis of the above statement is that
   A. job training, to be valuable, should be a continuous process
   B. most clerks have the same general intelligence but differ only in the amount of training they have received
   C. skill in an occupation can be acquired as a result of instruction by others
   D. employees with similar training will produce similar quality and quantity of work

43.____

44. Sometimes the term "clerical work" is used synonymously with the term "office work" to indicate that the work is clerical work, whether done by a clerk in a place called "the office," by the foreman in the shop, or by an investigator in the field. The essential feature is the work itself, not who does it or where it is done. If it is clerical work in one place, it is clerical work everywhere.

44.____

Of the following, the LEAST DIRECT implication of the above statement is that
A. many jobs have clerical aspects
B. some clerical work is done in offices
C. the term "clerical work" is used in place of the term "office work" to emphasize the nature of the work done rather than by whom it is done
D. clerks are not called upon to perform other than clerical work

45. Scheduling work within a unit involves the knowledge of how long the component parts of the routine take, and the precedence which certain routines should take over others. Usually, the important functions should be attended to on a schedule, and less important work can be handled as fill-in.
The one of the following which is the VALID statement on the basis of the above statement is that
A. only employees engaged in routine assignments should have their work scheduled
B. the work of an employee should be so scheduled that occasional absences will not upset his routine
C. a proper scheduling of work takes the importance of the various functions of a unit into consideration
D. if office work is not properly scheduled, important functions will be neglected

46. A filing system is unquestionably an effective tool for the systematic executive, and it use in office practice is indispensable, but a casual examination of almost any filing drawer in any office will show that hundreds of letters and papers which have no value whatever are being preserved.
The LEAST accurate of the following statements on the basis of the above statement is that
A. it is generally considered to be good office practice to destroy letters or papers which are of no value
B. many files are cluttered with useless paper
C. a filing system is a valuable aid in effective office management
D. every office executive should personally make a thorough examination of the files at regular intervals

47. As a supervisor, you may receive requests for information which you know should not be divulged.
Of the following replies you may give to such a request received over the telephone, the BEST one is:
A. "I regret to advise you that it is the policy of the department not to give out this information over the telephone."
B. "If you hold on a moment, I'll have you connected with the chief of the division."
C. "I am sorry that I cannot help you, but we are not permitted to give out any information regarding such matters."
D. "I am sorry but I know nothing regarding this matter."

48. Training promotes cooperation and teamwork, and results in lowered unit costs of operation.
The one of the following which is the MOST valid implication of the above statement is that
   A. training is of most value to new employees
   B. training is a factor in increasing efficiency and morale
   C. the actual cost of training employees may be small
   D. training is unnecessary in offices where personnel costs cannot be reduced

49. A government employee should understand how his particular duties contribute to the achievement of the objectives of his department.
This statement means MOST NEARLY that
   A. an employee who understands the functions of his department will perform his work efficiently
   B. all employees contribute equally in carrying out the objectives of their department
   C. an employee should realize the significance of his work in relation to the aims of his department
   D. all employees should be able to assist in setting up the objectives of a department

50. Many office managers have a tendency to overuse form letters and are prone to print form letters for every occasion, regardless of the number of copies of these letters which is needed.
On the basis of this statement, it is MOST logical to state that the determination of the need for a form letter should depend upon the
   A. length of the period during which the form letter may be used
   B. number of form letters presently being used in the office
   C. frequency with which the form letter may be used
   D. number of typists who may use the form letter

KEY (CORRECT ANSWERS)

1.	A	11.	B	21.	B	31.	A	41.	B
2.	C	12.	A	22.	B	32.	C	42.	C
3.	C	13.	D	23.	A	33.	B	43.	C
4.	B	14.	A	24.	A	34.	C	44.	D
5.	A	15.	D	25.	D	35.	D	45.	C
6.	A	16.	B	26.	D	36.	B	46.	D
7.	B	17.	B	27.	B	37.	C	47.	C
8.	D	18.	C	28.	D	38.	B	48.	B
9.	B	19.	C	29.	A	39.	B	49.	C
10.	D	20.	D	30.	B	40.	C	50.	C

TEST 2

DIRECTIONS: Each question or incomplete statement is followed by several suggested answers or completions. Select the one that BEST answers the question or completes the statement. *PRINT THE LETTER OF THE CORRECT ANSWER IN THE SPACE AT THE RIGHT.*

1. Your bureau is assigned an important task.
   Of the following, the function that you, as an administrative officer, can LEAST reasonably be expected to perform under these circumstances is the
   A. division of the large job into individual tasks
   B. establishment of "production lines" within the bureau
   C. performance personally of a substantial share of all the work
   D. checkup to see that the work has been well done

   1.____

2. Suppose that you have broken a complex job into its smaller components before making assignments to the employees under your jurisdiction.
   Of the following, the LEAST advisable procedure to follow from that point is to
   A. give each employee a picture of the importance of his work for the success of the total job
   B. establish a definite line of work flow and responsibility
   C. post a written memorandum of the best method for performing each job
   D. teach a number of alternative methods for doing each job

   2.____

3. As an administrative officer, you are requested to draw up an organization chart of the whole department.
   Of the following, the MOST important characteristic of such a chart is that it will
   A. include all details of the organization which distinguish it from any other
   B. be a schematic representation of purely administrative functions within the department
   C. present a modification of the actual departmental organization in light of principles of scientific management
   D. present an accurate picture of the lines of authority and responsibility

   3.____

4. Of the following, the MOST important principle in respect to delegation of authority that should guide you in your work as supervisor in charge of a bureau is that you should
   A. delegate as much authority as you effectively can
   B. make certain that all administrative details clear through your desk
   C. have all decisions confirmed by you
   D. discourage the practice of consulting you on matters of basic policy

   4.____

5. Of the following, the LEAST valid criterion to be applied in evaluating the organization of the department in which you are employed as a supervisor is:
   A. Is authority for making decisions centralized?
   B. Is authority for formulating policy centralized?
   C. Is authority granted commensurate with the responsibility involved?
   D. Is each position and its relation to other positions from the standpoint of responsibility clearly defined?

   5.____

6. Functional centralization is the bringing together of employees doing the same kind of work and performing similar tasks.
   Of the following, the one which is NOT an important advantage flowing from the introduction of functional centralization in a large city department is that
   A. inter-bureau communication and traffic are reduced
   B. standardized work procedures are introduced more easily
   C. evaluation of employee performances is facilitated
   D. inequalities in working conditions are reduced

7. As a supervisor, you find that a probationary employee under your supervision is consistently below a reasonable standard of performance for the job he is assigned to do.
   Of the following, the MOST appropriate action for you to take FIRST is to
   A. give him an easier job to do
   B. advise him to transfer to another department
   C. recommend to your superior that he be discouraged at the end of his probationary period
   D. determine whether the cause for his below-standard performance can be readily remedied

8. Certain administrative functions, such as those concerned with budgetary and personnel selection activities, have been delegated to central agencies separated from the operating departments.
   Of the following, the PRINCIPAL reason for such separation is that
   A. a central agency is generally better able to secure funds for performing these functions
   B. decentralization increases executive control
   C. greater economy, efficiency, and uniformity can be obtained by establishing central staff of experts to perform these functions
   D. the problems involved in performing these functions vary significantly from one operating department to another

9. The one of the following which is LEAST valid as a guiding principle for you, in your work as supervisor, in building team spirit and teamwork in your bureau is that you should attempt to
   A. convince the personnel of the bureau that public administration is a worthwhile endeavor
   B. lead every employee to visualize the integration of his own individual function with the program of the whole bureau
   C. develop a favorable public attitude toward the work of the bureau
   D. maintain impartiality by convenient delegation of authority in controversial matters

10. Of the following, the LEAST desirable procedure for the competent supervisor to follow is to
    A. organize his work before taking responsibility for helping others with theirs
    B. avoid schedules and routines when he is busy
    C. be flexible in planning and carrying out his responsibilities
    D. secure the support of his staff in organizing the total job of the unit

11. The responsibility for making judgment about staff members which is inherent in the supervisor's position may arouse hostilities toward the supervisor.
    Of the following, the BEST suggestion to the supervisor for handling this responsibility is for the supervisor to avoid
    A. individual criticism by taking up problems directly through group meetings
    B. any personal feeling or action that would imply that the supervisor has any power over the staff
    C. making critical judgments without accompanying them with reassurance to the staff member concerned

12. To carry out MOST effectively his responsibility for holding to a standard of quantity and quality, the supervisor should
    A. demand much more from himself than he does from his staff
    B. provide a clearly defined statement of what is expected of the staff
    C. teach the staff to assume responsible attitudes
    D. help the staff out when they get into unavoidable difficulties

13. The supervisor should inspire confidence and respect.
    This objective is MOST likely to be attained by the supervisor if he endeavors always to
    A. know the answers to the workers' questions
    B. be fair and just
    C. know what is going on in the office
    D. behave like a supervisor

14. Two chief reasons for the centralization of office functions are to eliminate costly duplication and to bring about greater coordination.
    The MOST direct implication of this statement is that
    A. greater coordination of office work will result in centralization of office functions
    B. where there is no centralization of office functions, there can be no coordination of work
    C. centralization of office functions may reduce duplication of work
    D. decentralization of office functions may be a result of costly duplication

15. The efficient administrative assistant arranges a definite schedule of the regular work of his division, but assigns the occasional and emergency tasks when they arise to the employees available at the time to handle these tasks.
    The management procedure described in this statement is desirable MAINLY because it
    A. relieves the administrative assistant of the responsibility of supervising the work of his staff
    B. enables more of the staff to become experienced in handling different types of problems
    C. enables the administrative assistant to anticipate problems which may arise
    D. provides for consideration of current work load when making special assignments

16. Well-organized training courses for office employees are regarded by most administrators as a fundamental and essential part of a well-balanced personnel program.
Such training of clerical employees results LEAST directly in
    A. providing a reservoir of trained employees who can carry on the duties of other clerks during the absence of these clerks
    B. reducing the individual differences in the innate ability of clerical employees to perform complex duties
    C. bringing about a standardization throughout the department of operational methods found to be highly effective in one of its units
    D. preparing clerical employees for promotion to more responsible positions

17. The average typing speed of a typist is not necessarily a true indication of her efficiency.
Of the following, the BEST justification for this statement is that
    A. the typist may not maintain her maximum typing speed at all times
    B. a rapid typist will ordinarily type more letters than a slow one
    C. a typist's assignments usually include other operations in addition to actual typing
    D. typing speed has no significant relationship to the difficulty of material being typed

18. Although the use of labor-saving machinery and the simplification of procedures tend to decrease unit clerical labor costs, there is, nevertheless, a contrary tendency in the overall cost of office work. This contrary tendency, evidenced by the increase in size of the office staffs, has developed from the increasingly extensive use of systems of analysis and methods of research.
Of the following, the MOST accurate statement on the basis of the above statement is that
    A. the tendency for the overall costs of office work to increase is bringing about a counter-tendency to decrease unit costs of office work
    B. office machines are of little value in reducing the unit costs of the work of offices in which the overall costs are increasing
    C. The increasing use of systems of analysis and methods of research is bringing about a condition which will necessitate a curtailment of the use of these techniques in the office
    D. expanded office functions tend to offset savings resulting from increased efficiency in office management

19. The most successful supervisor wins his victories through preventive rather than through curative action.
The one of the following which is the MOST accurate statement on the basis of this statement is that
    A. success in supervision may be measured more accurately in terms of errors corrected than in terms of errors prevented
    B. anticipating problems makes for better supervision than waiting until these problems arise

5 (#2)

    C. difficulties that cannot be prevented by the supervisor cannot be overcome
    D. the solution of problems in supervision is best achieved by scientific methods

20. Assume that you have been requested to design an office form which is to be duplicated by the mimeograph process.
In planning the layout of the various items appearing on the form, it is LEAST important for you to know the
    A. amount of information which the form is to contain
    B. purpose for which the form will be used
    C. size of the form
    D. number of copies of the form which are required

20.____

21. The supervisor is responsible for the accuracy of the work performed by her subordinates.
Of the following procedures which she might adopt to insure the accurate copying of long reports from rough draft originals, the MOST effective one is to
    A. examine the rough draft for errors in grammar, punctuation, and spelling before assigning it to a typist to copy
    B. glance through each typed report before it leaves her bureau to detect any obvious errors made by the typist
    C. have another employee read the rough draft original to the typist who typed the report, and have the typist make whatever corrections are necessary
    D. rotate assignments involving the typing of long reports equally among all the typists in the unit

21.____

22. The total number of errors made during the month, or other period studied, indicates, in a general way, whether the work has been performed with reasonable accuracy. However, this is not in itself a true measure, but must be considered in relation to the total volume of work produced.
On the basis of this statement, the accuracy of work performed is MOST truly measured by the
    A. total number of errors made during a specified period
    B. comparison of the number of errors made and the quantity of work produced during a specified period
    C. average amount of work produced by the unit during each month or other designated period of time
    D. none of the above answers

22.____

23. In the course of your duties, you receive a letter which, you believe, should be called to the attention of your supervisor.
Of the following, the BEST reason for attaching previous correspondence to this letter before giving it to your supervisor is that
    A. there is less danger, if such a procedure is followed, of misplacing important letters
    B. this letter can probably be better understood in the light of previous correspondence

23.____

C. your supervisor is probably in a better position to understand the letter than you
D. this letter will have to be filed eventually so there is no additional work involved

24. Suppose that you are requested to transmit to the stenographers in your bureau an order curtailing certain privileges that they have been enjoying. You anticipate that your staff may resent curtailment of such privileges.
Of the following, the BEST action for you to take is to
   A. impress upon your staff that an order is an order and must be obeyed
   B. attempt to explain to your staff the probable reasons for curtailing their privileges
   C. excuse the curtailment of privileges by saying that the welfare of the staff was evidently not considered
   D. warn your staff that violation of an order may be considered sufficient cause for immediate dismissal

25. Suppose that a stenographer recently appointed to your bureau submits a memorandum suggesting a change in office procedure that has been tried before and has been found unsuccessful.
Of the following, the BEST action for you to take is to
   A. send the stenographer a note acknowledging receipt of the suggestion, but do not attempt to carry out the suggestion
   B. point out that suggestions should come from her supervisor, who has a better knowledge of the problems of the office
   C. try out the suggested change a second time, lest the stenographer lose interest in her work
   D. call the stenographer in, explain that the change if not practicable, and compliment her for her interest and alertness

26. Suppose that you are assistant to one of the important administrators in your department. You receive a note from the head of department asking your supervisor to assist with a pressing problem that has arisen by making an immediate recommendation. Your supervisor is out of town on official business for a few days and cannot be reached. The head of department, evidently, is not aware of his absence.
Of the following, the BEST action for you to take is to
   A. send the note back to the head of department without comment so as not to incriminate your supervisor
   B. forward the note to one of the administrators in another division of the department
   C. wait until your supervisor returns and bring the note to his attention immediately
   D. get in touch with the head of department immediately and inform him that your supervisor is out of town

27. One of your duties may be to estimate the budget of your unit for the next fiscal year. Suppose that you expect no important changes in the work of your unit during the next year.

Of the following, the MOST appropriate basis for estimating next year's budget is the
- A. average budget of your unit for the last five years
- B. budget of your unit for the current year plus fifty percent to allow for possible expansion
- C. average current budget of units in your department
- D. budget of your unit for the current fiscal year

28. As a supervisor, you should realize that the work of a stenographer ordinarily requires a higher level of intelligence than the work of a typist CHIEFLY because
    - A. the salary range of stenographers is, in most government and business offices, lower than the salary range of typists
    - B. greater accuracy and skill is ordinarily required of a typist
    - C. the stenographer must understand what is being dictated to enable her to write it out in shorthand
    - D. typists are required to do more technical and specialized work

29. Suppose that you are acting as assistant to an important administrator in your department.
    Of the following, the BEST reason for keeping a separate "pending" file of letters to which answers are expected very soon is that
    - A. important correspondence should be placed in a separate, readily accessible file
    - B. a periodic check of the "pending" file will indicate the possible need for follow-up letters
    - C. correspondence is never final, so provision should be made for keeping files open
    - D. there is seldom sufficient room in the permanent files to permit filing all letters

30. For a busy executive in a government department, the services of an assistant are valuable and almost indispensable.
    Of the following, the CHIEF value of an assistant PROBABLY lies in her
    - A. ability to assume responsibility for making major decisions
    - B. familiarity with the general purpose and functions of civil service
    - C. special education
    - D. familiarity with the work and detail involved in the duties of the executive whom she assists

31. The supervisor should set a good example.
    Of the following, the CHIEF implication of the above statement is that the supervisor should
    - A. behave as he expects his workers to behave
    - B. know as much about the worker as his workers do
    - C. keep his workers informed of what he is doing
    - D. keep ahead of his workers

32. Of the following, the LEAST desirable procedure for the competent supervisor to follow is to
    A. organize his work before taking responsibility for helping others with theirs
    B. avoid schedules and routines when he is busy
    C. be flexible in planning and carrying out his responsibilities
    D. secure the support of his staff in organizing the total job of the unit

33. Evaluation helps the worker by increasing his security.
    Of the following, the BEST justification for this statement is that
    A. security and growth depend upon knowledge by the worker of the agency's evaluation
    B. knowledge of his evaluation by agency and supervisor will stimulate the worker to better performance
    C. evaluation enables the supervisor and worker to determine the reasons for the worker's strengths and weaknesses
    D. the supervisor and worker together can usually recognize and deal with any worker's insecurity

34. Systematizing for efficiency means MOST NEARLY
    A. performing an assignment despite all interruptions
    B. leaving difficult assignments until the next day
    C. having a definite time schedule for certain daily duties
    D. trying to do as little work as possible

35. The CHIEF reason for an employee training program is to
    A. increase the efficiency of the employee's work
    B. train the employee for promotion examinations
    C. to meet and talk with each new employee
    D. to give the supervisor an opportunity to reprimand the employee for his lack of knowledge

36. A supervisor may encourage his subordinates to make suggestions by
    A. keeping a record of the number of suggestions an employee makes
    B. providing a suggestion box
    C. outlining a list of possible suggestions
    D. giving credit to a subordinate whose suggestion has been accepted and used

37. The statement that accuracy is of greater importation than speed means MOST NEARLY that
    A. slower work increases employment
    B. fast workers may be inferior workers
    C. there are many varieties of work to do in an office
    D. the slow worker is the most efficient person

38. To print tabular material is always much more expensive than to print straight text.
It follows MOST NEARLY that
    A. the more columns and subdivisions there are in a table, the more expensive is the printing
    B. the omission of the number and title from a table reduces printing costs
    C. it is always desirable to only print straight text
    D. do not print tabular material as it is too expensive

39. If you were required to give service ratings to employees under your supervision, you should consider as MOST important, during the current period, the
    A. personal characteristics and salary and grade of an employee
    B. length of service and the volume of work performed
    C. previous service rating given him
    D. personal characteristics and the quality of work of an employee

40. If a representative committee of employees in a large department is to meet with an administrative officer for the purpose of improving staff relations and of handling grievances, it is BEST that these meetings be held
    A. at regular intervals
    B. whenever requested b an aggrieved employee
    C. whenever the need arises
    D. at the discretion of the administrative officer

41. In order to be best able to teach a newly appointed employee who must learn to do a type of work which is unfamiliar to him, his supervisor should realize that during this first stage in the learning process the subordinate is GENERALLY characterized by
    A. acute consciousness of self
    B. acute consciousness of subject matter, with little interest in persons or personalities
    C. inertness or passive acceptance of assigned role
    D. understanding of problems without understanding of the means of solving them

42. The MOST accurate of the following principles of education and learning for a supervisor to keep in mind when planning a training program for the assistant supervisors under her supervision is that
    A. assistant supervisors, like all other individuals, vary in the rate at which they learn new material and in the degree to which they can retain what they do learn
    B. experienced assistant supervisors who have the same basic college education and agency experience will be able to learn new material at approximately the same rate of speed
    C. the speed with which assistant supervisors can learn new material after the age of forty is half as rapid as at ages twenty to thirty
    D. with regard to any specific task, it is easier and takes less time to break an experienced assistant supervisor of old, unsatisfactory work habits than it is to teach him new, acceptable ones

43. A supervisor has been transferred from supervision of one group of units to another group of units in the same center. She spends the first three weeks in her new assignment in getting acquainted with her new subordinates, their caseload problems and their work. In this process, she notices that some of the cash records and forms which are submitted to her by two of the assistant supervisors are carelessly or improperly prepared.
The BEST of the following actions for the supervisor to take in this situation is to
    A. carefully check the work submitted by these assistant supervisors during an additional three weeks before taking any more positive action
    B. confer with these offending workers and show each one where her work needs improvement and how to go about achieving it
    C. institute an in-service training program specifically designed to solve such a problem and instruct the entire subordinate staff in proper work methods
    D. make a note of these errors for documentary use in preparing the annual service rating reports and advise the workers involved to prepare their work more carefully

43.____

44. A supervisor, who was promoted to this position a year ago, has supervised a certain assistant supervisor for this one year. The work of the assistant supervisor has been very poor because he has done a minimum of work, refused to take sufficient responsibility, been difficult to handle, and required very close supervision. Apparently due to the increasing insistence by his supervisor that he improve the caliber of his work, the assistant supervisor tenders his resignation, stating that the demands of the job are too much for him. The opinion of the previous supervisor, who had supervised this assistant supervisor for two years, agrees substantially with that of the new supervisor.
Under such circumstances, the BEST of the following actions the supervisor can take, in general, is to
    A. recommend that the resignation be accepted and that he be rehired should he later apply when he feels able to do the job
    B. recommend that the resignation be accepted and that he not be rehired should he later so apply
    C. refuse to accept the resignation but try to persuade the assistant supervisor to accept psychiatric help
    D. refuse to accept the resignation, promising the assistant supervisor that he will be less closely supervised in the future since he is now so experienced

44.____

45. Rumors have arisen to the effect that one of the staff investigators under your supervision has been attending classes at a local university during afternoon hours when he is supposed to be making field visits.
The BEST of the following ways for you to approach this problem is to
    A. disregard the rumors since, like most rumors, they probably have no actual foundation in fact
    B. have a discreet investigation made in order to determine the actual facts prior to taking any other action

45.____

C. inform the investigator that you know what he has been doing and that such behavior is overt dereliction of duty and is punishable by dismissal
D. review the investigator's work record, spot check his cases, and take no further action unless the quality of his work is below average for the unit

46. A supervisor must consider many factors in evaluating a worker whom he has supervised for a considerable time.
In evaluating the capacity of such a worker to use independent judgment, the one of the following to which the supervisor should generally give MOST consideration is the worker's
    A. capacity to establish good relationships with people (clients, colleagues)
    B. educational background
    C. emotional stability
    D. the quality and judgment shown by the worker in previous work situations known to the supervisor

46.____

47. A supervisor is conducting a special meeting with the assistant supervisors under her supervision to read and discuss some major complex changes in the rules and procedures. She notices that one of the assistant supervisors who is normally attentive at meetings seems to be paying no attention to what is being said. The supervisor stops reading the rules and asks the assistant supervisor a couple of questions about the changed procedure, to which she gets satisfactory answers.
The BEST action of the following for the supervisor to take at the meeting is to
    A. advise the assistant supervisor gently but firmly that these changes are complex and that her undivided attention is required in order to fully comprehend them
    B. avoid further embarrassment to the assistant supervisor by asking the group as a whole to pay more attention to what is being read
    C. discontinue the questioning and resume reading the procedure
    D. politely request the assistant supervisor to stop giving those present the impression that she is uninterested in what goes on about her

47.____

48. A supervisor becomes aware that one of her very competent experienced workers never takes notes during an interview with a client except to note an occasional name, address, or date. When asked about this practice by the supervisor, the worker states that she has a good memory for important details and has always been able to satisfactorily record an interview after the client has left.
It would generally be BEST for the supervisor to handle this situation by
    A. discussing with her that more extensive note-taking may sometimes be desirable with a client who believes note-taking to be evidence that his problem will receive serious consideration
    B. agreeing with this practice since note-taking interferes with the establishment of a proper worker-client relationship
    C. explaining that, since interviewing is an art form rather than an exact science, a good worker must devise her own personal rules for interviewing and not be bound by general principles

48.____

D. warning the worker that memory is too uncertain a thing to be relied upon and, therefore, notes should be taken during an interview of all matters

49. When an experienced subordinate who has the authority and information necessary to make a decision on a certain difficult matter brings the matter to his supervisor without having made the decision, it would generally be BEST for the supervisor to
    A. agree to make the decision for the subordinate after the subordinate has explained why he finds it difficult to make the decision and after he has made a recommendation
    B. make the decision for the subordinate, explaining to him the reasons for arriving at the decision
    C. refuse to make the decision, but discuss the various alternatives with the subordinate in order to clarify the issues involved
    D. refuse to make the decision, explaining to the subordinate that he is deemed to be fully qualified and competent to make the decision

49._____

50. The one of the following instances when it is MOST important for an upper level supervisor to follow the chain of command is when he is
    A. communicating decisions   B. communicating information
    C. receiving suggestions   D. seeking information

50._____

KEY (CORRECT ANSWERS)

1.	C	11.	D	21.	C	31.	A	41.	A
2.	D	12.	B	22.	B	32.	B	42.	A
3.	D	13.	B	23.	B	33.	C	43.	B
4.	A	14.	C	24.	B	34.	C	44.	B
5.	D	15.	D	25.	D	35.	A	45.	B
6.	A	16.	B	26.	D	36.	D	46.	D
7.	D	17.	C	27.	D	37.	B	47.	C
8.	C	18.	D	28.	C	38.	A	48.	A
9.	D	19.	B	29.	B	39.	D	49.	C
10.	B	20.	D	30.	D	40.	A	50.	A

TEST 3

DIRECTIONS: Each question or incomplete statement is followed by several suggested answers or completions. Select the one that BEST answers the question or completes the statement. *PRINT THE LETTER OF THE CORRECT ANSWER IN THE SPACE AT THE RIGHT.*

1. Experts in the field of personnel relations feel that it is generally bad practice for subordinate employees to become aware of pending or contemplated changes in policy or organizational set-up via the "grapevine" CHIEFLY because
   A. evidence that one or more responsible officials have proved untrustworthy will undermine confidence in the agency
   B. the information disseminated by this method is seldom entirely accurate and generally spreads needless unrest among the subordinate staff
   C. the subordinate staff may conclude that the administration feels the staff cannot be trusted with the true information
   D. the subordinate staff may conclude that the administration lacks the courage to make an unpopular announcement through officials channels

1.____

2. In order to maintain a proper relationship with a worker who is assigned to staff rather than line functions, a line supervisor should
   A. accept all recommendations of the staff worker
   B. include the staff worker in the conferences called by the supervisor for his subordinates
   C. keep the staff worker informed of developments in the area of his staff assignment
   D. require that the staff worker's recommendations be communicated to the supervisor through the supervisor's own superior

2.____

3. Of the following, the GREATEST disadvantage of placing a worker in a staff position under the direct supervision of the supervisor whom he advises is the possibility that the
   A. staff worker will tend to be insubordinate because of a feeling of superiority over the supervisor
   B. staff worker will tend to give advice of the type which the supervisor wants to hear or finds acceptable
   C. supervisor will tend to be mistrustful of the advice of a worker of subordinate rank
   D. supervisor will tend to derive little benefit from the advice because to supervise properly he should know at least as much as his subordinate

3.____

4. One factor which might be given consideration in deciding upon the optimum span of control of a supervisor over his immediate subordinates is the position of the supervisor in the hierarchy of the organization. It is generally considered proper that the number of subordinates immediately supervised by a higher, upper echelon, supervisor
   A. is unrelated to and tends to form no pattern with the number supervised by lower level supervisors
   B. should be about the same as the number supervised by a lower level supervisor

4.____

25

C. should be larger than the number supervised by a lower level supervisor
D. should be smaller than the number supervised by a lower level supervisor

5. An important administrative problem is how precisely to define the limits on authority that is delegated to subordinate supervisors.
Such definition of limits of authority should be
   A. as precise as possible and practicable in all areas
   B. as precise as possible and practicable in areas of function, but should allow considerable flexibility in the area of personnel management
   C. as precise as possible and practicable in the area of personnel management, but should allow considerable flexibility in the areas of function
   D. in general terms so as to allow considerable flexibility both in the areas of function and in the areas of personnel management

6. The LEAST important of the following reasons why a particular activity should be assigned to a unit which performs activities dissimilar to it is that
   A. close coordination is needed between the particular activity and other activities performed by the unit
   B. it will enhance the reputation and prestige of the unit supervisor
   C. the unit makes frequent use of the results of this particular activity
   D. the unit supervisor has a sound knowledge and understanding of the particular activity

7. A supervisor is put in charge of a special unit. She is exceptionally well-qualified for this assignment by her training and experience. One of her very close personal friends has been working for some time as a field investigator in this unit. Both the supervisor and investigator are certain that the rest of the investigators in the unit, many of whom have been in the bureau for a long time, know of this close relationship.
Under these circumstances, the MOST advisable action for the supervisor to take is to
   A. ask that either she be allowed to return to her old assignment, or, if that cannot be arranged, that her friend be transferred to another unit in the center
   B. avoid any overt sign of favoritism by acting impartially and with greater reserve when dealing with this investigator than the rest of the staff
   C. discontinue any socializing with this investigator either inside or outside the office so as to eliminate any gossip or dissatisfaction
   D. talk the situation over with the other investigators and arrive at a mutually acceptable plan of proper office decorum

8. The one of the following causes of clerical error which is usually considered to be LEAST attributable to faulty supervision or inefficient management is
   A. inability to carry out instructions
   B. too much work to do
   C. an inappropriate record-keeping system
   D. continual interruptions

9. Assume that you are the supervisor of a clerical unit in a government agency. One of your subordinates violates a rule of the agency, a violation which requires that the employee be suspended from his work for one day. The violated rule is one that you have found to be unduly strict and you have recommended to the management of the agency that the rule be changed or abolished. The management has been considering your recommendation but has not yet reached a decision on the matter.
   In these circumstances, you should
   A. not initiate disciplinary action, but, instead explain to the employee that the rule may be changed shortly
   B. delay disciplinary action on the violation until the management has reached a decision on changing the rule
   C. modify the disciplinary action by reprimanding the employee and informing him that further action may be taken when the management has reached a decision on changing the rule
   D. initiate the prescribed disciplinary action without commenting on the strictness of the rule or on your recommendation

10. Assume that a supervisor praises his subordinates for satisfactory aspects of their work only when he is about to criticize them for unsatisfactory aspects of their work.
    Such a practice is undesirable PRIMARILY because
    A. his subordinates may expect to be praised for their work even if it is unsatisfactory
    B. praising his subordinates for some aspects of their work while criticizing other aspects will weaken the effects of the criticisms
    C. his subordinates would be more receptive to criticism if it were followed by praise
    D. his subordinates may come to disregard praise and wait for criticism to be given

11. The one of the following which would be the BEST reason for an agency to eliminate a procedure for obtaining and recording certain information is that
    A. it is no longer legally required to obtain the information
    B. there is an advantage in obtaining the information
    C. the information could be compiled on the basis of other information available
    D. the information obtained is sometimes incorrect

12. In determining the type and number of records to be kept in an agency, it is important to recognize that records are of value PRIMARILY as
    A. raw material to be used in statistical analysis
    B. sources of information about the agency's activities
    C. by-products of the activities carried on by the agency
    D. data for evaluating the effectiveness of the agency

Questions 13-17.

DIRECTIONS: Each of Questions 13 through 17 consists of a statement which contains one word that is incorrectly used because it is not in keeping with the meaning that the statement is evidently intended to convey. For each of these questions, you are to select the incorrectly used word and substitute for it one of the words lettered A, B, C, or D, which helps BEST to convey the meaning of the statement.

13. There has developed in recent years an increasing awareness of the need to measure the quality of management in all enterprises and to seek the principles that can serve as a basis for this improvement.
    A. growth   B. raise   C. efficiency   D. define

14. It is hardly an exaggeration to deny that the permanence, productivity, and humanity of any industrial system depend upon its ability to utilize the positive and constructive impulses of all who work and upon its ability to arouse and continue interest in the necessary activities.
    A. develop   B. efficiency   C. state   D. inspiration

15. The selection of managers on the basis of technical knowledge alone seems to recognize that the essential characteristic of management is getting things done through others, thereby demanding skills that are essential in coordinating the activities of subordinates.
    A. training   B. fails
    C. organization   D. improving

16. Only when it is deliberate and when it is clearly understood what impressions the ease of communication will probably create in the minds of employees and subordinate management, should top management refrain from commenting on a subject that is of general concern.
    A. obvious   B. benefit   C. doubt   D. absence

17. Scientific planning of work requires careful analysis of facts and a precise plan of action for the whims and fancies of executives that often provide only a vague indication of work to be done.
    A. substitutes   B. development
    C. preliminary   D. comprehensive

18. Assume that you are a supervisor. One of the workers under your supervision is careless about the routine aspects of his work.
    Of the following, the action MOST likely to develop in this worker a better attitude toward job routines is to demonstrate that
    A. it is just as easy to do his job the right way
    B. organization of his job will leave more time for field work
    C. the routine part of the job is essential to performing a good piece of work
    D. job routines are a responsibility of the worker

19. A supervisor can MOST effectively secure necessary improvement in a worker's office work by
    A. encouraging the worker to keep abreast of his work
    B. relating the routine part of his job to the total job to be done
    C. helping the worker to establish a good system for covering his office work and holding him to it
    D. informing the worker that he will be required to organize his work more efficiently

20. A supervisor should offer criticism in such a manner that the criticisms is helpful and not overwhelming.
    Of the following, the LEAST valid inference that can be drawn on the basis of the above statement is that a supervisor should
    A. demonstrate that the criticism is partial and not total
    B. give criticism in such a way that it does not undermine the worker's self-confidence
    C. keep his relationships with the worker objective
    D. keep criticism directed towards general work performance

21. The one of the following areas in which a worker may LEAST reasonably expect direct assistance from the supervisor is in
    A. building up rapport with all clients
    B. gaining insight into the unmet needs of clients
    C. developing an understanding of community resources
    D. interpreting agency policies and procedures

22. You are informed that a worker under your supervision has submitted a letter complaining of unfair service rating.
    Of the following, the MOST valid assumption for you to make concerning this worker is that he should be
    A. more adequately supervised in the future
    B. called in for a supervisory conference
    C. given a transfer to some other unit where he may be more happy
    D. given no more consideration than any other inefficient worker

23. Assume that you are a supervisor. You find that a somewhat bewildered worker, newly appointed to the department, hesitates to ask questions for fear of showing his ignorance and jeopardizing his position.
    Of the following, the BEST procedure for you to follow is to
    A. try to discover the reason for his evident fear of authority
    B. tell him that when he is in doubt about a procedure or a policy he should consult his fellow workers
    C. develop with the worker a plan for more frequent supervisory conferences
    D. explain why each staff member is eager to give him available information that will help him do a good job

24. Of the following, the MOST effective method of helping a newly-appointed employee adjust to his new job is to
    A. assure him that with experience his uncertain attitudes will be replaced by a professional approach
    B. help him, by accepting him as he is, to have confidence in his ability to handle the job
    C. help him to be on guard against the development of punitive attitudes
    D. help him to recognize the mutability of the agency's policies and procedures

25. Suppose that, as a supervisor, you have scheduled an individual conference with an experienced employee under your supervision.
    Of the following, the BEST plan of action for this conference is to
    A. discuss the work that the employee is most interested in
    B. plan with the employee to cover any problems that are difficult for him
    C. advise the employee that the conference is his to do with as he sees fit
    D. spot check the employee's work in advance and select those areas for discussion in which the employee has done poor work

26. Of the following, the CHIEF function of a supervisor should be to
    A. assist in the planning of new policies and the evaluation of existing ones
    B. promote congenial relationships among members of the staff
    C. achieve optimum functioning of each unit and each worker
    D. promote the smooth functioning of job routines

27. The competent supervisor must realize the importance of planning.
    Of the following, the aspect of planning which is LEAST appropriately considered a responsibility of the supervisor is
    A. long-range planning for the proper functioning of his unit
    B. planning to take care of peak and slack periods
    C. planning to cover agency policies in group conferences
    D. long-range planning to develop community resources

28. The one of the following objectives which should be of LEAST concern to the supervisor in the performance of his duties is to
    A. help the worker to make friends with all of his fellow employees
    B. be impartial and fair to all members of the staff
    C. stimulate the worker's growth on the job
    D. meet the needs of the individual employee

29. The one of the following which is LEAST properly considered a direct responsibility of the supervisor is
    A. liaison between the staff and the administrator
    B. interpreting administrative orders and procedures to the employees
    C. training new employees
    D. maintaining staff morale at a high level

30. In order to teach the employee to develop an objective approach, the BEST action for the supervisor to take is to help the worker to
    A. develop a sincere interest in his job
    B. understand the varied responsibilities that are an integral part of his job
    C. differentiate clearly between himself as a friend and as an employee
    D. find satisfaction in his work

31. If the employee shows excessive submission which indicates a need for dependence on the supervisor in handling an assignment, it would be MOST advisable for the supervisor to
    A. indicate firmly that the employee-supervisor relationship does not call for submission
    B. define areas of responsibility of employee and supervisor
    C. recognize the employee's need and of supervisor
    D. recognize the employee's need to be sustained and supported and help him by making decisions for him

32. Assume that, as a supervisor, you are conducting a group conference.
    Of the following, the BEST procedure for you to follow in order to stimulate group discussion is to
    A. permit the active participation of all members
    B. direct the discussion to an acceptable conclusion
    C. resolve conflicts of opinion among members of the group
    D. present a question for discussion on which the group members have some knowledge or experience

33. Suppose that, as a new supervisor, you wish to inform the staff under your supervision of your methods of operation.
    Of the following, the BEST procedure for you to follow is to
    A. advise the staff that they will learn gradually from experience
    B. inform each employee in an individual conference
    C. call a group conference for this purpose
    D. distribute a written memorandum among all members of the staff

34. The MOST constructive and effective method of correcting an employee who has made a mistake is, in general, to
    A. explain that his evaluation is related to his errors
    B. point out immediately where he erred and tell him how it should have been done
    C. show him how to readjust his methods so as to avoid similar errors in the future
    D. try to discover by an indirect method why the error was made

35. The MOST effective method for the supervisor to follow in order to obtain the cooperation of an employee under his supervision is, wherever possible, to
    A. maintain a careful record of performance in order to keep the employee on his toes
    B. give the employee recognition in order to promote greater effort and give him more satisfaction in his work

C. try to gain the employee's cooperation for the good of the service
D. advise the employee that his advancement on the job depends on his cooperation

36. Of the following, the MOST appropriate initial course for an employee to take when he is unable to clarify a policy with his supervisor is to
    A. bring up the problem at the next group conference
    B. discuss the policy immediately with his fellow employees
    C. accept the supervisor's interpretation as final
    D. determine what responsibility he has for putting the policy into effect

37. Good administration allows for different treatment of different workers.
Of the following, the CHIEF implication of this statement is that
    A. it would be unfair for the supervisor not to treat all staff members alike
    B. fear of favoritism tends to undermine staff morale
    C. best results are obtained by individualization within the limits of fair treatment
    D. difficult problems call for a different kind of approach

38. The MOST effective and appropriate method of building efficiency and morale in a group of employees is, in general,
    A. by stressing the economic motive
    B. through use of the authority inherent in the position
    C. by a friendly approach to all
    D. by a discipline that is fair but strict

39. Of the following, the LEAST valid basis for the assignment of work to an employee is the
    A. kind of service to be rendered
    B. experience and training of the employee
    C. health and capacity of the employee
    D. racial composition of the community where the office is located

40. The CHIEF justification for staff education, consisting of in-service training, lies in its contribution to
    A. improvement in the quality of work performed
    B. recruitment of a better type of employee
    C. employee morale, accruing from a feeling of growth on the job
    D. the satisfaction that the employee gets on his job

41. Suppose that you are a supervisor. An employee no longer with your department requests you, as his former supervisor, to write a letter recommending him for a position with a private organization.
Of the following the BEST procedure for you to follow is to include in the letter only information that
    A. will help the applicant get the job
    B. is clear, factual, and substantiated
    C. is known to you personally
    D. can readily be corroborated by personal interview

42. Of the following, the MOST important item on which to base the efficiency evaluation of an employee under your supervision is
    A. the nature of the relationship that he has built up with his fellow employees
    B. how he gets along with his supervisors
    C. his personal habits and skills
    D. the effectiveness of his control over his work

43. According to generally accepted personnel practice, the MOST effective method of building morale in a new employee is to
    A. exercise caution in praising the employee, lest he become overconfident
    B. give sincere and frank recommendation whenever possible in order to stimulate interest and effort
    C. praise the employee highly even for mediocre performance so that he will be stimulated to do better
    D. warn the employee frequently that he cannot hope to succeed unless he puts forth his best efforts

44. Errors made by newly-appointed employees often follow a predictable pattern. The one of the following errors likely to have LEAST serious consequences is the tendency of a new employee to
    A. discuss problems that are outside his province with the client
    B. persuade the client to accept the worker's solution of a problem
    C. be two strict in carrying out departmental policy and procedure
    D. depend upon the use of authority due to his inexperience and lack of skill in working with people

45. The MOST effective way for a supervisor to break down a worker's defensive stand against supervisory guidance is to
    A. come to an understanding with him on the mutual responsibilities involved in the job of the employee and that of the supervisor
    B. tell him he must feel free to express his opinions and to discuss basic problems
    C. show him how to develop toward greater objectivity, sensitivity, and understanding
    D. advise him that it is necessary to carry out agency policy and procedures in order to do a good job

46. Of the following, the LEAST essential function of the supervisor who is conducting a group conference should be to
    A. keep attention focused on the purpose of the conference
    B. encourage discussion of controversial points
    C. make certain that all possible viewpoints are discussed
    D. be thoroughly prepared in advance

47. When conducting a group conference, the supervisor should be LEAST concerned with
    A. providing an opportunity for the free interchange of ideas
    B. imparting knowledge and understanding of the work

C. leading the discussion toward a planned goal
D. pointing out where individual workers have erred in work practice

48. If the participants in a group conference are unable to agree on the proper application of a concept to the work of a department, the MOST suitable temporary procedure for the supervisor to follow is to
    A. suggest that each member think the subject through before the next meeting
    B. tell the group to examine their differences for possible conflicts with present policies
    C. suggest that practices can be changed because of new conditions
    D. state the acceptable practice in the agency and whether deviations from such practice can be permitted

49. If an employee is to participate constructively in any group discussion, it is MOST important that he have
    A. advance notice of the agenda for the meeting
    B. long experience in the department
    C. knowledge and experience in the particular work
    D. the ability to assume a leadership role

50. Of the following, the MOST important principle for the supervisor to follow when conducting a group discussion is that he should
    A. move the discussion toward acceptance by the group of a particular point of view
    B. express his ideas clearly and succinctly
    C. lead the group to accept the authority inherent in his position
    D. contribute to the discussion from his knowledge and experience

KEY (CORRECT ANSWERS)

1.	B	11.	C	21.	A	31.	B	41.	B
2.	C	12.	B	22.	B	32.	D	42.	D
3.	B	13.	B	23.	C	33.	C	43.	B
4.	D	14.	C	24.	B	34.	C	44.	C
5.	A	15.	B	25.	B	35.	B	45.	A
6.	B	16.	D	26.	C	36.	D	46.	B
7.	A	17.	A	27.	D	37.	C	47.	D
8.	A	18.	D	28.	A	38.	D	48.	D
9.	D	19.	B	29.	A	39.	D	49.	A
10.	D	20.	D	30.	C	40.	A	50.	D

EXAMINATION SECTION
TEST 1

DIRECTIONS: Each question or incomplete statement is followed by several suggested answers or completions. Select the one that BEST answers the question or completes the statement. *PRINT THE LETTER OF THE CORRECT ANSWER IN THE SPACE AT THE RIGHT.*

1. A supervisor notices that one of his more competent subordinates has recently been showing less interest in his work. The work performed by this employee has also fallen off and he seems to want to do no more than the minimum acceptable amount of work. When his supervisor questions the subordinate about his decreased interest and his mediocre work performance, the subordinate replies: *Sure, I've lost interest in my work. I don' see any reason why I should do more than I have to. When I do a good job, nobody notices it. But, let me fall down on one minor job and the whole place knows about it! So why should I put myself out on this job?*
    If the subordinate's contentions are true, it would be correct to assume that the
    A. subordinate has not received adequate training
    B. subordinate's workload should be decreased
    C. supervisor must share responsibility for this employee's reaction
    D. supervisor has not been properly enforcing work standards

1._____

2. How many subordinates should report directly to each supervisor? While there is agreement that there are limits to the number of subordinates that a manager can supervise well, this limit is determined by a number of important factors. Which of the following factors is MOST likely to increase the number of subordinates that can be effectively supervised by one supervisor in a particular unit?
    A. The unit has a great variety of activities.
    B. A staff assistant handles the supervisor's routine duties.
    C. The unit has a relatively inexperienced staff.
    D. The office layout is being rearranged to make room for more employees.

2._____

3. Mary Smith, an Administrative Assistant, heads the Inspection Records Unit of Department Y. She is a dedicated supervisor who not only strives to maintain an efficient operation, but she also tries to improve the competence of each individual member of her staff. She keeps these considerations in mind when assigning work to her staff. Her bureau chief asks her to compile some data based on information contained in her records. She feels that any member of her staff should be able to do this job.
    The one of the following members of her staff who would probably be given LEAST consideration for this assignment is
    A. Jane Abel, a capable Supervising Clerk with considerable experience in the unit
    B. Kenneth Brown, a Senior Clerk recently transferred to the unit who has not had an opportunity to demonstrate his capabilities

3._____

C. Laura Chance, a Clerk who spends full time on a single routine assignment
D. Michael Dunn, a Clerk who works on several minor jobs but still has the lightest workload

4. There are very few aspects of a supervisor's job that do not involve communication, either in writing or orally.
Which of the following statements regarding oral and written orders is NOT correct?
   A. Oral orders usually permit more immediate feedback than do written orders.
   B. Written orders, rather than oral orders, should generally be given when the subordinate will be held strictly accountable.
   C. Oral orders are usually preferable when the order contains lengthy detailed instructions.
   D. Written orders, rather than oral orders, should usually be given to a subordinate who is slow to understand or is forgetful.

5. Assume that you are the head of a large clerical unit in Department R. Your department's personnel office has appointed a Clerk, Roberta Rowe, to fill a vacancy in your unit. Before bringing this appointee to your office, the personnel office has given Roberta the standard orientation on salary, fringe benefits, working conditions, attendance, and the department's personnel rules. In addition, he has supplied her with literature covering these areas.
Of the following, the action that you should take FIRST after Roberta has been brought to your office is to
   A. give her an opportunity to read the literature furnished by the personnel office so that she can ask you questions about it
   B. escort her to the desk she will use and assign her to work with an experienced employee who will act as her trainer
   C. explain the duties and responsibilities of her job and its relationship with the jobs being performed by the other employees of the unit
   D. summon the employee who is currently doing the work that will be performed by Roberta and have him explain and demonstrate how to perform the required tasks

6. Your superior informs you that the employee turnover rate in your office is well above the norm and must be reduced.
Which one of the following initial steps would be LEAST appropriate in attempting to overcome this problem?
   A. Decide to be more lenient about performance standards and about employee requests for time off, so that your office will gain a reputation as an easy place to work
   B. Discuss the problem with a few of your key people whose judgment you trust to see if they can shed some light on the underlying causes of the problem

C. Review the records of employees who have left during the past year to see if there is a pattern that will help you understand the problem
D. Carefully review your training procedures to see whether they can be improved

7. In issuing instructions to a subordinate on a job assignment, the supervisor should ordinarily explain why the assignment is being made.
Omission of such an explanation is BEST justified when the

7._____

A. subordinate is restricted in the amount of discretion he can exercise in carrying out the assignment
B. assignment is one that will be unpopular with the subordinate
C. subordinate understands the reason as a result of previous similar assignments
D. assignment is given to an employee who is in need of further training

8. When a supervisor allows sufficient time for training and makes an appropriate effort in the training of his subordinates, his CHIEF goal is to

8._____

A. increase the dependence of one subordinate upon another in their everyday work activities
B. spend more time with his subordinates in order to become more involved in their work
C. increase the capability and independence of his subordinates in carrying out their work
D. increase his frequency of contact with his subordinates in order to better evaluate their performance

9. In preparing an evaluation of a subordinate's performance, which one of the following items is usually irrelevant?

9._____

A. Remarks about tardiness or absenteeism
B. Mention of any unusual contributions or accomplishments
C. A summary of the employee's previous job experience
D. An assessment of the employee's attitude toward the job

10. The ability to delegate responsibility while maintaining adequate controls is one key to a supervisor's success.
Which one of the following methods of control would minimize the amount of responsibility assumed by the subordinate?

10._____

A. Asking for a monthly status report in writing
B. Asking to receive copies of important correspondence so that you can be aware of potential problems
C. Scheduling periodic project status conferences with your subordinate
D. Requiring that your subordinate confer with you before making decisions on a project

11. You wish to assign an important project to a subordinate who you think has good potential.
    Which one of the following approaches would be MOST effective in successfully completing the project while developing the subordinate's abilities?
    A. Describe the project to the subordinate in general terms and emphasize that it must be completed as quickly as possible
    B. Outline the project in detail to the subordinate and emphasize that its successful completion could lead to career advancement
    C. Develop a detailed project outline and timetable, discuss the details and timing with him and assign the subordinate to carry out the plan on his own
    D. Discuss the project objectives and suggested approaches with the subordinate, and ask the subordinate to develop a detailed project outline and timetable of your approval

12. Research studies reveal that an important difference between high-production and low-production supervisors lies not in their interest in eliminating mistakes, but in their manner of handling mistakes.
    High-production supervisors are MOST likely to look upon mistakes as primarily
    A. an opportunity to provide training
    B. a byproduct of subordinate negligence
    C. an opportunity to fix blame in a situation
    D. a result of their own incompetence

13. Supervisors should try to establish what has been called *positive discipline*, an atmosphere in which subordinates willingly abide by rules which they consider fair.
    When a supervisor notices a subordinate violating an important rule, his FIRST course of action should be to
    A. stop the subordinate and tell him what he is doing wrong
    B. wait a day or two before approaching the employee involved
    C. call a meeting of all subordinates to discuss the rule
    D. forget the matter in the hope that it will not happen again

14. The working climate is the feeling, degree of freedom, the tone and the mood of the working environment.
    Which of the following contributes MOST to determining the working climate in a unit or group?
    A. The rules set for rest periods
    B. The example set by the supervisor
    C. The rules set for morning check-in
    D. The wages paid to the employee

15. John Polk is a bright, ingenious clerk with a lot of initiative. He has made many good suggestions to his supervisor in the Training Division of Department T, where he is employed. However, last week one of his bright ideas literally *blew up*. In setting up some electronic equipment in the training classroom, he cross some wires resulting in a damaged tape recorder and a classroom so filled with smoke that the training class had to be held in another room. When Mr. Brown, his supervisor, learned of this occurrence, he immediately summoned John to his private office. There Mr. Brown spent five minutes bawling John out, calling him an overzealous, overgrown kid, and send him back to his job without letting John speak once.
Of the following, the action of Mr. Brown that MOST deserves approval is that he
    A. took disciplinary action immediately without regard for past performance
    B. kept the disciplinary interview to a brief period
    C. concentrated his criticism on the root cause of the occurrence
    D. held the disciplinary interview in his private office

16. Typically, when the technique of *supervision by results* is practiced, higher management sets down, either implicitly or explicitly, certain performance standards or goals that the subordinate is expected to meet. So long as these standards are met, management interferes very little.
The MOST likely result of the use of this technique is that it will
    A. lead to ambiguity in terms of goals
    B. be successful only to the extent that close direct supervision is practiced
    C. make it possible to evaluate both employee and supervisory effectiveness
    D. allow for complete autonomy on the subordinate's part

17. Assume that you, an Administrative Assistant, are the supervisor of a large clerical unit performing routine clerical operations. One of your clerks consistently produces much less work than other members of our staff performing similar tasks.
Of the following, the action you should take FIRST is to
    A. ask the clerk if he wants to be transferred to another unit
    B. reprimand the clerk for his poor performance and warn him that further disciplinary action will be taken if his work does not improve
    C. quietly ask the clerk's co-workers whether they know why his performance is poor
    D. discuss this matter with the clerk to work out plans for improving his performance

18. When making written evaluations and reviews of the performance of subordinates, it is usually ADVISABLE to
    A. avoid informing the employee of the evaluation if it is critical because it may create hard feelings
    B. avoid informing the employee of the evaluation whether critical or favorable because it is tension-producing

C. permit the employee to see the evaluation but not to discuss it with him because the supervisor cannot be certain where the discussion might lead
D. discuss the evaluation openly with the employee because it helps the employee understand what is expected of him

19. There are a number of well-known and respected human relations principles that successful supervisors have been using for years in building good relationships with their employees.
Which of the following does NOT illustrate such a principle?
    A. Give clear and complete instructions
    B. Let each person know how he is getting along
    C. Keep an open-door policy
    D. Make all relationships personal ones

19.____

20. Assume that it is your responsibility as an Administrative Assistant to maintain certain personnel records that are continually being updated. You have three senior clerks assigned specifically to this task. Recently, you have noticed that the volume of work has increased substantially, and the processing of personnel records by the clerks is backlogged. Your supervisor is now receiving complaints due to the processing delay.
Of the following, the BEST course of action for you to take FIRST is to
    A. have a meeting with the clerks, advise them of the problem, and ask that they do their work faster; then confirm your meeting in writing for the record
    B. request that an additional position be authorized for your unit
    C. review the procedures being used for processing the work, and try to determine if you can improve the flow of work
    D. get the system moving faster by spending some of your own time processing the backlog

20.____

21. Assume that you are in charge of a payroll unit consisting of four clerks. It is Friday, November 14. You have just arrived in the office after a conference. Your staff is preparing a payroll that must be forwarded the following Monday. Which of the following new items on your desk should you attend to FIRST?
    A. A telephone message regarding very important information needed for the statistical summary of salaries paid for the month of November
    B. A memorandum regarding a new procedure that should be followed in preparing the payroll
    C. A telephone message from an employee who is threatening to endorse his paycheck *Under Protest* because he is dissatisfied with the amount
    D. A memorandum from your supervisor reminding you to submit the probationary period report on a new employee

21.____

22. You are an Administrative Assistant in charge of a unit that orders and issues supplies. On a particular day you are faced with the following four situations. Which one should you take care of FIRST?

22.____

A. One of your employees who is in the process of taking the quarterly inventory of supplies has telephoned and asked that you return his call as soon as possible
B. A representative of a company that is noted for producing excellent office supplies will soon arrive with samples for you to distribute to the various offices in your agency
C. A large order of supplies which was delivered this morning has been checked and counted and a deliveryman is waiting for you to sign the receipt
D. A clerk from the purchase division asks you to search for a bill you failed to send to them which is urgently needed in order for them to complete a report due this morning

23. As an Administrative Assistant, assume that it is necessary for you to give an unpleasant assignment to one of your subordinates. You expect this employee to raise some objections to this assignment.
The MOST appropriate of the following actions for you to take FIRST is to issue the assignment
    A. orally, with the further statement that you will not listen to any complaints
    B. in writing, to forestall any complaints by the employee
    C. orally, permitting the employee to express his feelings
    D. in writing, with a note that any comments should be submitted in writing

24. Assume that you are an Administrative Assistant supervising the Duplicating and Reproduction Unit of Department B. One of your responsibilities is to prepare a daily schedule showing when and on which of your unit's four duplicating machine jobs are to be run off.
Of the following, the factor that should be given LEAST consideration in preparing the schedule is the
    A. priority of each of the jobs to be run off
    B. production speed of the different machines that will be used
    C. staff available to operate the machines
    D. date on which the job order was received

25. Cycling is an arrangement where papers are processed throughout a period according to an orderly plan rather than as a group all at one time. This technique has been used for a long time by public utilities in their cycle billing.
Of the following practices, the one that BEST illustrates this technique is that in which
    A. paychecks for per annum employees are issued bi-weekly and those for per diem employees are issued weekly
    B. field inspectors report in person to their offices one day a week, on Fridays, when they do all their paperwork and also pick up their paychecks
    C. the dates for issuing relief checks to clients vary depending on the last digit of the clients' social security numbers
    D. the last day for filing and paying income taxes is the same for Federal, State, and City income taxes

26. The employees in your division have recently been given an excellent up-to-date office manual, but you find that a good number of employees are not following the procedures outlined in it.
    Which one of the following would be MOST likely to ensure that employees begin using the manual effectively?
    A. Require each employee to keep a copy of the manual in plain sight on his desk
    B. Issue warnings periodically to those employees who deviate most from procedures prescribed in the manual
    C. Tell an employee to check his manual when he does not follow the proper procedures
    D. Suggest to the employees that the manual be studied thoroughly

27. The one of the following factors which should be considered FIRST in the design of office forms is the
    A. information to be included in the form
    B. sequence of the information
    C. purpose of the form
    D. persons who will be using the form

28. Window envelopes are being used to an increasing extent by government and private industry.
    The one of the following that is NOT an advantage of window envelopes is that they
    A. cut down on addressing costs
    B. eliminate the need to attach envelopes to letters being sent forward for signature by a superior
    C. are less costly to buy than regular envelopes

29. Your bureau head asks you to prepare the office layouts for several of his units being moved to a higher floor in your office building.
    Of the following possibilities, the one that you should AVOID in preparing the layouts is to
    A. place the desks of the first-line supervisors near those of the staffs they supervise
    B. place the desks of employees whose work is most closely related near one another
    C. arrange the desks so that employees do not face one another
    D. locate desks with many outside visitors farthest from the office entrance

30. Which one of the following conditions would be LEAST important in considering a change of the layout in a particular office?
    A. Installation of a new office machine
    B. Assignment of five additional employees to your office
    C. Poor flow of work
    D. Employees' personal preferences of desk location

31. Suppose Mr. Bloom, an Administrative Assistant, is dictating a letter to a stenographer. His dictation begins with the name of the addressee and continues to the body of the letter. However, Mr. Bloom does not dictate the address of the recipient of the letter. He expects the stenographer to locate it. The use of this practice by Mr. Bloom is
    A. *acceptable*, especially if he gives the stenographer the letter to which he is responding
    B. *acceptable*, especially if the letter is lengthy and detailed
    C. *unacceptable*, because it is not part of a stenographer's duties to search for information
    D. *unacceptable*, because he should not rely on the accuracy of the stenographer

32. Assume that there are no rules, directives or instructions concerning the filing of materials in your office or the retention of such files. A system is now being followed of placing in inactive files any materials that are more than one year old.
    Of the following, the MOST appropriate thing to do with material that has been in an inactive file in your office for more than one year is to
    A. inspect the contents of the files to decide how to dispose of them
    B. transfer the material to a remote location, where it can be obtained if necessary
    C. keep the material intact for a minimum of another three years
    D. destroy the material which has not been needed for at least a year

33. Suppose you, an Administrative Assistant, have just returned to your desk after engaging in an all-morning conference. Joe Burns, a Clerk, informs you that Clara McClough, an administrator in another agency, telephoned during the morning and that, although she requested to speak with you, he was able to give her the desired information.
    Of the following, the MOST appropriate action for you to take in regard to Mr. Burns' action is to
    A. thank him for assisting Ms. McClough in your absence
    B. explain to him the proper telephone practice to use in the future
    C. reprimand him for not properly channeling Ms. McClough's call
    D. issue a memo to all clerical employees regarding proper telephone practices

34. When interviewing subordinates with problems, supervisors frequently find that asking direct questions of the employee results only in evasive responses. The supervisor may, therefore, resort to the non-directive interview technique. In this technique, the supervisor avoids pointed questions; he leads the employee to continue talking freely uninfluenced by the supervisor's preconceived notions. This technique often enables the employee to bring his problem into sharp focus and to reach a solution to his problem. Suppose that you are a supervisor interviewing a subordinate about his recent poor attendance record.

On calling his attention to his excessive lateness record, he replies: *I just don't seem to be able to get up in the morning. Frankly, I've lost interest in this job. don't care about it. When I get up in the morning, I have to skip breakfast and I'm still late. I don't care about this job.*
If you are using the non-directive technique in this interview, the MOST appropriate of the following responses for you to make is
- A. You don't care about this job?
- B. Don't you think you are letting your department down?
- C. Are you having trouble at home?
- D. Don't you realize your actions are childish?

35. An employee in a work group made the following comment to a co-worker: *It's great to be a lowly employee instead of an Administrative Assistant because you can work without thinking. The Administrative Assistant is getting paid to plan, schedule, and think. Let him see to it that you have a productive day.*
Which one of the following statements about his quotation BEST reflects an understanding of good personnel management techniques and the role of the supervising Administrative Assistant?
- A. The employee is wrong in attitude and in his perception of the role of the Administrative Assistant.
- B. The employee is correct in attitude but is wrong in his perception of the role of the Administrative Assistant.
- C. The employee is correct in attitude and in his perception of the role of the Administrative Assistant.
- D. The employee is wrong in attitude but is right in his perception of the role of the Administrative Assistant.

KEY (CORRECT ANSWERS)

1.	C	11.	D	21.	B	31.	A
2.	B	12.	A	22.	C	32.	A/B
3.	A	13.	A	23.	C	33.	A
4.	C	14.	B	24.	D	34.	A
5.	C	15.	D	25.	C	35.	D
6.	A	16.	C/D	26.	C		
7.	C	17.	D	27.	C		
8.	C	18.	D	28.	C		
9.	C	19.	D	29.	D		
10.	D	20.	C	30.	D		

TEST 2

DIRECTIONS: Each question or incomplete statement is followed by several suggested answers or completions. Select the one that BEST answers the question or completes the statement. *PRINT THE LETTER OF THE CORRECT ANSWER IN THE SPACE AT THE RIGHT.*

Questions 1-5.

DIRECTIONS: Questions 1 through 5 are to be answered SOLELY on the basis of the following passage.

General supervision, in contrast to close supervision, involves a high degree of delegation of authority and requires some indirect means to ensure that employee behavior conforms to management needs. Not everyone works well under general supervision; however, general supervision works best where subordinates desire responsibility. General supervision also works well where individuals in work groups have strong feelings about the quality of the finished work products. Strong identification with management goals is another trait of persons who work well under general supervision. There are substantial differences in the amount of responsibility people are willing to accept on the job. One person lay flourish under supervision that another might find extremely restrictive.

Psychological research provides evidence that the nature of a person's personality affects his attitude toward supervision. There are some employees with a low need for achievement and high fear of failure who shy away from challenges and responsibilities. Many seek self-expression off the job and ask only to be allowed to daydream on it. There are others who have become so accustomed to the authoritarian approach in their culture, family and previous work experience that they regard general supervision as no supervision at all. They abuse the privileges it bestows on them and refuse to accept the responsibilities it demands.

Different groups develop different attitudes toward work. Most college graduates, for example, expect a great deal of responsibility and freedom. People with limited education, on the other hand, often have trouble accepting the concept that people should make decisions for themselves, particularly decisions concerning work. Therefore, the extent to which general supervision will be effective varies greatly with the subordinates involved.

1. According to the above passage, which one of the following is a NECESSARY part of management policy regarding general supervision?
   A. Most employees should formulate their own work goals.
   B. Deserving employees should be rewarded periodically.
   C. Some controls on employee work patterns should be established.
   D. Responsibility among employees should generally be equalized.

1.____

2. It can be inferred from the above passage that an employee who avoids responsibilities and challenges is MOST likely to
   A. gain independence under general supervision
   B. work better under close supervision than under general supervision
   C. abuse the liberal guidelines of general supervision
   D. become more restricted and cautious under general supervision

2.____

3. Based on the above passage, employees who succeed under general supervision are MOST likely to
   A. have a strong identification with people and their problems
   B. accept work obligations without fear
   C. seek self-expression off the job
   D. value the intellectual aspects of life

4. Of the following, the BEST title for the passage is
   A. Benefits and Disadvantages of General Supervision
   B. Production Levels of Employees Under General Supervision
   C. Employee Attitudes Toward Work and the Work Environment
   D. Employee Background and Personality as a Factor in Utilizing General Supervision

5. It can be inferred from the above passage that the one of the following employees who is MOST likely to work best under general supervision is one who
   A. is a part-time graduate student
   B. was raised by very strict parents
   C. has little confidence
   D. has been closely supervised in past jobs

Questions 6-10.

DIRECTIONS: Questions 6 through 10 are to be answered SOLELY on the basis of the following passage.

The concept of *program management* was first developed in order to handle some of the complex projects undertaken by the U.S. Department of Defense in the 1950's. Program management is an administrative system combining planning and control techniques to guide and coordinate all the activities which contribute to one overall program or project. It has been used by the federal government to manage space exploration and other programs involving many contributing organizations. It is also used by state and local governments and by some large firms to provide administrative integration of work from a number of sources, be they individuals, departments or outside companies.

One of the specific administrative techniques for program management is Program Evaluation Review Technique (PERT). PERT begins with the assembling of a list of all the activities needed to accomplish an overall task. The next step consists of arranging these activities in a sequential network showing both how much time each activity will take and which activities must be completed before others can begin. The time required for each activity is estimated by simple statistical techniques by the persons who will be responsible for the work, and the time required to complete the entire string of activities along each sequential path through the network is then calculated. There may be dozens or hundreds of these paths, so the calculation is usually done by computer. The longest path is then labeled the *critical path* because no matter how quickly events not on this path are completed, the events long the longest path must be finished before the project can be terminated. The overall starting and completion dates are then pinpointed, and target dates are established for each task. Actual progress can later be checked by comparison to the network plan.

3 (#2)

6. Judging from the information in the above passage, which one of the following projects is MOST suitable for handling by a program management technique?
   A. Review and improvement of the filing system used by a city office
   B. Computerization of accounting data already on file in an office
   C. Planning and construction of an urban renewal project
   D. Announcing a change in city tax regulations to thousands of business firms

7. The above passage indicates that program management methods are now in wide use by various kinds of organizations.
   Which one of the following organizations would you LEAST expect to make much use of such methods today?
   A. An automobile manufacturer
   B. A company in the aerospace business
   C. The government of a large city
   D. A library reference department

8. In making use of the PERT technique, the FIRST step is to determine
   A. every activity that must take place in order to complete the project
   B. a target date for completion of the project
   C. the estimated time required to complete each activity which is related to the whole
   D. which activities will make up the longest path on the chart

9. Who estimates the time required to complete a particular activity in a PERT program?
   A. The people responsible for the particular activity
   B. The statistician assigned to the program
   C. The organization that has commissioned the project
   D. The operator who programs the computer

10. Which one of the following titles BEST describes the contents of the passage?
    A. The Need For Computers in Today's Projects
    B. One Technique For Program Management
    C. Local Governments Can Now Use Space-Age Techniques
    D. Why Planning Is Necessary For Complex Projects

11. An Administrative Assistant has been criticized for the low productivity in the group which he supervises.
    Which of the following BEST reflects an understanding of supervisory responsibilities in the area of productivity?
    An Administrative Assistant should be held responsible for his own
    A. individual productivity and the productivity of the group he supervises, because he is in a position where he maintains or increases production through others
    B. personal productivity only, because the supervisor is not likely to have any effect on the productivity of subordinates

C. individual productivity but only for a drop in the productivity of the group he supervises, since subordinates will receive credit for increased productivity individually
D. personal productivity only, because this is how he would be evaluated if he were not a supervisor

12. A supervisor has held a meeting in his office with an employee about the employee's grievance. The grievance concerned the sharp way in which the supervisor reprimanded the employee for an error the employee made in the performance of a task assigned to him. The problem was not resolved.
Which one of the following statements about this meeting BEST reflects an understanding of good supervisory techniques?
    A. It is awkward for a supervisor to handle a grievance involving himself. The supervisor should not have held the meeting.
    B. It would have been better is the supervisor had held the meeting at the employee's workplace, even though there would have been frequent distractions, because the employee would have been more relaxed.
    C. The resolution of a problem is not the only sign of a successful meeting. The achievement of communication was worthwhile.
    D. The supervisor should have been forceful. There is nothing wrong with raising your voice to an employee every once in a while.

13. John Hayden, the owner of a single-family house, complains that he submitted an application for reduction of assessment that obviously was not acted upon before his final assessment notice was sent to him. The timely receipt of the application has been verified in a departmental log book.
As the supervisor of the clerical unit through which this application was processed and where this delay occurred, you should be LEAST concerned with
    A. what happened
    B. who is responsible
    C. why it happened
    D. what can be learned from it

14. The one of the following that applies MOST appropriate to the role of the first-line supervisor is that usually he is
    A. called upon to help determine agency policy
    B. involved in long-range agency planning
    C. responsible for determining some aspects of basic organization structure
    D. a participant in developing procedures and methods

15. Sally Jones, an Administrative Assistant, gives clear and precise instructions to Robert Warren, a Senior Clerk. In these instructions, Ms. Jones clearly delegates authority to Mr. Warren to undertake a well-defined task.
In this situation, Ms. Jones should expect Mr. Warren to
    A. come to her to check out details as he progresses with the task
    B. come to her only with exceptional problems
    C. ask her permission if he wishes to use his delegated authority
    D. use his authority to redefine the task and its related activities

16. Planning involves establishing departmental goals and programs and determining ways of reaching them.
The MAIN advantage of such planning is that
    A. there will be no need for adjustments once a plan is put into operation
    B. it ensures that everyone is working on schedule
    C. it provides the framework for an effective operation
    D. unexpected work problems are easily overcome

17. As a result of reorganization, the jobs in a large clerical unit were broken down into highly specialized tasks. Each specialized task was then assigned to a particular employee to perform.
This action will probably lead to an increase in
    A. flexibility
    B. job satisfaction
    C. need for coordination
    D. employee initiative

18. Your office carries on a large volume of correspondence concerned with the purchase of supplies and equipment for city offices. You use form letters to deal with many common situations.
In which one of the following situations would use of a form letter be LEAST appropriate?
    A. Informing suppliers of a change in city regulations concerning purchase contracts
    B. Telling a new supplier the standard procedures to be followed in billing
    C. Acknowledging receipt of a complaint and saying that the complaint will be investigated
    D. Answering a city councilman's request for additional information on a particular regulation affecting suppliers

19. Assume that you are an Administrative Assistant heading a large clerical unit. Because of the great demands being made on your time, you have designated Tom Smith, a Supervising Clerk, to be your assistant and to assume some of your duties.
Of the following duties performed by you, the MOST appropriate one to assign to Tom Smith is to
    A. conduct the on-the-job training of new employees
    B. prepare the performance appraisal reports on your staff members
    C. represent your unit in dealings with the heads of other units
    D. handle matters that require exception to general policy

20. In establishing rules for his subordinates, a superior should be PRIMARILY concerned with
    A. creating sufficient flexibility to allow for exceptions
    B. making employees aware of the reasons for the rules and the penalties for infractions
    C. establishing the strength of his own position in relation to his subordinates
    D. having his subordinates know that such rules will be imposed in a personal manner

21. The practice of conducting staff training sessions on a periodic basis is generally considered
    A. *poor;* it takes employees away from their work assignments
    B. *poor;* all staff training should be done on an individual basis
    C. *good;* it permits the regular introduction of new methods and techniques
    D. *good;* it ensures a high employee productivity rate

22. Suppose, as an Administrative Assistant, you have just announced at a staff meeting with your subordinates that a radical reorganization of work will take place next week. Your subordinates at the meeting appear to be excited, tense, and worried.
    Of the following, the BEST action for you to take at that time is to
    A. schedule private conferences with each subordinate to obtain his reaction to the meeting
    B. close the meeting and tell your subordinates to return immediately to their work assignments
    C. give your subordinates some time to ask questions and discuss your announcement
    D. insist that your subordinates do not discuss your announcement among themselves or with other members of the agency

23. Suppose that as an Administrative Assistant you were recently placed in charge of the Duplicating and Stock Unit of Department Y. From your observation of the operations of your unit during your first week as its head, you get the impression that there are inefficiencies in its operations causing low productivity.
    To obtain an increase in its productivity, the FIRST of the following actions you should take is to
    A. seek the advice of your immediate superior on how he would tackle this problem
    B. develop plans to correct any unsatisfactory conditions arising from other than manpower deficiencies
    C. identify the problems causing low productivity
    D. discuss your productivity problem with other unit heads to find out how they handled similar problems

24. Assume that you are an Administrative Assistant recently placed in charge of a large clerical unit. At a meeting, the head of another unit tells you: *My practice is to give a worker more than he can finish. In that way you can be sure that you are getting the most out of him.*
    For you to accept this practice would be
    A. *advisable,* since your actions would be consistent with those practiced in your agency
    B. *inadvisable,* since such a practice is apt to create frustration and lower staff morals
    C. *advisable* since a high goal stimulates people to strive to attain it
    D. *inadvisable,* since management may, in turn, set too high a productivity goal for the unit

7 (#2)

25. Suppose that you are the supervisor of a unit in which there is an increasing amount of friction among several of your staff members. One of the reasons for this friction is that the work of some of these staff members cannot be completed until other staff members complete related work.
Of the following, the MOST appropriate action for you to take is to
   A. summon these employees to a meeting to discuss the responsibilities each has and to devise better methods of coordination
   B. have a private talk with each employee involved and make each understand that there must be more cooperation among the employees
   C. arrange for interviews with each of the employees involved to determine what his problems are
   D. shift the assignments of these employees so that each will be doing a job different from his current one

25.____

26. An office supervisor has a number of responsibilities with regard to his subordinates.
Which one of the following functions should NOT be regarded as a basic responsibility of the office supervisor?
   A. Telling employees how to solve personal problems that may be interfering with their work
   B. Training new employees to do the work assigned to them
   C. Evaluating employees' performance periodically and discussing the evaluation with each employee
   D. Bringing employee grievances to the attention of higher-level administrators and seeking satisfactory resolutions

26.____

27. One of your most productive subordinates frequently demonstrates a poor attitude toward his job. He seems unsure of himself, and he annoys his co-workers because he is continually belittling himself and the work that he is doing.
In trying to help him overcome this problem, which of the following approaches is LEAST likely to be effective?
   A. Compliment him on his work and assign him some additional responsibilities, telling him that he is being given these responsibilities because of his demonstrated ability
   B. Discuss with him the problem of his attitude, and warn him that you will have to report it on his next performance evaluation
   C. Assign him a particularly important and difficult project, stressing your confidence in his ability to complete it successfully
   D. Discuss with him the problem of his attitude, and ask him for suggestions as to how you can help him overcome it

27.____

28. You come to realize that a personality conflict between you and one of your subordinates is adversely affecting his performance.
Which one of the following would be the MOST appropriate FIRST step to take?
   A. Report the problem to your superior and request assistance. His experience may be helpful in resolving this problem.

28.____

8 (#2)

    B. Discuss the situation with several of the subordinate's co-workers to see if they can suggest any remedy
    C. Suggest to the subordinate that he get professional counseling or therapy
    D. Discuss the situation candidly with the subordinate, with the objective of resolving the problem between yourselves

29. Assume that you are an Administrative Assistant supervising the Payroll Records Section in Department G. Your section has been requested to prepare and submit to the department's budget officer a detailed report giving a breakdown of labor costs under various departmental programs and sub-programs. You have assigned this task to a Supervising Clerk, giving him full authority for seeing that this job is performed satisfactorily. You have given him a written statement of the job to be done and explained the purpose and use of this report.
The next step that you should take in connection with this delegated task is to
    A. assist the Supervising Clerk in the step-by-step performance of the job
    B. assure the Supervising Clerk that you will be understanding of mistakes if made at the beginning
    C. require him to receive your approval for interim reports submitted at key points before he can proceed further with his task
    D. give him a target date for the completion of this report

30. Assume that you are an Administrative Assistant heading a unit staffed with six clerical employees. One Clerk, John Snell, is a probationary employee appointed four months ago. During the first three months, John learned his job quickly, performed his work accurately and diligently, and was cooperative and enthusiastic in his attitude. However, during the past few weeks his enthusiasm seems dampened, he is beginning to make mistakes and at times appears bored.
Of the following, the MOST appropriate action for you to take is to
    A. check with John's co-workers to find out whether they can explain John's change in attitude and work habits
    B. wait a few more weeks before taking any action, so that John will have an opportunity to make the needed changes on his own initiative
    C. talk to John about the change in his work performance and his decreased enthusiasm
    D. change John's assignment since this may be the basic cause of John's change in attitude and performance

31. The supervisor of a clerical unit, on returning from a meeting, finds that one of his subordinates is performing work not assigned by him. The subordinate explains that the group supervisor had come into the office while the unit supervisor was out and directed the employee to work on an urgent assignment. This is the first time the group supervisor had bypassed the unit supervisor.
Of the following, the MOST appropriate action for the unit supervisor to take is to

A. explain to the group supervisor that bypassing the unit supervisor is an undesirable practice
B. have the subordinate stop work on the assignment until the entire matter can be clarified with the group supervisor
C. raise the matter of bypassing a supervisor at the next staff conference held by the group supervisor
D. forget about the incident

32. Assume that you are an Administrative Assistant in charge of the Mail and Records Unit of Department K. On returning from a meeting, you notice that Jane Smith is not at her regular work location. You learn that another employee, Ruth Reed, had become faint, and that Jane took Ruth outdoors for some fresh air. It is a long-standing rule in your unit that no employee is to leave the building during office hours except on official business or with the unit head's approval. Only a few weeks ago, John Duncan was reprimanded by you for going out at 10:00 A.M. for a cup of coffee.
With respect to Jane Smith's violation of this rule, the MOST appropriate of the following actions for you to take is to
    A. issue a reprimand to Jane Smith, with an explanation that all employees must be treated in exactly the same way
    B. tell Jane that you should reprimand her, but you will not do so in this instance
    C. overlook this rule violation in view of the extenuating circumstances
    D. issue the reprimand with no further explanation, treating her in the same manner that you treated John Duncan

33. Assume that you are an Administrative Assistant recently assigned as supervisor of Department X's Mail and Special Services Unit. In addition to processing your department's mail, your clerical employees are often sent on errands in the city. You have learned that, while on such official errands, these clerks sometimes take care of their own personal matters or those of their co-workers. The previous supervisor had tolerated this practice even though it violated a departmental personnel rule.
The MOST appropriate of the following actions for you to take is to
    A. continue to tolerate this practice so long as it does not interfere with the work of your unit
    B. take no action until you have proof that an employee has violated this rule; then give a mild reprimand
    C. wait until an employee has committed a gross violation of this rule; then bring him up on charges
    D. discuss this rule with your staff and caution them that its violation might necessitate disciplinary action

34. Supervisor who exercise "close supervision" over their subordinate usually check up on their employees frequently, give them frequent instructions and, in general, limit their freedom to do their work in their own way. Those who exercise "general supervision" usually set forth the objectives of a job, tell their subordinates what they want accomplished, fix the limits within which the subordinates can work and let the employees (if they are capable) decide how the job is to be done.
Which one of the following conditions would contribute LEAST to the success of the general supervision approach in an organization?
    A. Employees in the unit welcome increased responsibilities
    B. Work assignments in the unit are often challenging
    C. Work procedures must conform with those of other units
    D. Staff members support the objectives of the unit

35. Assume that you are an Administrative Assistant assigned as supervisor of the Clerical Services Unit of a large agency's Labor Relations Division. A member of your staff comes to you with a criticism of a policy followed by the Labor Relations Division. You also have similar views regarding this policy.
Of the following, the MOST appropriate action for you to take in response to his criticism is to
    A. agree with him, but tell him that nothing can be done about it at your level
    B. suggest to him that it is not wise for him to express criticism of policy
    C. tell the employee that he should direct his criticism to the head of your agency if he wants quick action
    D. ask the employee if he has suggestions for revising the policy

KEY (CORRECT ANSWERS)

1.	C	11.	A	21.	C	31.	D
2.	B	12.	C	22.	C	32.	C
3.	B	13.	B	23.	C	33.	D
4.	D	14.	D	24.	B	34.	C
5.	A	15.	B	25.	A	35.	D
6.	C	16.	C	26.	A		
7.	D	17.	C	27.	B		
8.	A	18.	D	28.	D		
9.	A	19.	A	29.	D		
10.	B	20.	B	30.	C		

TEST 3

DIRECTIONS: Each question or incomplete statement is followed by several suggested answers or completions. Select the one that BEST answers the question or completes the statement. *PRINT THE LETTER OF THE CORRECT ANSWER IN THE SPACE AT THE RIGHT.*

1. At the request of your bureau head, you have designed a simple visitor's referral form. The form will be cut from 8½" x 11" stock.
   Which of the following should be the dimensions of the form if you want to be sure that there is no waste of paper?
   A. 2¾" x 4¼"   B. 3¼" x 4¾"   C. 3¾" x 4¾"   D. 4½" x 5½"

   1.____

2. An office contains six file cabinets, each containing three drawers. One of your responsibilities as a new Administrative Assistant is to see that there is sufficient filing space. At the present time, 1/4 of the file space contains forms, 2/9 contains personnel records, 1/3 contains reports, and 1/7 of the remaining space contains budget records.
   If each drawer may contain more than one type of record, how much drawer space is now empty?
   A. 0 drawers   B. $^{13}/_{14}$ of a drawer
   C. 3 drawers   D. 3½ drawers

   2.____

3. Assume that there were 21 working days in March. The five clerks in your unit had the following number of absences in March:
   Clerk H: 2 absences
   Clerk J: 1 absence
   Clerk K: 6 absences
   Clerk L: 0 absences
   Clerk M: 10 absences
   To the nearest day, what was the AVERAGE attendance in March for the five clerks in your unit?
   A. 4   B. 17   C. 18   D. 21

   3.____

Questions 4-12.

DIRECTIONS: Questions 4 through 12 each consist of a sentence which may or may not be an example of good English usage. Consider grammar, punctuation, spelling, capitalization, verbosity, awkwardness, etc. Examine each sentence, and then choose the CORRECT statement about it from the four choices below it. If the English usage in the sentence is better as given than with any of the changes suggested in options B, C, or D, choose option A.

4. The stenographers who are secretaries to commissioners have more varied duties than the stenographic pool.
   A. This is an example of effective writing.
   B. In this sentence there would be a comma after *commissioners* in order to break up the sentence into clauses.
   C. In this sentence, the words *stenographers in* should be inserted after the word "than".
   D. In this sentence, the word *commissioners* is misspelled.

5. A person who becomes an administrative assistant will be called upon to provide leadership, to insure proper quantity and quality of production, and many administrative chores must be performed.
   A. This sentence is an example of effective writing.
   B. The sentence should be divided into three separate sentences, each describing a duty.
   C. The words *many administrative chores must be performed* should be changed to *to perform many administrative chores*.
   D. The words *to provide leadership* should be changed to *to be a leader*.

6. A complete report has been submitted by our branch office, giving details about this transaction.
   A. This sentence is an example of effective writing.
   B. The phrase *giving details about this transaction* should be placed between the words *report* and *has*.
   C. A semi-colon should replace the comma after the word *office* to indicate independent clauses.
   D. A colon should replace the comma after the word *office* since the second clause provides further explanation.

7. The report was delayed because of the fact that the writer lost his rough draft two days before the deadline.
   A. This sentence is an example of effective writing.
   B. In this sentence the words *of the fact that* are unnecessary and should be deleted.
   C. In this sentence the words *because of the fact that* should be shortened to *due to*.
   D. In this sentence the word *before* should be replaced by *prior to*.

8. Included in this offer are a six months' guarantee, a complete set of instructions, and one free inspection of the equipment.
   A. This sentence is an example of effective writing.
   B. The word *is* should be substituted for the word *are*.
   C. The word *months* should have been spelled *month's*.
   D. The word *months* should be spelled *months*.

9. Certain employees come to the attention of their employers. Especially those with poor work records and excessive absences.
   A. This sentence is an example of effective writing.
   B. The period after the word *employers* should be changed to a comma, and the first letter of the word *Especially* should be changed to a small *e*.
   C. The period after the word *employers* should be changed to a semicolon, and the first letter of the word *Especially* should be changed to a small *e*.
   D. The period after the word *employers* should be changed to a colon.

9.____

10. The applicant had decided to decline the appointment by the time he was called for the interview.
    A. This sentence is an example of effective writing.
    B. In this sentence the word *had* should be deleted.
    C. In this sentence the phrase *was called* should be replaced by *had been called*.
    D. In this sentence the phrase *had decided to decline* should be replaced by *declined*.

10.____

11. There are two elevaters, each accommodating ten people
    A. This sentence is correct.
    B. In this sentence the word *elevaters* should be spelled *elevators*.
    C. In this sentence the word *each* should be replaced by the word *both*.
    D. In this sentence the word *accommodating* should be spelled *accomodating*.

11.____

12. With the aid of a special device, it was possible to alter the letterhead on the department's stationary.
    A. This sentence is correct.
    B. The word *aid* should be spelled *aide*.
    C. The word *device* should be spelled *devise*.
    D. The word *stationary* should be spelled *stationery*.

12.____

13. Examine the following sentence and then choose from the options below the correct word to be inserted in the blank space.
    Everybody in both offices _____ involved in the project.
    A. are   B. feel   C. is

13.____

Questions 14-18.

DIRECTIONS: Questions 14 through 18 are to be answered SOLELY on the basis of the information in the following passage.

A new way of looking at job performance promises to be a major advance in measuring and increasing a person's true effectiveness in business. The fact that individuals differ enormously in their judgment of when a piece of work is actually finished is significant. It is believed that more than half of all people in the business world are defective in the *sense of closure*, that is they do not know the proper time to throw the switch that turns off their effort in one direction and diverts it to a new job. Only a minority of workers at any level have the required judgment and the feeling of responsibility to work on a job to the point of maximum effectiveness. The vast majority let go of each task far short of the completion point.

Very often, a defective sense of closure exists in an entire staff. When that occurs, it usually stems from a long-standing laxness on the part of higher management. A low degree of responsibility has been accepted and ithas come to e standard. Combating this requires implementation of a few basic policies. Firstly, it is important to make each responsibility completely clear and to set certain guideposts as to what constitutes complete performance. Secondly, excuses for delays and failures should not be dealt with too sympathetically, but interest should be shown in the encountered obstacles. Lastly, a checklist should be used periodically to determine whether new levels of expectancy and new closure values have been set.

14. According to the above passage, a *majority of* people in the business world   14.____
    A. do not complete their work on time
    B. cannot properly determine when a particular job is completed
    C. make lame excuses for not completing a job on time
    D. can adequately judge their own effectiveness at work

15. It can be *inferred* from the above passage that when a poor sense of closure is observed among all the employees in a unit, the responsibility for raising the performance level belongs to   15.____
    A. non-supervisory employees   B. the staff as a whole
    C. management   D. first-line supervisors

16. It is *implied* by the above passage that, by the establishment of work guideposts, employees may develop a   16.____
    A. better understanding of expected performances
    B. greater interest in their work relationships
    C. defective sense of closure
    D. lower level of performance

17. It can be *inferred* from the above passage that an individual's idea of whether a job is finished is MOST closely associated with his   17.____
    A. loyalty to management
    B. desire to overcome obstacles
    C. ability to recognize his own defects
    D. sense of responsibility

18. Of the following, the BEST heading for the above passage is   18.____
    A. Management's Role in a Large Bureaucracy
    B. Knowing When a Job is Finished
    C. The Checklist, a Supervisor's Tool For Effectiveness
    D. Supervisory Techniques

Questions 19-25.

DIRECTIONS: Answer Questions 19 through 25 assuming that you are in charge of public information for an office which issues report and answers questions from other offices and from the public on changes in land use. The charts below represent comparative land use in four neighborhood. The area of each neighborhood is expressed in city blocks. Assume that all city blocks are the same size.

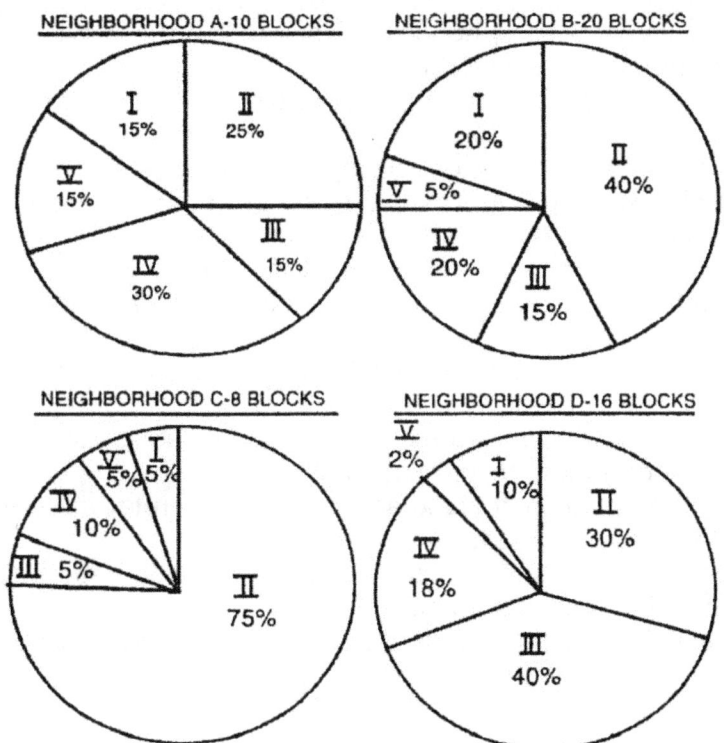

KEY: I – One- and two-family houses
II – Apartment buildings
III – Office buildings
IV – Retail stores
V - Factories and warehouses

19. In how many of these neighborhoods does residential use (categories I and II together) account for *more than 50%* of the land use?
A. 1   B. 2   C. 3   D. 4

19._____

20. How many of the neighborhoods have an area of land occupied by apartment buildings which is GREATER than the area of land occupied by apartment buildings in Neighborhood C?
A. None   B. 1   C. 2   D. 3

20._____

21. Which neighborhood has the LARGEST land area occupied by factories and warehouses?   21.____
    A. A   B. B   C. C   D. D

22. In which neighborhood is the LARGEST percentage of the land devoted to *both* office buildings and retail stores?   22.____
    A. A   B. B   C. C   D. D

23. What is the difference, to the nearest city block, between the amount of land devoted to one- and two-family houses in Neighborhood A and the amount devoted to similar use in Neighborhood C?   23.____
    A. 1 block   B. 2 blocks   C. 5 blocks   D. 10 blocks

24. Which one of the following types of buildings occupies the same amount of land area in Neighborhood B as the amount of land area occupied by retail stores in Neighborhood A?   24.____
    A. Apartment buildings   B. Office buildings
    C. Retail stores   D. Factories and warehouses

25. Based on the information in the charts, which one of the following statements must be TRUE?   25.____
    A. Factories and warehouses are gradually disappearing from all the neighborhoods except Neighborhood A.
    B. Neighborhood B has more land area occupied by retail stores than any of the other neighborhoods.
    C. There are more apartment dwellers living in Neighborhood C than in any of the other neighborhoods.
    D. All four of these neighborhoods are predominantly residential.

KEY (CORRECT ANSWERS)

1.	A	11.	B
2.	C	12.	D
3.	B	13.	C
4.	C	14.	B
5.	C	15.	C
6.	B	16.	A
7.	B	17.	D
8.	A	18.	B
9.	B	19.	B
10.	A	20.	B

21. A
22. D
23. A
24. B
25. B

EXAMINATION SECTION
TEST 1

DIRECTIONS: Each question or incomplete statement is followed by several suggested answers or completions. Select the one that BEST answers the question or completes the statement. *PRINT THE LETTER OF THE CORRECT ANSWER IN THE SPACE AT THE RIGHT.*

1. You have recently been assigned to a new office and are expected to supervise six clerks.
   All of the following would be good introductory steps to take EXCEPT

   A. giving a clear presentation of yourself to the clerks, including a short summary of your recent work experience
   B. initiating informal discussions with each clerk concerning his work
   C. making a general survey of all the functions which each clerk has been performing
   D. making a list of the duties each clerk is required to perform and giving it to the clerk

2. Your supervisor has advised you that a specific aspect of a job is being done incorrectly and you acknowledge the mistake.
   Of the following, the MOST efficient way of dealing with this situation is to

   A. call a meeting of the clerks who are performing this particular function and explain the correct method
   B. assume the blame and correct the errors as they are given to you
   C. speak with each clerk individually and carefully show each one the proper method
   D. distribute a set of written instructions covering all clerical procedures to the employees doing that particular job

3. A new department regulation calls for a change in a particular method of processing new applications. Two clerks have complained to you that the new method is more time-consuming, and they prefer to do it the original way.
   Of the following, what is the MOST advisable thing to do?

   A. Discuss the situation with them and attempt to determine whether they are utilizing the method properly.
   B. Discuss the advantages of both methods with them and let them use the one that is more practical.
   C. Firmly instruct the clerks to proceed with the new method since it is not up to them to refute department policy.
   D. Tell them to survey the opinions of the other clerks on this matter and inform you of the results.

4. A member of the clerical staff has recently begun reporting late for work rather regularly. On each occasion, the individual presented an excuse, but the latenesses continue.
   Of the following, the MOST advisable action for her supervisor to take is to

   A. have a staff meeting and stress the importance of being on time for work, without singling out the specific individual
   B. put a notice on the departmental office bulletin board, specifying and stressing that lateness can not be tolerated

C. talk privately with the individual to determine whether there are any unusual circumstances that might be causing the lateness
D. send the individual a memorandum clearly indicating that continual lateness will result in disciplinary action

5. Assume that, as the supervisor of a unit, you have been asked to prepare a vacation schedule for your subordinate employees. The employees have had different lengths of service. Some of them have already submitted requests for certain weeks.
Of the following, which factor would be LEAST important in setting up this schedule?

   A. Your opinion of each employee's past work performance
   B. Each employee's preference for a vacation period
   C. The amount of work the unit is expected to accomplish during the vacation period
   D. The number of employees who have requested to go on vacation at the same time

6. Your superior finds that he must leave the office one day before he has had time to check and sign the day's correspondence. He asks you to proofread the letters, have corrections made where necessary, and then sign his name. You have never signed his name before.
Of the following, the BEST thing for you to do is to

   A. sign your superior's name in full, making it look as much like his handwriting as possible
   B. sign your superior's name and your own name in full as proof that you signed for him
   C. sign your superior's name in full and add your initials to show that the signature is not his own
   D. politely refuse to sign his name because it is forgery

7. The head of your office sometimes makes handwritten notations on original letters which he receives and requests that you mail the letters back to the sender. Of the following, the BEST action for you to take FIRST is to

   A. request that this practice be stopped because it does not provide for a record in the files
   B. request that this practice be stopped because it is not the customary way to respond to letters
   C. photocopy the letters so that there are copies for the file and then send the letters out
   D. ask the head of your office if he wants you to keep any record of the letters

8. The main function of most agency administrative offices is *information management*. Information that is received by an administrative office may be classified as active (information which requires the recipient to take some action) or passive (information which does not require action).
Which one of the following items received must clearly be treated as ACTIVE information?
A(n)

   A. confirmation of payment
   B. press release concerning an agency event
   C. advertisement for a new restaurant opening near the agency
   D. request for a student transcript

9. Which of the following statements about the use of the photocopy process is CORRECT?   9._____

   A. It is difficult to use.
   B. It can be used to reproduce color.
   C. It does not print well on colored paper.
   D. Once source documents have been used, they cannot be used again.

10. In order to get the BEST estimate of how long a repetitive office procedure should take, a supervisor should find out how   10._____

    A. long it takes her best worker to do the procedure once on a typical day
    B. long it takes her best and worst workers to do the procedure once on a typical day
    C. much time her best worker spends on the procedure during a typical week and the total number of times the worker executes the procedure during the same week
    D. much time all her subordinates spend on the procedure during a typical week and the total number of times the procedure was executed during the same week by all employees

11. Of the following, the MOST suitable and appropriate way to make 250 copies of a particular form is to   11._____

    A. print all 250 copies on the office computer
    B. delegate the work to someone else
    C. reproduce it on a photocopying machine
    D. use an offset printing process

Questions 12-18.

DIRECTIONS: Questions 12 through 18 are to be answered on the basis of the extracts shown below from Federal withholding tables. These tables indicate the amounts which must be withheld from the employee's salary by his employer for Federal income tax and for social security. They are based on weekly earnings.

4 (#1)

INCOME TAX WITHHOLDING TABLE

The wages are -		And the number of withholding exemptions claimed is-					
At least	But less than	0	1	2	3	4	5
		The amount of income tax to be withheld shall be -					
$200	$205	$14.10	$11.80	$9.50	$7.20	$4.90	$2.80
205	210	14.90	12.60	10.30	8.00	5.70	3.50
210	215	15.70	13.40	11.10	8.80	6.50	4.20
215	220	16.50	14.20	11.90	9.60	7.30	5.00
220	225	17.30	15.00	12.70	10.40	8.10	5.80
225	230	18.10	15.80	13.50	11.20	8.90	6.60
230	235	18.90	16.60	14.30	12.00	9.70	7.40
235	240	19.70	17.40	15.10	12.80	10.50	8.20
240	245	20.50	18.20	15.90	13.60	11.30	9.00
245	250	21.30	19.00	16.70	14.40	12.10	9.80

SOCIAL SECURITY EMPLOYEE TAX TABLE

Wages		Tax to be withheld	Wages		Tax to be withheld
At least	But less than		At least	But less than	
$202.79	$202.99	$15.35	$229.72	$229.91	$16.75
202.99	203.18	15.36	229.91	230.10	16.76
203.18	203.37	15.37	230.10	230.29	16.77
203.37	203.56	15.38	230.29	230.49	16.78
203.56	203.75	15.39	230.49	230.68	16.79
203.75	203.95	15.40	230.68	230.87	16.80
203.95	204.14	15.41	230.87	231.06	16.81
204.14	204.33	15.42	231.06	231.25	16.82
204.33	204.52	15.43	231.25	231.45	16.83
204.52	204.72	15.44	231.45	231.64	16.84

Wages		Tax to be withheld	Wages		Tax to be withheld
At least	But less than		At least	But less than	
$222.02	$222.22	$16.35	$234.52	$234.72	$17.00
222.22	222.41	16.36	234.72	234.91	17.01
222.41	222.60	16.37	234.91	235.10	17.02
222.60	222.79	16.38	235.10	235.29	17.03
222.79	222.99	16.39	235.29	235.49	17.04
222.99	223.18	16.40	235.49	235.68	17.05
223.18	223.37	16.41	235.68	235.87	17.06
223.37	223.56	16.42	235.87	236.06	17.07
223.56	223.75	16.43	236.06	236.25	17.08
223.75	223.95	16.44	236.25	236.45	17.09

12. Dave Andes has wages of $242.75 for one week. He has claimed three withholding exemptions.
    What is the Federal income tax which should be withheld?

    A. $13.60   B. $15.90   C. $18.20   D. $20.50

    12._____

13. Mary Hodes has wages of $229.95 for one week.
    What is the Social Security tax which should be withheld?

    A. $16.75   B. $16.76   C. $16.77   D. $16.78

    13._____

14. Joe Jones had wages of $235.63 for one week. He has claimed two withholding exemptions.
    What is the Federal income tax which should be withheld?

    A. $12.80   B. $14.30   C. $15.10   D. $17.40

    14._____

15. Tom Stein had wages of $203.95 for one week. What is the Social Security tax which should be withheld?

    A. $15.40   B. $15.41   C. $16.05   D. $16.06

    15._____

16. Robert Helman had wages of $222.80 for one week. He has claimed one withholding exemption.
    If only Federal income tax and Social Security tax were deducted from his earnings for the same week, how much *take-home* pay should he have for the week?

    A. $191.41   B. $193.96   C. $194.12   D. $195.65

    16._____

17. Audrey Stein has wages of $203.00 for one week. She claimed no withholding exemptions.
    If only Federal income tax and Social Security tax were deducted from her earnings for the same week, how much *take-home* pay should she have for the week?

    A. $171.84   B. $172.34   C. $173.54   D. $175.84

    17._____

18. Anthony Covallo, who worked 28 hours in the past week, has a regular hourly rate of $7.25 per hour and earns a premium of time and a half for hours over 40. He has claimed four withholding exemptions.
    After Social Security tax and Federal income tax are deducted from his wages for the past week, how much pay does he have left?

    A. $180.98   B. $181.13   C. $182.29   D. $182.74

    18._____

19. In judging the adequacy of a standard office form, which of the following is LEAST important?
    _____ of the form.

    A. Date   B. Legibility   C. Size   D. Design

    19._____

20. Clear and accurate telephone messages should be taken for employees who are out of the office.
    Which of the following is of LEAST importance when taking a telephone message?

    A. Name of the person called
    B. Name of the caller

    20._____

C. Details of the message
D. Time of the call

21. Suppose that all office supplies are kept in a centrally located cabinet in the office. Of the following, which is usually the BEST policy to adhere to for distribution of supplies?

    A. Permit employees to stock up on all supplies to avoid frequent trips to the cabinet.
    B. Assign one employee to be in charge of distributing all supplies to other employees at frequent intervals.
    C. Inform employees that supplies should be taken in large quantities and only when needed.
    D. Keep cabinet closed and instruct employees that they must check with you before taking supplies.

Questions 22-25.

DIRECTIONS: Questions 22 through 25 are to be answered SOLELY on the basis of the following passage.

Use of the systems and procedures approach to office management is revolutionizing the supervision of office work. This approach views an enterprise as an entity which seeks to fulfill definite objectives. Systems and procedures help to organize repetitive work into a routine, thus reducing the amount of decision-making required for its accomplishment. As a result, employees are guided in their efforts and perform only necessary work. Supervisors are relieved of any details of execution and are free to attend to more important work. Establishing work guides which require that identical tasks be performed the same way each, time permits standardization of forms, machine operations, work methods, and controls. This approach also reduces the probability of errors. Any error committed is usually discovered quickly because the incorrect work does not meet the requirement of the work guides. Errors are also reduced through work specialization which allows each employee to become thoroughly proficient in a particular type of work. Such proficiency also tends to improve the morale of the employees.

22. Of the following, which one BEST expresses the main theme of the above passage? The

    A. advantages and disadvantages of the systems and procedures approach to office management
    B. effectiveness of the systems and procedures approach to office management in developing skills
    C. systems and procedures approach to office management as it relates to office costs
    D. advantages of the systems and procedures approach to office management for supervisors and office workers

23. Work guides are LEAST likely to be used when

    A. standardized forms are used
    B. a particular office task is distinct and different from all others
    C. identical tasks are to be performed in identical ways
    D. similar work methods are expected from each employee

24. According to the above passage, when an employee makes a work error, it USUALLY   24._____

   A. is quickly corrected by the supervisor
   B. necessitates a change in the work guides
   C. can be detected quickly if work guides are in use
   D. increases the probability of further errors by that employee

25. The above passage states that the accuracy of an employee's work is INCREASED by   25._____

   A. using the work specialization approach
   B. employing a probability sample
   C. requiring him to shift at one time into different types of tasks
   D. having his supervisor check each detail of work execution

---

KEY (CORRECT ANSWERS)

1. D   11. C
2. A   12. A
3. A   13. B
4. C   14. C
5. A   15. B

6. C   16. A
7. D   17. C
8. D   18. D
9. B   19. A
10. D   20. D

   21. B
   22. D
   23. B
   24. C
   25. A

TEST 2

DIRECTIONS: Each question or incomplete statement is followed by several suggested answers or completions. Select the one that BEST answers the question or completes the statement. *PRINT THE LETTER OF THE CORRECT ANSWER IN THE SPACE AT THE RIGHT.*

1. A certain supervisor often holds group meetings with subordinates to discuss the goals of the unit and manpower requirements for meeting objectives.
   For the supervisor to hold such meetings is a

   A. *good* practice because it will aid both the supervisor and subordinates in planning and completing the unit's work
   B. *good* practice because it will prevent future problems from interfering with the unit's objectives
   C. *poor* practice because the supervisor has the sole responsibility for meeting objectives and should make manpower decisions without any advice
   D. *poor* practice because the subordinates will be allowed to set their own work quotas

   1.___

2. Assume that you are a supervisor who has been asked to evaluate the work of a clerk who was transferred to your unit about six months ago.
   Which one of the following, by itself, provides the BEST basis for making such an evaluation?

   A. Ask the clerk's former supervisor about the employee's previous work.
   B. Ask the clerk's co-workers for their opinions of the employee's work.
   C. Evaluate the quantity and quality of the employee's work over the six-month period.
   D. Observe the employee's performance from time to time during the next week and base your evaluation on these observations.

   2.___

3. Which of the following would be the MOST desirable way for a supervisor to help improve the job performance of a particular subordinate?

   A. Criticize the employee's performance in front of other employees.
   B. Privately warn the employee that failure to meet work standards may lead to dismissal.
   C. Hold a meeting with this employee and other subordinates in which the need to improve the unit's performance is stressed.
   D. Meet privately with the employee and discuss both positive and negative aspects of the employee's work

   3.___

4. Suppose that your office has a limited supply of a pamphlet which people may read in your office when they seek certain information, but another office in your building is supposed to have a large supply available for distribution to the public.
   Which of the following would be the BEST thing for you to do when someone states that he has not been able to obtain one of these pamphlets?

   A. Tell him that he misunderstood the directions that other employees have given him and carefully direct him to the other office.
   B. Ask whether he has visited the other office and requested a copy from them.
   C. Let him take one of your office's copies of the pamphlet and then call the other office and ask why they have run out of copies for distribution.

   4.___

D. Tell him that your office does its best to keep the public informed but that this might not be true of other offices.

5. On Monday, a clerk made many errors in completing a new daily record form. The supervisor explained the errors and had the clerk correct the form. On Tuesday, the clerk made fewer errors. Because he was very busy, the supervisor did not point out the errors to the clerk but corrected the errors himself. On Wednesday, the clerk made the same number of errors as on Tuesday. The supervisor reprimanded the clerk for making so many errors.
The supervisor's handling of this situation on Wednesday may be considered poor MAINLY because the

   A. clerk was not given enough time to complete each form properly
   B. supervisor should not have expected improvement without further training
   C. clerk was obviously incapable of completing the form
   D. supervisor should have continued to correct the errors himself

Questions 6-8.

DIRECTIONS: Questions 6 through 8 are to be answered SOLELY on the basis of the information contained in the following passage.

When using words like company, association, council, committee, and board in place of the full official name, the writer should not capitalize these short forms unless he intends them to invoke the full force of the institution's authority. In legal contracts, in minutes, or in formal correspondence where one is speaking formally and officially on behalf of the company, the term "Company" is usually capitalized, but in ordinary usage, where it is not essential to load the short form with this significance, capitalization would be excessive. (Example: The company will have many good openings for graduates this June.)

The treatment recommended for short forms of place names is essentially the same as that recommended for short forms of organizational names. In general, we capitalize the full form but not the short form. If Park Avenue is referred to in one sentence, then "the avenue" is sufficient in subsequent references. The same is true with words like building, hotel, station, and airport, which are capitalized when part of a proper name (Pan Am Building, Hotel Plaza, Union Station, O'Hare Airport) but are simply lower-cased when replacing these specific names.

6. The above passage states that USUALLY the short forms of names of organizations

   A. and places should not be capitalized
   B. and places should be capitalized
   C. should not be capitalized, but the short forms of names of places should be capitalized
   D. should be capitalized, but the short forms of names of places should not be capitalized

7. The above passage states that in legal contracts, in minutes, and in formal correspondence, the short forms of names of organizations should

   A. usually not be capitalized   B. usually be capitalized
   C. usually not be used   D. never be used

8. It can be INFERRED from the above passage that decisions regarding when to capitalize certain words

   A. should be left to the discretion of the writer
   B. should be based on generally accepted rules
   C. depend on the total number of words capitalized
   D. are of minor importance

9. The Central Terminal and the Gardens Terminal are located on Glover Street.
   In ordinary usage, if this sentence were to be followed by the sentence in the choices below, which form of the sentence would be CORRECT?

   A. Both Terminals are situated on the same street.
   B. Both terminals are situated on the same Street.
   C. Both terminals are situated on the same street.
   D. Both Terminals are situated on the same Street.

10. A stylus is a(n)

    A. implement for writing containing a cylinder of graphite
    B. implement for writing with ink or a similar fluid
    C. pointed implement used to write
    D. stick of colored wax used for writing

11. As a supervisor, you have the responsibility of teaching new employees the functions and procedures of your office after their orientation by the personnel office.
    Of the following, the BEST way to begin such instruction is to

    A. advise the new employee of the benefits and services available to him, over and above his salary
    B. discuss the negative aspects of the departmental procedures and indicate methods available to overcome them
    C. assist the new employee in understanding the general purpose of the office procedures and how they fit in with the overall operation
    D. give a detailed briefing of the operations of your office, its functions and procedures

12. Assume that you are the supervisor of a clerical unit. One of the duties of the employees in your unit is to conduct a brief interview with persons using the services of your agency for the first time. The purpose of the interview is to get general background information in order to best direct them to the appropriate division.
    A clerk comes to your office and says that a prospective client has just called her some rather unpleasant names, accused her of being nosey and meddlesome, and has stated emphatically that she refuses to talk with an *underling,* meaning the clerk. The young woman is almost in tears. Of the following, what is the FIRST action you should take?

    A. Immediately call the agency's protection officer, have him advise the client of the regulations, and tell her that she will be removed if she is not more polite.
    B. Calm the clerk, introduce yourself to the client, and quietly discuss the agency's services, regulations, and informational needs, and request that she complete the interview with the clerk.

C. Calm the clerk, have her return and firmly advise the client of the agency's rules concerning the need for this first interview.
D. Introduce yourself to the client and advise her that without an apology to the clerk and completion of the interview, she will not be given any service.

13. A recent high school graduate has just been assigned to the unit which you supervise. Which of the following would be the LEAST desirable technique to use with this employee?

   A. At any one time, give the new employee only as much detail about the job as the employee can absorb.
   B. Always tell the new employee the correct procedure, then demonstrate how it is accomplished.
   C. Assign the employee the same quantity and type of work that the other employees are doing to see if the employee can handle the job.
   D. Assume the employee is tense and be prepared to repeat procedures and descriptions.

13._____

14. Assume that you supervise a work unit of several employees. Which of the following is LEAST essential in assuring that the goals which you set for the unit are achieved?

   A. Establishing objectives and standards for the staff
   B. Providing justification for disciplinary action
   C. Measuring performance or progress of individuals against standards
   D. Taking corrective action where performance is less than expected

14._____

15. One of the clerks you supervise is often reluctant to accept assignments and usually complains about the amount of work expected, although the other clerks with the same assignments and workload seem quite happy.
Of the following, the MOST accurate assumption that you can make about this clerk is that she

   A. will require additional observation and help
   B. will eventually have to be discharged or transferred
   C. is incompetent
   D. is overworked

15._____

Questions 16-21.

DIRECTIONS: Questions 16 through 21 are to be answered SOLELY on the basis of the airline timetable and the information appearing on the last page of this test.

Fact Situation:
An administrator wants you to purchase airline tickets for him so that he can attend a meeting being held in Chicago on Monday. He must leave from LaGuardia Airport in New York on Monday morning as late as possible but with arrival in Chicago no later than 9:00 A.M. He wishes to fly coach/economy class both ways. The meeting is due to end at 5:30 P.M., and he wishes to obtain the first plane after 6:45 P.M. going back to LaGuardia Airport. If all these requirements have been met, he would, if possible, also like to fly to and leave from Midway Airport in Chicago and go non-stop both ways.

16. You should obtain a ticket for the administrator from New York to Chicago on flight number

    A. 483 B. 201 C. 277 D. 539

17. You should obtain a ticket for the administrator from Chicago to New York on flight number

    A. 588 B. 692 C. 268 D. 334

18. The administrator decides to take limousines to and from both airports.
    If the limousine charge in Chicago is $52.50. and there is no reduced rate for a round-trip flight, what is the cost of the administrator's round-trip air fare PLUS limousine service?

    A. $827.50 B. $931.00 C. $963.00 D. $967.00

19. The administrator asked you whether he would be able to get breakfast on his flight to Chicago or whether he should go to the airport early and eat there before boarding the plane. He prefers to eat on the plane.
    Of the following, the BEST reply to make is:

    A. I will have to telephone the airport to find out
    B. You should eat at the airport
    C. A meal is served on the plane
    D. Only certain passengers get a meal on the plane

20. Of the following requests of the administrator concerning his travel arrangements, which one is IMPOSSIBLE to meet?

    A. Chicago arrival no later than 9 A.M.
    B. New York departure from LaGuardia Airport
    C. Non-stop flights both ways
    D. Chicago departure from Midway Airport

21. Suppose that it is necessary to take a first-class seat on the trip to Chicago although you have no problem reserving a coach/economy seat on the return trip.
    If there is no reduction in fare for round-trip flights, how much MORE will this trip cost than round-trip coach/ economy?

    A. $209 B. $236 C. $318 D. $636

22. Ms. X, a clerk under your supervision, has been working in the unit for a few weeks. Some of the other employees have complained to you that Ms. X has an annoying habit of constantly tapping her feet on the floor and it disturbs their work.
    The BEST thing for you to do is to

    A. ignore the complaints because the employees should be concerned only with their own habits
    B. speak with Ms. X privately and discuss the situation with her
    C. make a general announcement that employees should control their nervous habits
    D. observe Ms. X for a few weeks to see if the employees are correct, and then take action

23. Suppose you answer a telephone call from someone who states that he is a friend of one of your co-workers and needs the employee's new address in order to send an invitation. Your co-worker is on vacation but you know her address.
Which of the following is the BEST action for you to take?

    A. Give the caller the address but ask the caller not to mention that you are the one who gave it out.
    B. Give the caller the address and leave a note for your co-worker stating what you did.
    C. Tell the caller you do not know the address but will give the employee's phone number if that will help.
    D. Offer to take his name and address and have your co-worker contact him.

24. Assume that you receive a telephone call in which the caller requests information which you know is posted in the office next to yours. You start to tell the caller you will transfer her call to the right office, but she interrupts you and says she has been transferred from office to office and is tired of getting a *run-around*. Of the following, the BEST thing for you to do is to

    A. give the caller the phone number of the office next to yours and quickly end the conversation
    B. give her the phone number of the office next to yours and tell her you will try to transfer her call
    C. ask her if she wants to hold on while you get the information for her
    D. tell the caller that she could have avoided the *run-around* by asking for the right office, and suggest that she come in person

25. Assume that your unit processes confidential forms which are submitted by persons seeking financial assistance. An individual comes to your office, gives you his name, and states that he would like to look over a form which he sent in about a week ago because he believes he omitted some important information.
Of the following, the BEST thing for you to do FIRST is to

    A. locate the proper form
    B. call the individual's home telephone number to verify his identity
    C. ask the individual if he has proof of his identity
    D. call the security office

KEY (CORRECT ANSWERS)

1. A
2. C
3. D
4. B
5. B

6. A
7. B
8. B
9. C
10. C

11. C
12. B
13. C
14. B
15. A

16. A
17. D
18. B
19. C
20. D

21. C
22. B
23. D
24. C
25. C

EXAMINATION SECTION
TEST 1

DIRECTIONS: Each question or incomplete statement is followed by several suggested answers or completions. Select the one that BEST answers the question or completes the statement. *PRINT THE LETTER OF THE CORRECT ANSWER IN THE SPACE AT THE RIGHT.*

Questions 1-4.

DIRECTIONS: Questions 1 through 4 are to be answered SOLELY on the basis of the following passage.

    Job analysis combined with performance appraisal is an excellent method of determining training needs of individuals. The steps in this method are to determine the specific duties of the job, to evaluate the adequacy with which the employee performs each of these duties, and finally to determine what significant improvements can be made by training.
    The list of duties can be obtained in a number of ways: asking the employee, asking the supervisor, observing the employee, etc. Adequacy of performance can be estimated by the employee, but the supervisor's evaluation must also be obtained. This evaluation will usually be based on observation.
    What does the supervisor observe? The employee, while he is working; the employee's work relationships; the ease, speed, and sureness of the employee's actions; the way he applies himself to the job; the accuracy and amount of completed work; its conformity with established procedures and standards; the appearance of the work; the soundness of judgment it shows; and, finally, signs of good or poor communication, understanding, and cooperation among employees.
    Such observation is a normal and inseparable part of the everyday job of supervision. Systematically, recorded, evaluated, and summarized, it highlights both general and individual training needs.

1. According to the passage, job analysis may be used by the supervisor in
   A. increasing his own understanding of tasks performed in his unit
   B. increasing efficiency of communication within the organization
   C. assisting personnel experts in the classification of positions
   D. determining in which areas an employee needs more instruction

2. According to the passage, the FIRST step in determining the training needs of employees is to
   A. locate the significant improvements that can be made by training
   B. determine the specific duties required in a job
   C. evaluate the employee's performance
   D. motivate the employee to want to improve himself

2 (#1)

3. On the basis of the above passage, which of the following is the BEST way for a supervisor to determine the adequacy of employee performance?
   A. Check the accuracy and amount of completed work
   B. Ask the training officer
   C. Observe all aspects of the employee's work
   D. Obtain the employee's own estimate

3.____

4. Which of the following is NOT mentioned by the passage as a factor to be taken into consideration in judging the adequacy of employee performance?
   A. Accuracy of completed work
   B. Appearance of completed work
   C. Cooperation among employees
   D. Attitude of the employee toward his supervisor

4.____

5. In indexing names of business firms and other organizations, ONE of the rules to be followed is:
   A. The word *and* is considered an indexing unit.
   B. When a firm name includes the full name of a person who is not well-known, the person's first name is considered as the first indexing unit.
   C. Usually the units in a firm name are indexed in the order in which they are written.
   D. When a firm's name is made up of single letters (such as ABC Corp.), the letters taken together are considered more than one indexing unit.

5.____

6. Assume that people often come to your office with complaints of errors in your agency's handling of their clients. The employees in your office have the job of listening to these complaints and investigating them. One day, when it is almost closing time, a person comes into your office, apparently very angry, and demands that you take care of his complaint at once.
   Your IMMEDIATE reaction should be to
   A. suggest that he return the following day
   B. find out his name and the nature of his complaint
   C. tell him to write a letter
   D. call over your supervisor

6.____

7. Assume that part of your job is to notify people concerning whether their applications for a certain program have been approved or disapproved. However, you do not actually make the decision on approval or disapproval. One day, you answer a telephone call from a woman who states that she has not yet received any word on her application. She goes on to tell you her qualifications for the program. From what she has said, you know that persons with such qualifications are usually approved.
   Of the following, which one is the BEST thing for you to say to her?
   A. "You probably will be accepted, but wait until you receive a letter before trying to join the program."
   B. "Since you seem well qualified, I am sure that your application will be approved."

7.____

C. "If you can write us a letter emphasizing your qualifications, it may speed up the process."
D. "You will be notified of the results of your application as soon as a decision has been made."

8. Suppose that one of your duties includes answering specific telephone inquiries. Your superior refers a call to you from an irate person who claims that your agency is inefficient and is wasting taxpayers' money.
Of the following, the BEST way to handle such a call is to
   A. listen briefly and then hang up without answering
   B. note the caller's comments and tell him that you will transmit them to your superiors
   C. connect the caller with the head of your agency
   D. discuss your own opinions with the caller

8._____

9. An employee has been assigned to open her division head's mail and place it on his desk. One day, the employee opens a letter which she then notices is marked *Personal*.
Of the following, the BEST action for her to take is to
   A. write *Personal* on the letter and staple the envelope to the back of the letter
   B. ignore the matter and treat the letter the same way as the others
   C. give it to another division head to hold until her own division head comes into the office
   D. leave the letter in the envelope and write *Sorry opened by mistake* on the envelope and initial it

9._____

Questions 10-14.

DIRECTIONS: Questions 10 through 14 each consist of a quotation which contains one word that is incorrectly used because it is not in keeping with the meaning that the quotation is evidently intended to convey. Of the words underlined in each quotation, determine which word is incorrectly used. Then select from among the words lettered A, B, C, and D the word which, when substituted for the incorrectly used word, would BEST help to convey the meaning of the quotation. (Do not indicate a change for an underlined word unless the underlined word is incorrectly used.)

10. Unless reasonable managerial supervision is exercised over office supplies, it is certain that there will be extravagance, rejected items out of stock, excessive prices paid for certain items, and obsolete material in the stockroom.
   A. overlooked   B. immoderate   C. needed   D. instituted

10._____

11. Since office supplies are in such common use, an attitude of indifference about their handling is not unusual. Their importance is often recognized only when they are utilized or out of stock, for office employees must have proper supplies if maximum productivity is to be attained.
   A. plentiful   B. unavailable   C. reduced   D. expected

11._____

12. Anyone <u>effected</u> by paperwork, <u>interested</u> in or engaged in office work, or desiring to improve <u>informational</u> activities can find materials <u>keyed</u> to his needs. 12.____
    A. attentive   B. available   C. affected   D. ambitious

13. Information is <u>homogeneous</u> and must therefore be properly classified so that each type may be <u>employed</u> in ways <u>appropriate</u> to its <u>own peculiar</u> properties. 13.____
    A. apparent
    B. heterogeneous
    C. consistent
    D. idiosyncratic

14. <u>Intellectual</u> training may seem a <u>formidable</u> phrase, but it means nothing more than the <u>deliberate</u> cultivation of the ability to think, and there is no <u>dark</u> contrast between the intellectual and the practical. 14.____
    A. subjective   B. objective   C. sharp   D. vocational

15. The MOST important reason for having a filing system is to 15.____
    A. get papers out of the way
    B. have a record of everything that has happened
    C. retain information to justify your actions
    D. enable rapid retrieval of information

16. The system of filing which is used MOST frequently is called _____ filing. 16.____
    A. alphabetic
    B. alphanumeric
    C. geographic
    D. numeric

17. One of the clerks under your supervision has been telephoning frequently to tell you that he was taking the day off. Unless there is a real need for it, taking leave which is not scheduled is frowned upon because it upsets the work schedule. 17.____
    Under these circumstances, which of the following reasons for taking the day off is MOST acceptable?
    A. "I can't work when my arthritis bothers me."
    B. "I've been pressured with work from my night job and needed the extra time to catch up."
    C. "My family just moved to a new house, and I needed the time to start the repairs."
    D. "Work here has not been challenging, and I've been looking for another job."

18. One of the employees under your supervision, previously a very satisfactory worker, has begun arriving late one or two mornings each week. No explanation has been offered for this change. You call her to your office for a conference. As you are explaining the purpose of the conference and your need to understand this sudden lateness problem, she becomes very angry and states that you have no right to question her. 18.____
    Of the following, the BEST course of action for you to take at this point is to

A. inform her in your most authoritarian tone that you are the supervisor and that you have every right to question her
B. end the conference and advise the employee that you will have no further discussion with her until she controls her temper
C. remain calm, try to calm her down, and when she has quieted, explain the reasons for your questions and the need for answers
D. hold your temper; when she has calmed down, tell her that you will not have a tardy worker in your unit and will have her transferred at once

19. Assume that, in the branch of the agency for which you work, you are the only clerical person on the staff with a supervisory title and, in addition, that you are the office manager. On a particular day when all members of the professional staff are away from the building attending an important meeting, an urgent call comes through requesting some confidential information ordinarily released only by professional staff.
Of the following, the MOST reasonable action for you to take is to
   A. decline to give the information because you are not a member of the professional staff
   B. offer to call back after you get permission from the agency director at the main office
   C. advise the caller that you will supply the information as soon as your chief returns
   D. supply the information requested and inform your chief when she returns

20. As a supervisor, you are scheduled to attend an important conference with your superior. However, that day you learn that your very capable assistant is ill and unable to come to work. Several highly sensitive tasks are scheduled for completion on this day.
Of the following, the BEST way to handle this situation is to
   A. tell your supervisor you cannot attend the meeting and ask that it be postponed
   B. assign one of your staff to see that the jobs are completed and turned in
   C. advise your supervisor of the situation and ask what you should do
   D. call the departments for which the work is being done and ask for an extension of time

21. When a decision needs to be made which is likely to affect units other than his own, a supervisor should USUALLY
   A. make such a decision quickly and then discuss it with his supervisor
   B. make such a decision only after careful consultation with his subordinates
   C. discuss the problem with his immediate superior before making such a decision
   D. have his subordinates arrive at such a decision in conference with the subordinates in the other units

22. Assume that, as a supervisor in Division X, you are training Ms. Y, a new employee, to answer the telephone properly.
You should explain that the BEST way to answer is to pick up the receiver and say:

A. "What is your name, please?"   B. "May I help you?"
C. "Ms. Y speaking."   D. "Division X, Ms. Y speaking."

Questions 23-25.

DIRECTIONS: Questions 23 through 25 consist of sentences in which two words are missing. Examine each sentence, and then choose from below it the words which should be inserted in the blank spaces in order to create a coherent and well-written sentence.

23. Human behavior is far _____ variable, and therefore _____ predictable, than that of any other species.
    A. less; as   B. less; not   C. more; not   D. more; less

24. The _____ limitation of this method is that the results are based _____ a narrow sample.
    A. chief; with   B. chief; on   C. only; for   D. only; to

25. Although there _____ a standard procedure for handling these problems, each case often has _____ own unique features.
    A. are; its   B. are; their   C. is; its   D. is; their

KEY (CORRECT ANSWERS)

1.	D		11.	B
2.	B		12.	C
3.	C		13.	B
4.	D		14.	C
5.	C		15.	D
6.	B		16.	A
7.	D		17.	A
8.	B		18.	C
9.	D		19.	B
10.	C		20.	C

21. C
22. D
23. D
24. B
25. C

TEST 2

DIRECTIONS: Each question or incomplete statement is followed by several suggested answers or completions. Select the one that BEST answers the question or completes the statement. *PRINT THE LETTER OF THE CORRECT ANSWER IN THE SPACE AT THE RIGHT.*

Questions 1-3.

DIRECTIONS: Questions 1 through 3 each consist of a group of four sentences. Read each sentence carefully, and select the one of the four in each group which represents the BEST English usage for business letters and reports.

1.
   A. The chairman himself, rather than his aides, has reviewed the report.
   B. The chairman himself, rather than his aides, have reviewed the report.
   C. The chairmen, not the aide, has reviewed the report.
   D. The aide, not the chairmen, have reviewed the report.

   1.____

2.
   A. Various proposals were submitted but the decision is not been made.
   B. Various proposals has been submitted but the decision has not been made.
   C. Various proposals were submitted but the decision is not been made.
   D. Various proposals have been submitted but the decision has not been made.

   2.____

3.
   A. Everyone were rewarded for his successful attempt.
   B. They were successful in their attempts and each of them was rewarded.
   C. Each of them are rewarded for their successful attempts.
   D. The reward for their successful attempts were made to each of them.

   3.____

4. Which of the following is MOST suited to arrangement in chronological order?
   A. Applications for various types and levels of jobs
   B. Issues of a weekly publication
   C. Weekly time cards for all employees for the week of April 21
   D. Personnel records for all employees

   4.____

5. Words that are *synonymous* with a given word ALWAYS _____ the given word.
   A. have the same meaning as
   B. have the same pronunciation as
   C. have the opposite meaning of
   D. can be rhymed with

   5.____

Questions 6-11.

DIRECTIONS: Questions 6 through 11 are to be answered on the basis of the following chart showing numbers of errors made by four clerks in one work unit for a half-year period.

	Allan	Barry	Cary	David
July	5	4	1	7
August	8	3	9	8
September	7	8	7	5
October	3	6	5	3
November	2	4	4	6
December	5	2	8	4

6. The clerk with the HIGHEST number of errors for the six-month period was
   A. Allan   B. Barry   C. Cary   D. David

7. If the number of errors made by Allan in the six months shown represented one-eighth of the total errors made by the unit during the entire year, what was the TOTAL number of errors made by the unit for the year?
   A. 124   B. 180   C. 240   D. 360

8. The number of errors made by David in November was what FRACTION of the total errors made in November?
   A. 1/3   B. 1/6   C. 3/8   D. 3/16

9. The average number of errors made per month per clerk was MOST NEARLY
   A. 4   B. 5   C. 6   D. 7

10. Of the total number of errors made during the six-month period, the percentage made in August was MOST NEARLY
    A. 2%   B. 4%   C. 23%   D. 4%

11. If the number of errors in the unit were to decrease in the next six months by 30%, what would be MOST NEARLY the total number of errors for the unit for the next six months?
    A. 87   B. 94   C. 120   D. 137

12. The arithmetic mean salary for five employees earning $18,500, $18,300, $18,600, $18,400, and $18,500, respectively is
    A. $18,450   B. $18,460   C. $18,475   D. $18,500

13. Last year, a city department which is responsible for purchasing supplies ordered bond paper in equal quantities from 22 different companies. The price was exactly the same for each company, and the total cost for the 22 orders was $693,113.
    Assuming prices did not change during the year, the cost of EACH order was MOST NEARLY
    A. $31,490   B. $31,495   C. $31,500   D. $31,505

14. A city agency engaged in repair work uses a small part which the city purchases for $0.14 each. Assume that, in a certain year, the total expenditure of the city for this part was $700.
    How MANY of these parts were purchased that year?
    A. 50   B. 200   C. 2,000   D. 5,000

15. The work unit which you supervise is responsible for processing fifteen reports per month.
    If your unit has four clerks and the best worker completes 40% of the reports himself, how many reports would each of the other clerks have to complete if they all do an equal number?
    A. 1   B. 2   C. 3   D. 4

16. Assume that the work unit in which you work has 24 clerks and 18 stenographers. In order to change the ratio of stenographers to clerks so that there is one stenographer for every four clerks, it would be necessary to REDUCE the number of stenographers by
    A. 3   B. 6   C. 9   D. 12

17. Assume that your office is responsible for opening and distributing all the mail of the division. After opening a letter, one of your subordinates notices that it states that there should be an enclosure in the envelope. However, there is no enclosure in the envelope.
    Of the following, the BEST instruction that you can give the clerk is to
    A. call the sender to obtain the enclosure
    B. call the addressee to inform him that the enclosure is missing
    C. note the omission in the margin of the letter
    D. forward the letter without taking any action

18. While opening the envelope containing official correspondence, you accidentally cut the enclosed letter.
    Of the following, the BEST action for you to take is to
    A. leave the material as it is
    B. put it together by using transparent mending tape
    C. keep it together by putting it back in the envelope
    D. keep it together by using paper clips

19. Suppose your supervisor is on the telephone in his office and an applicant arrives for a scheduled interview with him.
    Of the following, the BEST procedure to follow ordinarily is to
    A. informally chat with the applicant in your office until your supervisor has finished his phone conversation
    B. escort him directly into your supervisor's office and have him wait for him there
    C. inform your supervisor of the applicant's arrival and try to make the applicant feel comfortable while waiting
    D. have him hang up his coat and tell him to go directly in to see your supervisor

20. The length of time that files should be kept is GENERALLY
    A. considered to be seven years
    B. dependent upon how much new material has accumulated in the files
    C. directly proportionate to the number of years the office has been in operation
    D. dependent upon the type and nature of the material in the files

21. Cross-referencing a document when you file it means
    A. making a copy of the document and putting the copy into a related file
    B. indicating on the front of the document the name of the person who wrote it, the date it was written, and for what purpose
    C. putting a special sheet or card in a related file to indicate where the document is filed
    D. indicating on the document where it is to be filed

22. Unnecessary handling and recording of incoming mail could be eliminated by
    A. having the person who opens it initial it
    B. indicating on the piece of mail the names of all the individuals who should see it
    C. sending all incoming mail to more than one central location
    D. making a photocopy of each piece of incoming mail

23. Of the following, the office tasks which lend themselves MOST readily to planning and study are
    A. repetitive, occur in volume, and extend over a period of time
    B. cyclical in nature, have small volume, and extend over a short period of time
    C. tasks which occur only once in a great while not according to any schedule, and have large volume
    D. special tasks which occur only once, regardless of their volume and length of time

24. A good recordkeeping system includes all of the following procedures EXCEPT the
    A. filing of useless records
    B. destruction of certain files
    C. transferring of records from one type of file to another
    D. creation of inactive files

25. Assume that, as a supervisor, you are responsible for orienting and training new employees in your unit.
    Which of the following can MOST properly be omitted from your discussions with a new employee?
    A. The purpose of commonly used office forms
    B. Time and leave regulations
    C. Procedures for required handling of routine business calls
    D. The reason the last employee was fired

KEY (CORRECT ANSWERS)

1.	A	11.	A
2.	D	12.	B
3.	B	13.	D
4.	B	14.	D
5.	A	15.	C
6.	C	16.	D
7.	C	17.	C
8.	C	18.	B
9.	B	19.	C
10.	C	20.	D

21. C
22. B
23. A
24. A
25. D

EXAMINATION SECTION
TEST 1

DIRECTIONS: Each question or incomplete statement is followed by several suggested answers or completions. Select the one that BEST answers the question or completes the statement. *PRINT THE LETTER OF THE CORRECT ANSWER IN THE SPACE AT THE RIGHT.*

1. A supervisor may be required to help train a newly appointed clerk. 1.____
   Which of the following is LEAST important for a newly appointed clerk to know in order to perform his work efficiently?
   A. Acceptable ways of answering and recording telephone calls
   B. The number of files in the storage files unit
   C. The filing methods used by his unit
   D. Proper techniques for handling visitors

2. In your agency you have the responsibility of processing clients who have 2.____
   appointments with agency representatives. On a particularly busy day, a client comes to your desk and insists that she must see the person handling her case although she has no appointment.
   Under the circumstances, your FIRST action should be to
   A. show her the full appointment schedule
   B. give her an appointment for another day
   C. ask her to explain the urgency
   D. tell her to return later in the day

3. Which of the following practices is BEST for a supervisor to use when assigning 3.____
   work to his staff?
   A. Give workers with seniority the most difficult jobs
   B. Assign all unimportant work to the slower workers
   C. Permit each employee to pick the job he prefers
   D. Make assignments based on the workers' abilities

4. In which of the following instances is a supervisor MOST justified in giving 4.____
   commands to people under his supervision? When
   A. they delay in following instructions which have been given to them clearly
   B. they become relaxed and slow about work, and he wants to speed up their production
   C. he must direct them in an emergency situation
   D. he is instructing them on jobs that are unfamiliar to them

5. Which of the following supervisory actions or attitudes is MOST likely to result 5.____
   in getting subordinates to try to do as much work as possible for a supervisor? He
   A. shows that his most important interest is in schedules and production goals
   B. consistently pressures his staff to get the work out

C. never fails to let them know he is in charge
D. considers their abilities and needs while requiring that production goals be met

6. Assume that a supervisor has been explaining certain regulations to a new clerk under his supervision.
The MOST efficient way for the supervisor to make sure that the clerk has understood the explanation is to
   A. give him written materials on the regulations
   B. ask him if he has any further questions about the regulations
   C. ask him specific questions based on what has just been explained to him
   D. watch the way he handles a situation involving these regulations

6.____

7. One of your unit clerks has been assigned to work for a Mr. Jones in another office for several days. At the end of the first day, Mr. Jones, saying the clerk was not satisfactory, asks that she not be assigned to him again. This clerk is one of your most dependable workers, and no previous complaints about her work have come to you from any other outside assignments.
To get to the root of this situation, your FIRST action should be to
   A. ask Mr. Jones to explain in what way her work was unsatisfactory
   B. ask the clerk what she did that Mr. Jones considered unsatisfactory
   C. check with supervisors for whom she previously worked to see if your own rating of her is in error
   D. tell Mr. Jones to pick the clerk he would prefer to have work for him the next time

7.____

8. A senior typist, still on probation, is instructed to type, as quickly as possible, one section of a draft of a long, complex report. Her part must be typed and readable before another part of the report can be written. Asked when she can have the report ready, she gives her supervisor an estimate of a day longer than she knows it will actually take. She then finishes the job a day sooner than the date given her supervisor.
The judgment shown by the senior typist in giving an overestimate of time in a situation like this is, in general,
   A. *good*, because it prevents the supervisor from thinking she works slowly
   B. *good*, because it keeps unrealistic supervisors from expecting too much
   C. *bad*, because she should have used the time left to further check and proofread her work
   D. *bad*, because schedules and plans for other parts of the project may have been based on her false estimate

8.____

9. Suppose a new clerk, still on probation, is placed under your supervision and refuses to do a job you ask him to do.
What is the FIRST thing you should do?
   A. Explain that you are the supervisor and he must follow your instructions
   B. Tell him he may be suspended if he refuses
   C. Ask someone else to do the job and rate him accordingly
   D. Ask for his reason for objecting to the request

9.____

10. As a supervisor of a small group of people, you have blamed worker A for something that you later find out was really done by worker B.
    The BEST thing for you to do now would be to
    A. say nothing to worker A but criticize worker B for his mistake while worker A is near so that A will realize that you know who made the mistake
    B. speak to each worker separately, apologize to worker A for your mistake, and discuss worker B's mistake with him
    C. bring both workers together, apologize to worker A for your mistake, and discuss worker B's mistake with him
    D. say nothing now but be careful about mixing up worker A with worker B in the future

11. You have just learned one of your staff is grumbling that she thinks you are not pleased with her work. As far as you're concerned, this isn't true at all. In fact, you've paid no particular attention to this worker lately because you've been very busy. You have just finished preparing an important report and *breaking in* a new clerk.
    Under the circumstances, the BEST thing to do is
    A. ignore her; after all, it's just a figment of her imagination
    B. discuss the matter with her now to try to find out and eliminate the cause of this problem
    C. tell her not to worry about it; you haven't had time to think about her work
    D. make a note to meet with her at a later date in order to straighten out the situation

12. A most important job of a supervisor is to positively motivate employees to increase their work production.
    Which of the following LEAST indicates that a group of workers has been positively motivated?
    A. Their work output becomes constant and stable.
    B. Their cooperation at work becomes greater.
    C. They begin to show pride in the product of their work.
    D. They show increased interest in their work

13. Which of the following traits would be LEAST important in considering a person for a merit increase?
    A. Punctuality
    B. Using initiative successfully
    C. High rate of production
    D. Resourcefulness

14. Of the following, the action LEAST likely to gain a supervisor the cooperation of his staff is for him to
    A. give each person consideration as an individual
    B. be as objective as possible when evaluating work performance
    C. rotate the least popular assignments
    D. expect subordinates to be equally competent

15. It has been said that, for the supervisor, nothing can beat the *face-to-face* communication of talking to one subordinate at a time.
This method is, however, LEAST appropriate to use when
   A. supervisor is explaining a change in general office procedure
   B. subject is of personal importance
   C. supervisor is conducting a yearly performance evaluation of all employees
   D. supervisor must talk to some of his employees concerning their poor attendance and punctuality

15.____

16. While you are on the telephone answering a question about your agency, a visitor comes to your desk and starts to ask you a question. There is no emergency or urgency in either situation, that of the phone call or that of answering the visitor's question.
In this case, you should
   A. continue to answer the person on the telephone until you are finished and then tell the visitor you are sorry to have kept him waiting
   B. excuse yourself to the person on the telephone and tell the visitor that you will be with him as soon as you have finished on the phone
   C. explain to the person on the telephone that you have a visitor and must shorten the conversation
   D. continue to answer the person on the phone while looking up occasionally at the visitor to let him know that you know he is waiting

16.____

17. While speaking on the telephone to someone who called, you are disconnected.
The FIRST thing you should do is
   A. hang up but try to keep your line free to receive the call back
   B. immediately get the dial tone and continually dial the person who called you until you reach him
   C. signal the switchboard operator and ask her to re-establish the connection
   D. dial O for Operator and explain that you were disconnected

17.____

18. The type of speech used by an office worker in telephone conversations greatly affects the communicator.
Of the following, the BEST way to express your ideas when telephoning is with a vocabulary that consists mainly of _____ words.
   A. formal, intellectual sounding   B. often used colloquial
   C. technical, emphatic   D. simple, descriptive

18.____

19. Suppose a clerk under your supervision has taken a personal phone call and is at the same time needed to answer a question regarding an assignment being handled by another member of your office. He appears confused as to what he should do. How should you instruct him later as to how to handle a similar situation?
You should tell him to
   A. tell the caller to hold on while he answers the question
   B. tell the caller to call back a little later

19.____

C. return the call during an assigned break
D. finish the conversation quickly and answer the question

20. You are asked to place a telephone call by your supervisor. When you place the call, you receive what appears to be a wrong number.
Of the following, you should FIRST
   A. check the number with your supervisor to see if the number he gave you is correct
   B. ask the person on the other end what his number is and who he is
   C. check with the person on the other end to see if the number you dialed is the number you received
   D. apologize to the person on the other end for disturbing him and hang up

20.____

Questions 21-30.

DIRECTIONS: WORD MEANING
Each of Questions 21 through 30 contains a word in capitals followed by four suggested meanings of the word. For each question, choose the BEST meaning and write the letter of the best meaning in the space at the right.

21. ACCURATE
   A. correct   B. useful   C. afraid   D. careless
21.____

22. ALTER
   A. copy   B. change   C. repeat   D. agree
22.____

23. DOCUMENT
   A. outline   B. agreement   C. blueprint   D. record
23.____

24. INDICATE
   A. listen   B. show   C. guess   D. try
24.____

25. INVENTORY
   A. custom   B. discovery   C. warning   D. list
25.____

26. ISSUE
   A. annoy   B. use up   C. give out   D. gain
26.____

27. NOTIFY
   A. inform   B. promise   C. approve   D. strength
27.____

28. ROUTINE
   A. path   B. mistake   C. habit   D. journey
28.____

29. TERMINATE
   A. rest   B. start   C. deny   D. end
29.____

30. TRANSMIT
   A. put in   B. send   C. stop   D. go across
30.____

Questions 31-35.

DIRECTIONS: READING COMPREHENSION
Questions 31 through 35 test how well you understand what you read. It will be necessary for you to read carefully because your answers to these questions should be based SOLELY on the information given in the following paragraphs.

The recipient gains an impression of a typewritten letter before he begins to read the message. Factors which provide for a good first impression include margins and spacing that are visually pleasing, formal parts of the letter which are correctly placed according to the style of the letter, copy which is free of obvious erasures and over-strikes, and transcript that is even and clear. The problem for the typist is that of how to produce that first, positive impression of her work.

There are several general rules which a typist can follow when she wishes to prepare a properly spaced letter on a sheet of letterhead. Ordinarily, the width of a letter should not be less than four inches nor more than six inches. The side margins should also have a desirable relation to the bottom margin and the space between the letterhead and the body of the letter. Usually the most appealing arrangement is when the side margins are even and the bottom margin is slightly wider than the side margins. In some offices, however, standard line length is used for all business letters, and the secretary then varies the spacing between the date line and the inside address according to the length of the letter.

31. The BEST title for the above paragraphs would be
    A. Writing Office Letters
    B. Making Good First Impressions
    C. Judging Well-Typed Letters
    D. Good Placing and Spacing for Office Letters

32. According to the above paragraphs, which of the following might be considered the way in which people very quickly judge the quality of work which has been typed?
    By
    A. measuring the margins to see if they are correct
    B. looking at the spacing and cleanliness of the typescript
    C. scanning the body of the letter for meaning
    D. reading the date line and address for errors

33. What, according to the above paragraphs, would be definitely UNDESIRABLE as the average line length of a typed letter?
    A. 4"   B. 5"   C. 6"   D. 7"

34. According to the above paragraphs, when the line length is kept standard, the secretary
    A. does not have to vary the spacing at all since this also is standard
    B. adjusts the spacing between the date line and inside address for different lengths of letters
    C. uses the longest line as a guideline for spacing between the date line and inside address
    D. varies the number of spaces between the lines

35. According to the above paragraphs, side margins are MOST pleasing when they 35.____
    A. are even and somewhat smaller than the bottom margin
    B. are slightly wider than the bottom margin
    C. vary with the length of the letter
    D. are figured independently from the letterhead and the body of the letter

Questions 36-40.

DIRECTIONS: CODING

    Name of Applicant   H A N G S B R U K E
    Test Code   c o m p l e x i t y
    File Number   0 1 2 3 4 5 6 7 8 9

Assume that each of the above capital letters is the first letter of the name of an applicant, that the small letter directly beneath each capital letter is the test code for the applicant, and that the number directly beneath each code letter is the file number for the applicant.

In each of the following Questions 36 through 40, the test code letters and the file numbers in Columns 2 and 3 should correspond to the capital letters in Column 1. For each question, look at each column carefully and mark your answer as follows:
    If there is an error only in Column 2, mark your answer A.
    If there is an error only in Column 3, mark your answer B.
    If there is an error in both Columns 2 and 3, mark your answer C.
    If both Columns 2 and 3 are correct, mark your answer D.

The following sample question is given to help you understand the procedure.

SAMPLE QUESTION

Column 1	Column 2	Column 3
AKEHN	otyci	18902

In Column 2, the final test code letter *i* should be *m*. Column 3 is correctly coded in Column 1. Since there is an error only in Column 2, the answer is A.

	Column 1	Column 2	Column 3	
36.	NEKKU	mytti	29987	36.____
37.	KRAEB	txlye	86095	37.____
38.	ENAUK	ymoit	92178	38.____
39.	REANA	xeomo	69121	39.____
40.	EKHSE	ytcxy	97049	

Questions 41-50.

DIRECTIONS: ARITHMETICAL REASONING
Solve the following problems.

41. If a secretary answered 28 phone calls and typed the addresses for 112 credit statements in one morning, what is the RATIO of phone calls answered to credit statements typed for that period of time?
    A. 1:4   B. 1:7   C. 2:3   D. 3:5

42. According to a suggested filing system, no more than 10 folders should be filed behind any one file guide, and from 15 to 25 file guides should be used in each file drawer for easy finding and filing.
    The MAXIMUM number of folders that a five-drawer file cabinet can hold to allow easy finding and filing is
    A. 550   B. 750   C. 1,100   D. 1,250

43. An employee had a starting salary of $32,902. He received a salary increase at the end of each year, and at the end of the seventh year, his salary was $36,738.
    What was his AVERAGE annual increase in salary over these seven years?
    A. $510   B. $538   C. $548   D. $572

44. The 55 typists and 28 senior clerks in a certain agency were paid a total of $1,943,200 in salaries for the year.
    If the average annual salary of a typist was $22,400, the average annual salary of a senior clerk was
    A. $25,400   B. $26,600   C. $26,800   D. $27,000

45. A typist has been given a three-page report to type. She has finished typing the first two pages. The first page has 283 words, and the second page has 366 words.
    If the total report consists of 954 words, how many words will she have to type on the third page of the report?
    A. 202   B. 287   C. 305   D. 313

46. In one day, Clerk A processed 30% more forms than Clerk B, and Clerk C processed 11/4 as many forms as Clerk A.
    If Clerk B processed 40 forms, how many MORE forms were processed by Clerk C?
    A. 12   B. 13   C. 21   D. 25

47. A clerk who earns a gross salary of $452 every week has the following deductions taken from her paycheck: 17½% for City, State, Federal taxes, and for Social Security, $1.20 for health insurance, and $6.10 for union dues.
    The amount of her take-home pay is
    A. $286.40   B. $312.40   C. $331.60   D. $365.60

48. In 2022 an agency spent $400 to buy pencils at a cost of $1 a dozen. If the agency used ¾ of these pencils in 2022 and used the same number of pencils in 2023, how many MORE pencils did it have to buy to have enough pencils for all of 2023?
    A. 1,200   B. 2,400   C. 3,600   D. 4,800

49. A clerk who worked in Agency X earned the following salaries: $30,070 the first year, $30,500 the second year, and $30,960 the third year. Another clerk who worked in Agency Y for three years earned $30,550 a year for two years and $30,724 the third year.
The DIFFERENCE between the average salaries received by both clerks over a three-year period is
    A. $98   B. $102   C. $174   D. $282

50. An employee who works over 40 hours in any week receives overtime payment for the extra hours at time and one-half (1½ times) his hourly rate of pay. An employee who earns $15.60 an hour works a total of 45 hours during a certain week.
His TOTAL pay for that week would be
    A. $624.00   B. $702.00   C. $741.00   D. $824.00

KEY (CORRECT ANSWERS)

1.	B	11.	B	21.	A	31.	D	41.	A
2.	C	12.	A	22.	B	32.	B	42.	D
3.	D	13.	A	23.	D	33.	D	43.	C
4.	C	14.	D	24.	B	34.	B	44.	A
5.	D	15.	A	25.	D	35.	A	45.	C
6.	C	16.	B	26.	C	36.	B	46.	D
7.	A	17.	A	27.	A	37.	C	47.	D
8.	D	18.	D	28.	C	38.	D	48.	B
9.	D	19.	C	29.	D	39.	A	49.	A
10.	B	20.	C	30.	B	40.	C	50.	C

TEST 2

DIRECTIONS: Each question or incomplete statement is followed by several suggested answers or completions. Select the one that BEST answers the question or completes the statement. *PRINT THE LETTER OF THE CORRECT ANSWER IN THE SPACE AT THE RIGHT.*

1. To tell a newly employed clerk to fill a top drawer of a four-drawer cabinet with heavy folders which will be often used and to keep lower drawers only partly filled is
   A. *good*, because a tall person would have to bend unnecessarily if he had to use a lower drawer
   B. *bad*, because the file cabinet may tip over when the top drawer is opened
   C. *good*, because it is the most easily reachable drawer for the average person
   D. *bad*, because a person bending down at another drawer may accidentally bang his head on the bottom of the drawer when he straightens up

   1.____

2. If you have requisitioned a ream of paper in order to duplicate a single page office announcement, how many announcements can be printed from the one package of paper?
   A. 200   B. 500   C. 700   D. 1,000

   2.____

3. In the operations of a government agency, a voucher is ORDINARILY used to
   A. refer someone to the agency for a position or assignment
   B. certify that an agency's records of financial transactions are accurate
   C. order payment from agency funds of a stated amount to an individual
   D. enter a statement of official opinion in the records of the agency

   3.____

4. Of the following types of cards used in filing systems, the one which is generally MOST helpful in locating records which might be filed under more than one subject is the _____ card.
   A. cut
   B. tickler
   C. cross-reference
   D. visible index

   4.____

5. The type of filing system in which one does NOT need to refer to a card index in order to find the folder is called
   A. alphabetic   B. geographic   C. subject   D. locational

   5.____

6. Of the following, records management is LEAST concerned with
   A. the development of the best method for retrieving important information
   B. deciding what records should be kept
   C. deciding the number of appointments a client will need
   D. determining the types of folders to be used

   6.____

2 (#2)

7. If records are continually removed from a set of files without *charging* them to the borrower, the filing system will soon become ineffective.
Of the following terms, the one which is NOT applied to a form used in a charge-out system is a
   A. requisition card
   B. out-folder
   C. record retrieval form
   D. substitution card

7.____

8. A new clerk has been told to put 500 cards in alphabetical order. Another clerk suggests that she divide the cards into four groups such as A to F, G to L, M to R, and S to Z, and then alphabetize these four smaller groups.
The suggested method is
   A. *poor*, because the clerk will have to handle the sheets more than once and will waste time
   B. *good*, because it saves time, is more accurate, and is less tiring
   C. *good*, because she will not have to concentrate on it so much when it is in smaller groups
   D. *bad*, because this method is much more tiring than straight alphabetizing

8.____

9. The term that describes the equipment attached to an office computer is
   A. interface   B. network   C. hardware   D. software

9.____

10. Suppose a clerk has been given pads of pre-printed forms to use when taking phone messages for others in her office. The clerk is then observed using scraps of paper and not the forms for writing her messages.
It should be explained that the BEST reason for using the forms is that
   A. they act as a checklist to make sure that the important information is taken
   B. she is expected to do her work in the same way as others in the office
   C. they make sure that unassigned paper is not wasted on phone messages
   D. learning to use these forms will help train her to use more difficult forms

10.____

11. Of the following, the one which is spelled INCORRECTLY is
   A. alphabetization
   B. reccommendation
   C. redaction
   D. synergy

11.____

12. Of the following, the MAIN reason a stock clerk keeps a perpetual inventory of supplies in the storeroom is that such an inventory will
   A. eliminate the need for a physical inventory
   B. provide a continuous record of supplies on hand
   C. indicate whether a shipment of supplies is satisfactory
   D. dictate the terms of the purchase order

12.____

13. As a supervisor, you may be required to handle different types of correspondence.
Of the following types of letters, it would be MOST important to promptly seal which kind of letters?

13.____

A. One marked *confidential*
B. Those containing enclosures
C. Any letter to be sent airmail
D. Those in which carbons will be sent along with the original

14. While opening incoming mail, you notice that one letter indicates that an enclosure was to be included but, even after careful inspection,, you are not able to find the information to which this refers.
Of the following, the thing that you should do FIRST is
A. replace the letter in its envelope and return it to the sender
B. file the letter until the sender's office mails the missing information
C. type out a letter to the sender informing them of their error
D. make a notation in the margin of the letter that the enclosure was omitted

14.____

15. You have been given a checklist and assigned the responsibility of inspecting certain equipment in the various offices of your agency.
Which of the following is the GREATEST advantage of the checklist?
A. It indicates which equipment is in greatest demand.
B. Each piece of equipment on the checklist will be checked only once.
C. It helps to insure that the equipment listed will not be overlooked.
D. The equipment listed suggests other equipment you should look for.

15.____

16. Your supervisor has asked you to locate a telephone number for an attorney named Jones, whose office is located at 311 Broadway and whose name is not already listed in your files.
The BEST method for finding the number would be for you to
A. call the information operator and have her get it for you
B. look in the alphabetical directory (white pages) under the name Jones at 311 Broadway
C. refer to the heading Attorney in the yellow pages for the name Jones at 311 Broadway
D. ask your supervisor who referred her to Mr. Jones, then call that person for the number

16.____

17. An example of material that should NOT be sent by first class mail is a
A. carbon copy of a letter   B. postcard
C. business reply card   D. large catalogue

17.____

18. Which of the following BEST describes *office work simplification*?
A. An attempt to increase the rate of production by speeding up the movements of employees
B. Eliminating wasteful steps in order to increase efficiency
C. Making jobs as easy as possible for employees so they will not be overworked
D. Eliminating all difficult tasks from an office and leaving only simple ones

18.____

19. The duties of a supervisor who is assigned the job of timekeeper may include all of the following EXCEPT
    A. computing and recording regular hours worked each day in accordance with the normal work schedule
    B. approving requests for vacation leave, sick leave, and annual leave
    C. computing and recording overtime hours worked beyond the normal schedule
    D. determining the total regular hours and total extra hours worked during the week

    19._____

20. Suppose a clerk under your supervision accidentally opens a personal letter while handling office mail.
    Under such circumstances, you should tell the clerk to put the letter back in the envelope and
    A. take the letter to the person to whom it belongs and make sure he understands that the clerk did not read it
    B. try to seal the envelope so it won't appear to have been opened
    C. write on the envelope *Sorry, opened by mistake*, and put his initials on it
    D. write on the envelope *Sorry, opened by mistake*, but not put his initials on it

    20._____

Questions 21-25.

DIRECTIONS: SPELLING
Each Question 21 through 25 consists of three words. In each question, one of the words may be spelled incorrectly or all three may be spelled correctly. For each question, if one of the words is spelled incorrectly, write the letter of the incorrect word in the space at the right. If all three words are spelled correctly, write the letter D in the space at the right.

SAMPLE I: (A) guide   (B) departmint   (C) stranger
SAMPLE II: (A) comply   (B) valuable   (C) window

In Sample Question I, *departmint* is incorrect. It should be spelled *department*. Therefore, B is the answer to Sample Question 1.
In Sample Question II, all three words are spelled correctly. Therefore D is the answer to Sample Question II.

21. A. argument   B. reciept   C. complain   21._____
22. A. sufficient   B. postpone   C. visible   22._____
23. A. expirience   B. dissatisfy   C. alternate   23._____
24. A. occurred   B. noticable   C. appendix   24._____
25. A. anxious   B. guarantee   C. calender   25._____

Questions 26-30.

DIRECTIONS: ENGLISH USAGE
Each Question 26 through 30 contains a sentence. Read each sentence carefully to decide whether it is correct. Then, in the space at the right, mark your answer:
A. if the sentence is incorrect because of bad grammar or sentence structure
B. of the sentence is incorrect because of bad punctuation
C. if the sentence is incorrect because of bad capitalization
D. if the sentence is correct

Each incorrect sentence has only one type of error. Consider a sentence correct if it has no errors, although there may be other correct ways of saying the same thing.

SAMPLE QUESTION I: One of our clerks were promoted yesterday.
The subject of this sentence is *one*, so the verb should be *was promoted* instead of *were promoted*. Since the sentence is incorrect because of bad grammar, the answer to Sample Question I is A.

SAMPLE QUESTION II: Between you and me, I would prefer not going there.
Since this sentence is correct, the answer to Sample Question II is D.

26. The National alliance of Businessmen is trying to persuade private businesses to hire youth in the summertime. 26.____

27. The supervisor who is on vacation, is in charge of processing vouchers. 27.____

28. The activity of the committee at its conferences is always stimulating. 28.____

29. After checking the addresses again, the letters went to the mailroom. 29.____

30. The director, as well as the employees, are interested in sharing the dividends. 30.____

Questions 31-40.

DIRECTIONS: FILING
Each Question 31 through 40 contains four names. For each question, choose the name that should be FIRST if the four names are to be arranged in alphabetical order in accordance with the Rules for Alphabetical Filing given below. Read these rules carefully. Then, for each question, indicate in the correspondingly numbered space at the right the letter before the name that should be FIRST in alphabetical order.

RULES FOR ALPHABETICAL FILING

Names of People

1. The names of people are filed in strict alphabetical order, first according to the last name, then according to first name or initial, and finally according to middle name or initial. For example: George Allen comes before Edward Bell, and Leonard P. Reston comes before Lucille B. Reston.

2. When last names are the same, for example A. Green and Agnes Green, the one with the initial comes before the one with the name written out when the first initials are identical.

3. When first and last names are alike and the middle initial is given, for example John David Doe and John Devoe Doe, the names should be filed in the alphabetical order of the middle names.

4. When first and last names are the same, a name without a middle initial comes before one with a middle name or initial. For example, John Doe comes before both John A. Doe and John Alan Doe.

5. When first and last names are the same, a name with a middle initial comes before one with a middle name beginning with the same initial. For example: Jack R. Herts comes before Jack Richard Hertz.

6. Prefixes such as De, O', Mac, Mc, and Van are filed as written and are treated as part of the names to which they are connected. For example: Robert O'Dea is filed before David Olsen.

7. Abbreviated names are treated as if they were spelled out. For example: Chas. is filed as Charles and Thos. is filed as Thomas.

8. Titles and designations such as Dr., Mr., and Prof. are disregarded in filing.

Names of Organizations

1. The names of business organizations are filed according to the order in which each word in the name appears. When an organization name bears the name of a person, it is filed according to the rules for filing names of people as given above. For example, William Smith Service Co. comes before Television Distributors, Inc.

2. Where bureau, board, office or department appears as the first part of the title of a governmental agency, that agency should be filed under the word in the title expressing the chief function of the agency. For example: Bureau of the Budget would be filed as if written Budget, (Bureau of the). The Department of Personnel would be filed as if written Personnel (Department of).

3. When the following words are part of an organization, they are disregarded: the, of, and.

7 (#2)

4. When there are numbers in a name, they are treated as if they were spelled out. For example: 10th Street Bootery is filed as Tenth Street Bootery.

SAMPLE QUESTION:
A. Jane Earl (2)
B. James A. Earle (4)
C. James Earl (1)
D. J. Earle (3)

The numbers in parentheses show the proper alphabetical order in which these names should be filed. Since the name that should be filed FIRST is James Earl, the answer to the sample question is C.

31. A. Majorca Leather Goods B. Robert Majorca and Sons 31.____
    C. Maintenance Management Corp. D. Majestic Carpet Mills

32. A. Municipal Telephone Service B. Municipal Reference Library 32.____
    C. Municipal Credit Union D. Municipal Broadcasting System

33. A. Robert B. Pierce B. R. Bruce Pierce 33.____
    C. Ronald Pierce D. Robert Bruce Pierce

34. A. Four Seasons Sports Club B. 14 Street Shopping Center 34.____
    C. Forty Thieves Restaurant D. 42nd St. Theaters

35. A. Franco Franceschini B. Amos Franchini 35.____
    C. Sandra Franceschia D. Lilie Franchinesca

36. A. Chas. A. Levine B. Kurt Levene 36.____
    C. Charles Levine D. Kurt E. Levene

37. A. Prof. Geo. Kinkaid B. Mr. Alan Kinkaid 37.____
    C. Dr. Albert A. Kinkade D. Kincade Liquors Inc.

38. A. Department of Public Events B. Office of the Public Administrator 38.____
    C. Queensborough Public Library D. Department of Public Health

39. A. Martin Luther King, Jr. Towers B. Metro North Plaza 39.____
    C. Manhattanville Houses D. Marble Hill Houses

40. A. Dr. Arthur Davids B. The David Check Cashing Service 40.____
    C. A.C. Davidsen D. Milton Davidoff

Questions 41-45.

DIRECTIONS: READING COMPREHENSION
Questions 41 through 45 test how well you understand what you read. It will be necessary for you to read carefully because your answers to these questions should be based SOLELY on the information given in the following paragraph.

8 (#2)

Work standards presuppose an ability to measure work. Measurement in office management is needed for several reasons. First, it is necessary to evaluate the overall efficiency of the office itself. It is then essential to measure the efficiency of each particular section or unit and that of the individual worker. To plan and control the work of sections and units, one must have measurement. A program of measurement goes hand in hand with a program of standards. One can have measurement without standards, but one cannot have work standards without measurement. Providing data on amount of work done and time expended, measurement does not deal with the amount of energy expended by an individual although in many cases such energy may be in direct proportion to work output. Usually from two-thirds to three fourths of all work can be measured. However, less than two-thirds of all work is actually measured because measurement difficulties are encountered when office work is non-repetitive and irregular, or when it is primarily mental rather than manual. These obstacles are often used as excuses for non-measurement far more frequently than is justified.

41. According to the paragraph, an office manager cannot set work standards unless he can
    A. plan the amount of work to be done
    B. control the amount of work that is done
    C. estimate accurately the quantity of work done
    D. delegate the amount of work to be done to efficient workers

42. According to the paragraph, the type of office work that would be MOST difficult to measure would be
    A. checking warrants for accuracy of information
    B. recording payroll changes
    C. processing applications
    D. making up a new system of giving out supplies

43. According to the paragraph, the actual amount of work that is measured is _____ of all work.
    A. less than two-thirds
    B. two-thirds to three-fourths
    C. less than three-sixths
    D. more than three-fourths

44. Which of the following would be MOST difficult to determine by using measurement techniques?
    A. The amount of work that is accomplished during a certain period of time
    B. The amount of work that should be planned for a period of time
    C. How much time is needed to do a certain task
    D. The amount of incentive a person must have to do his job

45. The one of the following which is the MOST suitable title for the paragraph is:
    A. How Measurement of Office Efficiency Depends on Work Standards
    B. Using Measurement for Office Management and Efficiency
    C. Work Standards and the Efficiency of the Office Worker
    D. Managing the Office Using Measured Work Standards

Questions 46-50.

DIRECTIONS: INTERPRETING STATISTICAL DATA
Questions 46 through 50 are to be answered using the information given in the following table.

AGE COMPOSITION IN THE LABOR FORCE IN CITY A
(2010-2020)

	Age Group	2010	2015	2020
Men	14-24	8,430	10,900	14,340
	25-44	22,200	22,350	26,065
	45+	17,550	19,800	21,970
Women	14-24	4,450	6,915	7,680
	25-44	9,080	10,010	11,550
	45+	7,325	9,470	13,180

46. The GREATEST increase in the number of people in the labor force between 2010 and 2015 occurred among
    A. men between the ages of 14 and 24
    B. men age 45 and over
    C. women between the ages of 14 and 24
    D. women age 45 and over

47. If the total number of women of all ages in the labor force increases from 2020 to 2025 by the same number as it did from 2015 to 2020, the TOTAL number of women of all ages in the labor force in 2025 will be
    A. 27,425   B. 29,675   C. 37,525   D. 38,425

48. The total increase in number of women in the labor force from 2010 to 2015 differs from the total increase of men in the same years by being _____ than that of men.
    A. 770 less   B. 670 more   C. 770 more   D. 1,670 more

49. In the year 2010, the proportion of married women in each group was as follows: 1/5 of the women in the 14-24 age group, 1/4 of those in the 25-44 age group, and 2/5 of those 45 and over.
    How many married women were in the labor force in 2010?
    A. 4,625   B. 5,990   C. 6,090   D. 7,910

50. The 14-24 age group of men in the labor force from 2010 to 2020 increased by APPROXIMATELY
    A. 40%   B. 65%   C. 70%   D. 75%

KEY (CORRECT ANSWERS)

1.	B	11.	B	21.	B	31.	C	41.	C
2.	B	12.	B	22.	D	32.	D	42.	D
3.	C	13.	A	23.	A	33.	B	43.	A
4.	C	14.	D	24.	B	34.	D	44.	D
5.	A	15.	C	25.	C	35.	C	45.	B
6.	C	16.	C	26.	C	36.	B	46.	A
7.	C	17.	D	27.	B	37.	D	47.	D
8.	B	18.	B	28.	D	38.	B	48.	B
9.	C	19.	B	29.	A	39.	A	49.	C
10.	A	20.	C	30.	A	40.	B	50.	C

EXAMINATION SECTION
TEST 1

DIRECTIONS: Each question or incomplete statement is followed by several suggested answers or completions. Select the one that BEST answers the question or completes the statement. *PRINT THE LETTER OF THE CORRECT ANSWER IN THE SPACE AT THE RIGHT.*

1. As the supervisor of a staff of clerical employees performing various types of work, you are responsible for the accuracy and efficiency with which their work is performed.
   Of the following actions you may take to insure the accuracy of their work, the MOST practical one is for you to

   A. review each operation completed by a staff member before permitting the employee to proceed to the next operation
   B. keep a record of every error made by an employee and use this record to determine whether a careless employee should be transferred or discharged
   C. assign work in such a way that every operation is performed independently by two employees
   D. determine what errors are likely to occur and set up safeguards to prevent the occurrence of these errors

2. Assume that you are the supervisor of a small clerical unit. One of your subordinates has violated a staff regulation by failing to inform you that he will be absent on a certain day.
   Of the following, the MOST appropriate action for you to take first is to

   A. discuss this matter with your immediate superior
   B. find out the reason for his failure to obey this staff regulation
   C. determine what disciplinary action other supervisors have taken in similar cases
   D. take no action if his absence did not interfere with the work of the unit; reprimand him if it did

3. A newly appointed clerk is assigned to a unit of an agency at a time when the supervisor of the unit is very busy and has little time to devote to instructing the new employee in the work he is to perform.
   Of the following, the MOST appropriate method of training this employee is for the supervisor to

   A. instruct the new employee to observe several experienced clerks at work and question them regarding any aspect of the work he does not understand
   B. delegate the job of training this employee to an employee in the unit who is qualified to instruct him
   C. assign the new employee a simple task and inform him that more complex and varied duties will be given him when the supervisor is less busy
   D. have the employee spend his time reading the agency's annual reports and the laws, rules, and regulations governing its work

4. As a supervisor, you may find it necessary to consult with your superior before taking action on some matters.
   Of the following, the action for which it is MOST important that you obtain the prior approval of your superior is one that involves

A. assuming additional functions for your unit
B. rotating assignments among your staff members
C. initiating regular meetings of your staff
D. assigning certain members of your staff to work overtime on an emergency job

5. Suppose that a clerk who is employed in a unit under your supervision performs his work quickly but carelessly. He is about to be transferred to another unit in your department. The chief of this other unit asks you for your opinion of this employee's work habits.
Of the following, the MOST appropriate reply for you to make is to

   A. point out this employee's good qualities only since he may correct his bad qualities after his transfer is effected
   B. say nothing good or bad about this employee, thus permitting him to start his new assignment with a clean slate
   C. inform the unit chief that this clerk performed his work speedily but was careless
   D. emphasize this employee's good points and minimize his bad points

6. When subordinates request his advice in solving problems encountered in their work, a certain bureau chief occasionally answers the request by first asking the subordinate what he thinks should be done.
This action by the bureau chief is, on the whole,

   A. *desirable* because it stimulates subordinates to give more thought to the solution of problems encountered
   B. *undesirable* because it discourages subordinates from asking questions
   C. *desirable* because it discourages subordinates from asking questions
   D. *undesirable* because it undermines the confidence of subordinates in the ability of their supervisor

7. Of the following factors that may be considered by a unit head in dealing with the tardy subordinate, the one which should be given LEAST consideration is the

   A. frequency with which the employee is tardy
   B. effect of the employee's tardiness upon the work of other employees
   C. willingness of the employee to work overtime when necessary
   D. cause of the employee's tardiness

8. Of the following, the action that is likely to contribute MOST to the prestige of a supervisor is for him to

   A. expect all his subordinates to perform with equal efficiency any tasks assigned to them
   B. observe the same rules of conduct that he expects his subordinates to observe
   C. seek their advice on his personal problems and offer them his advice on their personal problems
   D. be always frank and outspoken to his subordinates in pointing out their faults

9. Although an employee under your supervision frequently protests when receiving a monotonous assignment, he nevertheless performs the assigned task efficiently. His protests, however, disturb the other employees and interfere with their work.
Of the following actions you may take in handling this employee, the MOST desirable one is for you to

A. point out to him the effect of his conduct on the staff's work and request his cooperation in accepting such assignments
B. arrange to issue such assignments to him when the other members of his staff are not present
C. inform him that you will request his transfer to another unit unless he puts a halt to his unjustifiable protests
D. ask other members of the staff to tell him that he is disturbing them by his protests

10. Assume that you are the supervisor of a small clerical unit which tabulates data prepared by another unit. One of your employees calls your attention to what appears to be an erroneous figure.
Of the following, the MOST acceptable advice for you to give this employee is to tell him to

    A. omit the figure containing the apparent error and continue with the tabulation
    B. make whatever change in the erroneous figure that appears warranted and notify the supervisor of the unit which prepared the data that errors are being made by his staff
    C. accept the questionable figure as correct and continue with the tabulation since there is no certainty that an error has been made
    D. ask the supervisor of the unit that prepared the data to have the questionable figure checked for accuracy and corrected if it is erroneous

11. A clerk in an agency informs Mr. Brown, an applicant for a license issued by the agency, that the application filed by him was denied because he lacks a year and six months of required experience. Shortly after the applicant leaves the agency's office, the clerk realizes that Mr. Brown lacks only six months of required experience rather than a year and six months.
Of the following, the MOST desirable procedure to be followed in connection with this matter is that

    A. a printed copy of the requirements should be sent to Mr. Brown
    B. a letter explaining and correcting the error should be sent to Mr. Brown
    C. no action should be taken because Mr. Brown is not qualified at the present time for the license
    D. a report of this matter should be prepared and attached to Mr. Brown's application for reference if Mr. Brown should file another application

12. Mr. Stone, who has been recently placed in charge of a clerical unit staffed with ten employees, plans to institute several radical changes in the procedures of his unit.
Of the following actions he may take before adopting any of the revisions, the MOST desirable one is for Mr. Stone to

    A. distribute to each staff member a memorandum describing the revised procedures and requesting the staff's cooperation in giving the revised procedures a fair trial
    B. issue to each staff member a memorandum describing the proposed changes and inviting him to submit his written criticism of these proposed changes
    C. issue to each staff member a memorandum describing the proposed changes and notifying him of the time and date of a staff conference to be held on the merits of the proposed changes
    D. discuss the proposed changes with each staff member independently and obtain his opinion of the proposed changes

13. An assignment completed by Frank King is returned to him by his unit supervisor for certain changes. Frank King objects to making these changes.
    Of the following, the MOST appropriate action for the unit supervisor to take first is to

    A. permit Frank King to present his arguments against making these changes
    B. inform Frank King that he is free to take the matter up with a higher authority
    C. reprimand Frank King for objecting and assign another employee to make these changes
    D. state briefly that his decision is final and indicate by his manner that further discussion would be useless

14. A properly conducted job analysis will reveal the qualities essential for efficient job performance.
    Of the following, the MOST accurate implication of this statement is that job analysis

    A. enables the supervisor to standardize procedures
    B. aids the supervisor in fitting the man to the job
    C. is helpful to the supervisor in scheduling work
    D. assists the supervisor in estimating costs of jobs

15. All of us who are employed by a government agency are, figuratively speaking, living in glass houses.
    Of the following, this quotation MOST nearly means that employees of government agencies are

    A. basically secure in their positions
    B. more closely supervised than are those in private industry
    C. not free to exercise initiative
    D. subject to constant surveillance

16. So important to good supervision is effective leadership that some supervisors who are well equipped in this respect have compensated for deficiencies in other supervisory qualities.
    On the basis of this statement, the MOST accurate of the following statements is that

    A. supervisory ability is the most valuable attribute a leader can have
    B. effective leaders are generally deficient in other supervisory qualities
    C. other supervisory qualities may be substituted for leadership ability
    D. good leaders may make good supervisors even though lacking in other supervisory qualities

17. The improvement in skill and the development of proper attitudes are essential factors in the building of correct work habits.
    Of the following, the MOST valid implication of this statement for a supervisor is that

    A. the more skilled an employee is, the better will be his attitude toward his work
    B. developing proper attitudes in subordinates toward their work is more time-consuming for the supervisor than improving their skill
    C. the improvement of a worker's skill is only part of a supervisor's job
    D. correct work habits are established in order to either improve the skill of workers or develop in them a proper attitude toward their work

Questions 18-21.

DIRECTIONS: Questions 18 through 21 are based upon the situation described below. Consider the facts given in this situation when answering these questions.

SITUATION: You are the supervisor of a small unit in a large department. In order to assist your staff in handling a peak work load, ten temporary clerks have been hired for a period of two months.

18. Of the following actions you may take before assigning specific tasks to these temporary employees, the MOST appropriate action is for you to

   A. designate one of their number as your supervisory assistant
   B. find out what clerical experience and training each one has had
   C. ask each member of this group to indicate the type of work he prefers to do
   D. escort this group throughout the department, introducing each temporary employee to all the unit heads in the department

19. The ten temporary employees have been grouped into two teams of five employees each, and the two teams have been given different assignments. After working with his group for several days, an employee in one group asks to be transferred to the other group.
Of the following reasons for transferring this employee to the other group, the LEAST acceptable one is that

   A. there is a clash in temperament between him and some of the other members of his group
   B. he can perform the work assigned to the other group more efficiently than he can perform the work assigned to his group
   C. the work assigned to the other group is less monotonous than that assigned to his group
   D. the work assigned to his present group compels him to take frequent rest periods because of a physical disability

20. One of the temporary employees informs you that he has a suggestion for improving the method of performing the work assigned to his group.
Of the following actions, the MOST desirable one for you to take is to

   A. ignore his suggestion since he knows little about the purpose of the assignment
   B. ask him to try out the suggestion before submitting it to you
   C. have him discuss it with his co-workers before submitting it to you
   D. listen to his suggestion and take appropriate action

21. A temporary clerk who had been decreasing the amount of work he performed and who had also been attempting to induce other temporary clerks to reduce their production was twice cautioned by you to cease these practices. On each occasion, he promised to discontinue these improper practices and to perform his work conscientiously and cooperatively. Soon thereafter, he is detected for the third time attempting to persuade the other temporary clerks to shirk their duties.
Of the following, the MOST appropriate action for you to take is to

A. reprimand him for his improper conduct and have him transferred immediately to another unit
B. remind him that he may not be employed again as a temporary clerk if he continues his unethical practices
C. call a meeting of the temporary staff and warn them that anyone whose production falls below average will be discharged
D. report his improper practices to your immediate superior and recommend that this employee's services be terminated

22. As a supervisor in an agency, you receive a letter from the head of a civic organization requesting information which you are not permitted to divulge.
In preparing your letter of reply, it is MOST desirable that you

    A. begin with a pleasant phrase or statement and conclude with a brief statement denying the request
    B. limit your reply to a brief statement denying the request
    C. place the denial of the request between a pleasant opening phrase or statement and a cordial closing statement
    D. begin with a denial of the request and conclude with a pleasant closing statement

23. Of the following, it is LEAST essential for a supervisor, in assigning work to a subordinate, to issue written instructions when the

    A. supervisor will be on hand to check the work
    B. instructions are to be passed on to other employees
    C. assignment involves many details
    D. subordinate is to be held strictly accountable for the work performed

24. The suggestion is made that all the secretaries assigned to the bureau chiefs of a certain agency can be transferred to a newly established central transcribing unit which is to be staffed with stenographers and typists. Of the following, the MOST probable effect of reassigning these secretaries would be that

    A. the quality of the stenographic and typing work performed by the secretaries would deteriorate
    B. the bureau chiefs would be burdened with much of the routine work that is now performed by their secretaries
    C. typing and stenographic work would be performed less expeditiously and with frequent delays
    D. the development of understudies for bureau chiefs would be greatly hampered

25. In a large agency where both men and women are employed as clerks, certain duties may be assigned more appropriately to women than to men.
Of the following, the assignment that is generally MOST appropriate for a woman clerk is

    A. sorting and filing 3x5 index cards
    B. issuing supplies from the agency's stockroom to employees presenting requisitions
    C. serving at an information desk during the hours from 7:00 P.M. to 11:00 P.M. for a period of two months
    D. collecting outgoing mail from the various offices of the agency and delivering incoming mail to these offices

26. A unit supervisor discovers several errors in the work performed by a subordinate. In dealing with this subordinate, it is LEAST desirable for the supervisor to

    A. give his criticism immediately rather than at a later date
    B. make it clear to the subordinate that he is criticizing the subordinate and not the subordinate's work
    C. praise, when possible, some commendable aspect of the subordinate's work before making the adverse criticism
    D. make sure that his criticism is not overheard by other employees

27. The status of the morale of a staff is usually a good indication of the quality of the leadership displayed by the supervisor of the staff.
    Of the following, the BEST indication of the existence of high morale among a staff is that

    A. the employees are prompt in reporting for work
    B. the staff is always willing to subordinate personal desires to attain group objectives
    C. it is seldom necessary for the staff to work overtime
    D. the subordinates and their superior meet socially after working hours

28. The use of standard practices and procedures in large organizations is often essential in order to insure a smooth, efficient, and controlled flow of work. A strict adherence to standard practices and procedures to the extent that unnecessary delay is created is known, in general, as *red tape*.
    On the basis of this statement, the MOST accurate of the following statements is that

    A. although the use of standard practices and procedures promotes efficiency, it also creates unnecessary delays and *red tape*
    B. in order to insure a smooth, efficient, and controlled plan of work, *red tape* should be eliminated by a strict adherence to standard practices and procedures
    C. *red tape* is a necessary evil which invariably creeps into any large organization which uses standard practices and procedures
    D. *red tape* exists when delay takes place as a result of a too rigid conformity with standard practices and procedures

29. The tasks of government are imposed not only by law but also by public opinion, which at any time may be made into law. Government agencies must, therefore, strive to anticipate and fulfill the needs of the public.
    Of the following, the MOST valid implication of this statement is that the

    A. satisfaction of the needs of the public is one of the obligations of a government agency
    B. law prescribes what tasks government agencies should perform and public opinion determines how these tasks should be performed
    C. tasks imposed by law on a government agency have priority over those imposed by public opinion
    D. functions of a government agency should be carried out in accordance with the letter, rather than the spirit, of the law

30. The manner in which an employee performs on the job rather than his potential ability is the true test of his value to his employer.
    The one of the following which is NOT an implication of the above statement is a(n)

A. employee of great potential ability may be of little or no value to his employer
B. supervisor should observe the manner in which his subordinates perform their work
C. employee's potential ability is of no significance in determining his fitness for a specific job
D. employee should attempt to perform his work to the best of his ability

31. No routine will automatically bring itself into proper relation with changing conditions. Of the following situations, the one which MOST NEARLY exemplifies the truth of this statement is a

    A. change in the rules governing the submission or reports by employees working in the field is found to be impractical and the previous procedure is reinstituted
    B. long established method of filing papers in a bureau is found to be inadequate because of changes in the functions of the bureau
    C. long established method of distributing orders to the staff is found to work effectively when the size of the staff is considerably increased
    D. change in the rules governing hours of attendance at work proves distasteful to many employees

32. Interest is essentially an attitude of continuing attentiveness, found where activity is satisfactorily self-expressive. Whenever work is so circumscribed that the chance for self-expression or development is denied, monotony is present.
    On the basis of this statement, it is MOST accurate to state that

    A. tasks which are repetitive in nature do not permit self-expression and, therefore, create monotony
    B. interest in one's work is increased by financial and non-financial incentives
    C. jobs which are monotonous can be made self-expressive by substituting satisfactory working conditions
    D. workers whose tasks afford them no opportunity for self-expression find such tasks to be monotonous

33. The first step in an organizational study is the reading of the basic documents. There is some documentary basis for any governmental organization, outlining the purposes for which it was established, conferring certain powers, and imposing certain limitations on the conferred powers. This statement indicates that in making an organization study, one should FIRST

    A. review all the authoritative material in the field of government administration and organization
    B. arrange the functions of the organization on a functional chart in accordance with the official documents
    C. study the laws and authorities under which the organization operates
    D. outline the purposes for which the organization study was originally established

34. His attitude is as provincial as an isolationist country's unwillingness to engage in any international trade whatever, on the ground that it will be required to buy something from outsiders which could possibly be produced by local talent, although not as well and not as cheaply. This statement is MOST descriptive of the attitude of the division chief in a government agency who

A. wishes to restrict promotions to supervisory positions in his division exclusively to employees in his division
B. refuses to delegate responsible tasks to subordinates qualified to perform these tasks
C. believes that informal on-the-job training of new staff members is superior to formal training methods
D. frequently makes personal issues out of matters that should be handled on an impersonal basis

35. A trainee was paid a weekly wage of $480.00 for a 40-hour work week. As a result of a new labor contract, he is paid $494.00 a week for a 38-hour work week with time-and-one-half pay for time worked in excess of 38 hours in any work week.
If he continues to work 40 hours weekly under the new contract, the amount by which his average hourly rate for a 40-hour work week under the new contract exceeds the hourly rate previously paid him lies between _____ and _____, inclusive.

   A. $1.02; $1.06   B. $1.08; $1.16   C. $1.18; $1.26   D. $1.28; $1.36

36. The problem of inadequate storage space arising from the large number of inactive records stored in city agencies can be solved MOST satisfactorily with the aid of _____ equipment.

   A. photostat   B. microfilm
   C. IBM sorting   D. digital printing

37. To say that an employee is *erudite* means MOST NEARLY that he is

   A. scholarly
   B. insecure
   C. efficient
   D. punctual

38. The forms design section of a city agency recommended that the sizes of forms used by the agency be limited to the sizes that can be cut with the least amount of waste from either 17" x 22" or 17" x 28" sheets.
Of the following, the size that does NOT comply with this recommendation is

   A. 4 1/2" x 5 1/2"   B. 3 3/4" x 4 1/4"
   C. 3 1/2" x 4 1/4"   D. 4 1/4" x 2 3/4"

39. The number of investigations conducted by an agency in 2007 was 3,600. In 2008, the number of investigations conducted was one-third more than in 2007. The number of investigations conducted in 2009 was three-fourths of the number conducted in 2008. It is anticipated that the number of investigations conducted in 2010 will be equal to the average of the three preceding years.
On the basis of this information, the MOST accurate of the following statements is that the number of investigations conducted in

   A. 2007 is larger than the number anticipated for 2010
   B. 2008 is smaller than the number anticipated for 2010
   C. 2009 is equal to the number conducted in 2007
   D. 2009 is larger than the number anticipated for 2010

40. *The office manager thought it advisable to MOLLIFY his subordinate.*
    The word *mollify* as used in this sentence means MOST NEARLY

    A. reprimand   B. caution   C. calm   D. question

41. *The bureau chief adopted a DILATORY policy.* The word *dilatory* as used in this sentence means MOST NEARLY

    A. tending to cause delay   B. acceptable to all affected
    C. severe but fair   D. prepared with great care

42. *He complained about the PAUCITY of requests.* The word *paucity* as used in this sentence means MOST NEARLY

    A. great variety   B. unreasonableness
    C. unexpected increase   D. scarcity

43. To say that an event is *imminent* means MOST NEARLY that it is

    A. near at hand   B. unpredictable
    C. favorable or happy   D. very significant

44. *The general manager delivered a LAUDATORY speech.*
    The word *laudatory* as used in this sentence means MOST NEARLY

    A. clear and emphatic   B. lengthy
    C. introductory   D. expressing praise

45. *We all knew of his AVERSION for performing statistical work.*
    The word *aversion* as used in this sentence means MOST NEARLY

    A. training   B. dislike
    C. incentive   D. lack of preparation

46. *The engineer was CIRCUMSPECT in making his recommendations.* The word *circumspect* as used in this sentence means MOST NEARLY

    A. hostile   B. outspoken   C. biased   D. cautious

47. To say that certain clerical operations were *obviated* means MOST NEARLY that these operations were

    A. extremely distasteful   B. easily understood
    C. made unnecessary   D. very complicated

48. *The interviewer was impressed with the client's DEMEANOR.* The word *demeanor* as used in this sentence means MOST NEARLY

    A. outward manner   B. plan of action
    C. fluent speech   D. extensive knowledge

49. To say that the information was *gratuitous* means MOST NEARLY that it was

    A. given freely   B. deeply appreciated
    C. brief   D. valuable

50. *The supervisor was unaware of this EXIGENCY.*
    The word *exigency* as used in this sentence means MOST NEARLY

    A. unexplained absence   B. costly delay
    C. pressing need   D. final action

51. *She considered the supervisor's action to be ARBITRARY. The word arbitrary as used in this sentence means MOST NEARLY* 51._____

   A. inconsistent B. justifiable
   C. appeasing   D. dictatorial

52. *His report on the activities of the agency was VERBOSE.* 52._____
   The word verbose as used in this sentence means MOST NEARLY

   A. vivid B. wordy C. vague D. oral

Questions 53-61.

DIRECTIONS: Questions 53 through 61 are to be answered SOLELY on the basis of the following information.

Assume that the following rules for computing service ratings are to be used experimentally in determining the service ratings of seven permanent employees. (Note that these rules are hypothetical and are NOT to be confused with the existing method of computing service ratings for employees.) The personnel record of each of these seven employees is given in Table II. You are to determine the answer to each of the questions on the basis of the rules given below for computing service ratings and the data contained in the personnel records of these seven employees.

All computations should be made as of the close of the rating period ending March 31, 2007.

RULES FOR COMPUTING SERVICE RATINGS

Service Rating
The service rating of each permanent competitive class employee shall be computed by adding the following three scores: (1) a basic score, (2) the employee's seniority score, and (3) the employee's efficiency score.

Seniority Score
An employee's seniority score shall be computed by crediting him with 1/2% per year for each year of service starting with the date of the employee's entrance as a permanent employee into the competitive class, up to a maximum of 15 years (7 1/2%). A residual fractional period of eight months or more shall be considered as a full year and credited with 1/2%. A residual fraction of from four to, but not including, eight months shall be considered as a half-year and credited with 1/4%. A residual fraction of less than four months shall receive no credit in the seniority score. For example, a person who entered the competitive class as a permanent employee on August 1, 1999 would, as of March 31, 2002, be credited with a seniority score of 1 1/2% for his two years and 8 months of service.

Efficiency Score
An employee's efficiency score shall be computed by adding the annual efficiency ratings received by him during his service in his PRESENT position. (Where there are negative efficiency ratings, such ratings shall be subtracted from the sum of the positive efficiency ratings.) An employee's annual efficiency rating shall be based on the grade he receives from his supervisor for his work performance during the annual efficiency rating period.

Basic Score

A basic score of 70% shall be given to each employee upon permanent appointment to a competitive class position.

An employee shall receive a grade of "A" for performing work of the highest quality and shall be credited with an efficiency rating of plus (+) 3%, An employee shall receive a grade of "F" for performing work of the lowest quality and shall receive an efficiency rating of minus (-) 2%. Table I, entitled "Basis for Determining Annual Efficiency Ratings," lists the six grades of work performance with their equivalent annual efficiency ratings. Table I also lists the efficiency ratings to be assigned for service in a position for less than a year during the annual efficiency rating period. The annual efficiency rating period shall run from April 1 to March 31, inclusive.

TABLE I
BASIS FOE DETERMINING ANNUAL EFFICIENCY RATINGS

Quality of Work Performed	Grade Assigned A	Annual Efficiency Rating for Service in a Position for:		
		8 months to a full year	At least 4 months but less than 8 months	Less than 4 months
Highest Quality	A	+ 3%	+1½%	0%
Good Quality	B	+ 2%	+ 1%	0%
Standard Quality	C	+ 1%	+½%	0%
Substandard Quality	D	0%	0%	0%
Poor Quality	E	-1%	-½%	0%
Lowest Quality	F	-2%	-1%	0%

Appointment or Promotion during an Efficiency Rating Period

An employee who has been appointed or promoted during an efficiency rating period shall receive for that period an efficiency rating only for work performed by him during the portion of the period that he served in the position to which he was appointed or promoted. His efficiency rating for the period shall be determined in accordance with Table I.

Sample Computation of Service Rating

John Smith entered the competitive class as a permanent employee on December 1, 2002 and was promoted to his present position as a Clerk, Grade 3 on November 1, 2005. As a Clerk, Grade 3, he received a grade of "B" for work performed during the five-month period extending from November 1, 2005 to March 31, 2006 and a grade of "C" for work performed during the full annual period extending from April 1, 2006 to March 32, 2007.

On the basis of the Rules for Computing Service Ratings, John Smith should be credited with:

70 % basic score
2 1/4% seniority score - for 4 years and 4 months of service (from 12-1-02 to 3-31-07)
2 % efficiency score - for 5 months of "B" service and a full year of "C" service
74 1/4%

TABLE II
PERSONNEL RECORD OF SEVEN PERMANENT COMPETITIVE CLASS EMPLOYEES

Employee	Present Position	Date of Appointment or Promotion to Present Position	Date of Entry as Permanent Employee in Competitive Class
Allen	Clerk, Gr. 5	6-1-03	7-1-90
Brown	Clerk, Gr. 4	1-1-05	7-1-97
Cole	Clerk, Gr. 3	9-1-03	11-1-00
Fox	Clerk, Gr. 3	10-1-03	9-1-98
Green	Clerk, Gr. 2	12-1-01	12-1-01
Hunt	Clerk, Gr. 2	7-1-02	7-1-02
Kane	Steno, Gr. 3	11-16-04	3-1-01

Grades Received Annually for Work Performed in Present Position

Employee	4-1-01 to 3-31-02	4-1-02 to 3-31-03	4-1-03 to 3-31-04	4-1-04 to 3-31-05	4-1-05 to 3-31-06	4-1-06 to 3-31-07
Allen			C*	C	B	C
Brown				C*	C	B
Cole			A*	B	C	C
Fox			C*	C	D	C
Green	C*	D	C	D	C	C
Hunt		C*	C	E	C	C
Kane				B*	B	C

Explanatory Notes:
* Served in present position for less than a full year during this rating period. (Note date of appointment, or promotion, to present period.)

All seven employees have served continuously as permanent employees since their entry into the competitive class.

Questions 53 through 61 refer to the employees listed in Table II. You are to answer these questions SOLELY on the basis of the preceding Rules for Computing Service Ratings and on the information concerning these seven employees given in Table II. You are reminded that all computations are to be made as of the close of the rating period ending March 31, 2007. Candidates may find it helpful to arrange their computations on their scratch paper in an orderly manner since the computations for one question may also be utilized in answering another question.

53. The seniority score of Allen is   53.___
    A. 74%   B. 8 1/2%   C. 8%   D. 8 1/4%

54. The seniority score of Fox exceeds that of Cole by   54.___
    A. 1 1/2%   B. 2%   C. 1%   D. 3/4 1/4

55. The seniority score of Brown is   55.___
    A. equal to Hunt's   B. twice Hunt's
    C. more than Hunt's by 1 1/2%   D. less than Hunt's by 1/2%

56. Green's efficiency score is   56.___
    A. twice that of Kane   B. equal to that of Kane
    C. less than Kane's by 1/2%   D. less than Kane's by 1%

57. Of the following employees, the one who has the LOWEST efficiency score is   57.___
    A. Brown   B. Fox   C. Hunt   D. Kane

58. A comparison of Hunt's efficiency score with his seniority score reveals that his efficiency   58.___
    score is

    A. less than his seniority score by 1/2%
    B. less than his seniority score by 3/4%
    C. equal to his seniority score
    D. greater than his seniority score by 1/2%

59. Fox's service rating is   59.___
    A. 72 1/2%   B. 74%   C. 76 1/2%   D. 76 3/4%

60. Brown's service rating is   60.___
    A. less than 78%   B. 78%
    C. 78 1/4%   D. more than 78 1/4%

61. Cole's service rating exceeds Kane's by   61.___
    A. less than 2%   B. 2%
    C. 2 1/4%   D. more than 2 1/4%

Questions 62-71.

DIRECTIONS: Each of the sentences numbered 62 to 71 may be classified under one of the
              following four options:
              (A) faulty; contains an error in grammar only
              (B) faulty; contains an error in spelling only
              (C) faulty; contains an error in grammar and an error in spelling
              (D) correct; contains no error in grammar or in spelling

              Examine each sentence carefully to determine under which of the above four
              options it is best classified. Then, in the correspondingly numbered space at
              the right, write the letter preceding the option which is the BEST of the four
              listed above.

62. A recognized principle of good management is that an assignment should be given to whomever is best qualified to carry it out. 62.____

63. He considered it a privilege to be allowed to review and summarize the technical reports issued annually by your agency. 63.____

64. Because the warehouse was in an inaccessable location, deliveries of electric fixtures from the warehouse were made only in large lots. 64.____

65. Having requisitioned the office supplies, Miss Brown returned to her desk and resumed the computation of petty cash disbursements. 65.____

66. One of the advantages of this chemical solution is that records treated with it are not inflammable. 66.____

67. The complaint of this employee, in addition to the complaints of the other employees, were submitted to the grievance committee. 67.____

68. A study of the duties and responsibilities of each of the various categories of employees was conducted by an unprejudiced classification analyst. 68.____

69. Ties of friendship with this subordinate compels him to withold the censure that the subordinate deserves. 69.____

70. Neither of the agencies are affected by the decision to institute a program for rehabilitating physically handicaped men and women. 70.____

71. The chairman stated that the argument between you and he was creating an intolerable situation. 71.____

Questions 72-75.

DIRECTIONS: Each of Questions 72 through 75 consists of a statement containing five words in capital letters. One of these capitalized words is not in keeping with the meaning which the statement is evidently intended to convey. The five words in capital letters in each statement are reprinted after the statement. In the correspondingly numbered space at the right, write the letter preceding the one of the five words which does MOST to spoil the true meaning of the statement.

72. The alert employee will find, EVEN in the best managed offices, violations of some of the rules of good office management. However, further study will reveal that the correction of such violations is by ALL means a SIMPLE matter, BUT requires research, time, patience, and often a high degree of MANAGERIAL ability. 72.____

    A. Even   B. All   C. Simple   D. But   E. Managerial

73. The information clerk in any organization must DELEGATE tact, courtesy, and good judgment in DEALING with callers, many of whom, on the other hand, DISREGARD business ETIQUETTE in their CONTACT with the information clerk. 73.____

    A. Delegate   B. Dealing   C. Disregard
    D. Etiquette   E. Contact

74. When the supervisor gives advancement or other rewards only to SUBORDINATES who have REQUESTED them, or shows a sincere INTEREST in the welfare of his staff, he is building FAVORABLE ATTITUDES.

    A. Subordinates   B. Requested   C. Interest
    D. Favorable   E. Attitudes

74.___

75. An appointee to the City's civil service must be a bona fide resident of the City for at least three years immediately prior to his APPOINTMENT. An appointee who served in the Armed Forces retains as his legal address that place where he resided prior to his ENTRY into the MILITARY service, PROVIDED he has taken definite action to establish a new RESIDENCE.

    A. Appointment   B. Entry   C. Military
    D. Provided   E. Residence

75.___

KEY (CORRECT ANSWERS)

1. D	16. D	31. B	46. D	61. A
2. B	17. C	32. D	47. C	62. A
3. B	18. B	33. C	48. A	63. D
4. A	19. C	34. A	49. A	64. B
5. C	20. D	35. D	50. C	65. D
6. A	21. D	36. B	51. D	66. B
7. C	22. C	37. A	52. B	67. A
8. B	23. A	38. B	53. A	68. D
9. A	24. B	39. C	54. C	69. C
10. D	25. A	40. C	55. B	70. C
11. B	26. B	41. A	56. C	71. A
12. C	27. B	42. D	57. B	72. B
13. A	28. D	43. A	58. D	73. A
14. B	29. A	44. D	59. D	74. B
15. D	30. C	45. B	60. B	75. D

READING COMPREHENSION
UNDERSTANDING AND INTERPRETING WRITTEN MATERIAL
EXAMINATION SECTION
TEST 1

DIRECTIONS: Each question or incomplete statement is followed by several suggested answers or completions. Select the one that BEST answers the question or completes the statement. *PRINT THE LETTER OF THE CORRECT ANSWER IN THE SPACE AT THE RIGHT.*

Questions 1-3.

DIRECTIONS: Questions 1 through 3 are to be answered SOLELY on the basis of the following statement.

The equipment in a mailroom may include a mail metering machine. This machine simultaneously stamps, postmarks, seals, and counts letters as fast as the operator can feed them. It can also print the proper postage directly on a gummed strip to be affixed to bulky items. It is equipped with a meter which is removed from the machine and sent to the postmaster to be set for a given number of stampings of any denomination. The setting of the meter must be paid for in advance. One of the advantages of metered mail is that it bypasses the cancellation operation and thereby facilitates handling by the post office. Mail metering also makes the pilfering of stamps impossible, but does not prevent the passage of personal mail in company envelopes through the meters unless there is established a rigid control or censorship over outgoing mail.

1. According to this statement, the postmaster

    A. is responsible for training new clerks in the use of mail metering machines
    B. usually recommends that both large and small firms adopt the use of mail metering machines
    C. is responsible for setting the meter to print a fixed number of stampings
    D. examines the mail metering machine to see that they are properly installed in the mailroom

1.____

2. According to this statement, the use of mail metering machines

    A. requires the employment of more clerks in a mailroom than does the use of postage stamps
    B. interferes with the handling of large quantities of outgoing mail
    C. does not prevent employees from sending their personal letters at company expense
    D. usually involves smaller expenditures for mailroom equipment than does the use of postage stamps

2.____

3. On the basis of this statement, it is MOST accurate to state that

    A. mail metering machines are often used for opening envelopes
    B. postage stamps are generally used when bulky packages are to be mailed
    C. the use of metered mail tends to interfere with rapid mail handling by the post office
    D. mail metering machines can seal and count letters at the same time

3.____

125

Questions 4-5.

DIRECTIONS: Questions 4 and 5 are to be answered SOLELY on the basis of the following statement.

Forms are printed sheets of paper on which information is to be entered. While what is printed on the form is most important, the kind of paper used in making the form is also important. The kind of paper should be selected with regard to the use to which the form will be subjected. Printing a form on an unnecessarily expensive grade of papers is wasteful. On the other hand, using too cheap or flimsy a form can materially interfere with satisfactory performance of the work the form is being planned to do. Thus, a form printed on both sides normally requires a heavier paper than a form printed only on one side. Forms to be used as permanent records, or which are expected to have a very long life in files, requires a quality of paper which will not disintegrate or discolor with age. A form which will go through a great deal of handling requires a strong, tough paper, while thinness is a necessary qualification where the making of several copies of a form will be required.

4. According to this statement, the type of paper used for making forms

    A. should be chosen in accordance with the use to which the form will be put
    B. should be chosen before the type of printing to be used has been decided upon
    C. is as important as the information which is printed on it
    D. should be strong enough to be used for any purpose

5. According to this statement, forms that are

    A. printed on both sides are usually economical and desirable
    B. to be filed permanently should not deteriorate as time goes on
    C. expected to last for a long time should be handled carefully
    D. to be filed should not be printed on inexpensive paper

Questions 6-8.

DIRECTIONS: Questions 6 through 8 are to be answered SOLELY on the basis of the following paragraph.

The increase in the number of public documents in the last two centuries closely matches the increase in population in the United States. The great number of public documents has become a serious threat to their usefulness. It is necessary to have programs which will reduce the number of public documents that are kept and which will, at the same time, assure keeping those that have value. Such programs need a great deal of thought to have any success.

6. According to the above paragraph, public documents may be LESS useful if

    A. the files are open to the public
    B. the record room is too small
    C. the copying machine is operated only during normal working hours
    D. too many records are being kept

7. According to the above paragraph, the growth of the population in the United States has matched the growth in the quantity of public documents for a period of MOST NEARLY _____ years.

   A. 50 B. 100 C. 200 D. 300

8. According to the above paragraph, the increased number of public documents has made it necessary to

   A. find out which public documents are worth keeping
   B. reduce the great number of public documents by decreasing government services
   C. eliminate the copying of all original public documents
   D. avoid all new copying devices

Questions 9-10.

DIRECTIONS: Questions 9 and 10 are to be answered SOLELY on the basis of the following paragraph.

The work goals of an agency can best be reached if the employees understand and agree with these goals. One way to gain such understanding and agreement is for management to encourage and seriously consider suggestions from employees in the setting of agency goals.

9. On the basis of the above paragraph, the BEST way to achieve the work goals of an agency is to

   A. make certain that employees work as hard as possible
   B. study the organizational structure of the agency
   C. encourage employees to think seriously about the agency's problems
   D. stimulate employee understanding of the work goals

10. On the basis of the above paragraph, understanding and agreement with agency goals can be gained by

    A. allowing the employees to set agency goals
    B. reaching agency goals quickly
    C. legislative review of agency operations
    D. employee participation in setting agency goals

Questions 11-13.

DIRECTIONS: Questions 11 through 13 are to be answered SOLELY on the basis of the following paragraph.

In order to organize records properly, it is necessary to start from their very beginning and trace each copy of the record to find out how it is used, how long it is used, and what may finally be done with it. Although several copies of the record are made, one copy should be marked as the copy of record. This is the formal legal copy, held to meet the requirements of the law. The other copies may be retained for brief periods for reference purposes, but these copies should not be kept after their usefulness as reference ends. There is another reason for tracing records through the office and that is to determine how long it takes the copy of record to reach the central file. The copy of record must not be kept longer than necessary by the section of the office which has prepared it, but should be sent to the central file as soon as possible so that it can be available to the various sections of the office. The central file can make the copy of record available to the various sections of the office at an early date only if it arrives at the central file as quickly as possible. Just as soon as its immediate or active service period is ended, the copy of record should be removed from the central file and put into the inactive file in the office to be stored for whatever length of time may be necessary to meet legal requirements, and then destroyed.

11. According to the above paragraph, a reason for tracing records through an office is to   11.____

    A. determine how long the central file must keep the records
    B. organize records properly
    C. find out how many copies of each record are required
    D. identify the copy of record

12. According to the above paragraph, in order for the central file to have the copy of record available as soon as possible for the various sections of the office, it is MOST important that the   12.____

    A. copy of record to be sent to the central file meets the requirements of the law
    B. copy of record is not kept in the inactive file too long
    C. section preparing the copy of record does not unduly delay in sending it to the central file
    D. central file does not keep the copy of record beyond its active service period

13. According to the above paragraph, the length of time a copy of a record is kept in the inactive file of an office depends CHIEFLY on the   13.____

    A. requirements of the law
    B. length of time that is required to trace the copy of record through the office
    C. use that is made of the copy of record
    D. length of the period that the copy of record is used for reference purposes

Questions 14-16.

DIRECTIONS: Questions 14 through 16 are to be answered SOLELY on the basis of the following paragraph.

The office was once considered as nothing more than a focal point of internal and external correspondence. It was capable only of dispatching a few letters upon occasion and of preparing records of little practical value. Under such a concept, the vitality of the office force was impaired. Initiative became stagnant, and the lot of the office worker was not likely to be a happy one. However, under the new concept of office management, the possibilities of waste and mismanagement in office operation are now fully recognized, as are the possibilities for the modern office to assist in the direction and control of business operations. Fortunately, the modern concept of the office as a centralized service-rendering unit is gaining ever greater acceptance in today's complex business world, for without the modern office, the production wheels do not turn and the distribution of goods and services is not possible.

14. According to the above paragraph, the fundamental difference between the old and the new concept of the office is the change in the   14._____

    A. accepted functions of the office
    B. content and the value of the records kept
    C. office methods and systems
    D. vitality and morale of the office force

15. According to the above paragraph, an office operated today under the old concept of the office MOST likely would   15._____

    A. make older workers happy in their jobs
    B. be part of an old thriving business concern
    C. have a passive role in the conduct of a business enterprise
    D. attract workers who do not believe in modern methods

16. Of the following, the MOST important implication of the above paragraph is that a present-day business organization cannot function effectively without the   16._____

    A. use of modern office equipment
    B. participation and cooperation of the office
    C. continued modernization of office procedures
    D. employment of office workers with skill and initiative

Questions 17-20.

DIRECTIONS: Questions 17 through 20 are to be answered SOLELY on the basis of the following paragraph.

A report is frequently ineffective because the person writing it is not fully acquainted with all the necessary details before he actually starts to construct the report. All details pertaining to the subject should be known before the report is started. If the essential facts are not known, they should be investigated. It is wise to have essential facts written down rather than to depend too much on memory, especially if the facts pertain to such matters as amounts, dates, names of persons, or other specific data. When the necessary information has been gathered, the general plan and content of the report should be thought out before the writing is actually begun. A person with little or no experience in writing reports may find that it is wise to make a brief outline. Persons with more experience should not need a written outline, but they should make mental notes of the steps they are to follow. If writing reports without dictation is a regular part of an office worker's duties, he should set aside a certain time during the day when he is least likely to be interrupted. That may be difficult, but in most offices there are certain times in the day when the callers, telephone calls, and other interruptions are not numerous. During those times, it is best to write reports that need undivided concentration. Reports that are written amid a series of interruptions may be poorly done.

17. Before starting to write an effective report, it is necessary to   17._____

    A. memorize all specific information
    B. disregard ambiguous data
    C. know all pertinent information
    D. develop a general plan

18. Reports dealing with complex and difficult material should be
    A. prepared and written by the supervisor of the unit
    B. written when there is the least chance of interruption
    C. prepared and written as part of regular office routine
    D. outlined and then dictated

19. According to the paragraph, employees with no prior familiarity in writing reports may find it helpful to
    A. prepare a brief outline
    B. mentally prepare a synopsis of the report's content
    C. have a fellow employee help in writing the report
    D. consult previous reports

20. In writing a report, needed information which is unclear should be
    A. disregarded
    B. memorized
    C. investigated
    D. gathered

Questions 21-25.

DIRECTIONS: Questions 21 through 25 are to be answered SOLELY on the basis of the following passage.

Positive discipline minimizes the amount of personal supervision required and aids in the maintenance of standards. When a new employee has been properly introduced and carefully instructed, when he has come to know the supervisor and has confidence in the supervisor's ability to take care of him, when he willingly cooperates with the supervisor, that employee has been under positive discipline and can be put on his own to produce the quantity and quality of work desired. Negative discipline, the fear of transfer to a less desirable location, for example, to a limited extent may restrain certain individuals from overt violation of rules and regulations governing attendance and conduct which in governmental agencies are usually on at least an agency-wide basis. Negative discipline may prompt employees to perform according to certain rules to avoid a penalty such as, for example, docking for tardiness.

21. According to the above passage, it is reasonable to assume that in the area of discipline, the first-line supervisor in a governmental agency has GREATER scope for action in
    A. *positive* discipline, because negative discipline is largely taken care of by agency rules and regulations
    B. *negative* discipline, because rules and procedures are already fixed and the supervisor can rely on them
    C. *positive* discipline, because the supervisor is in a position to recommend transfers
    D. *negative* discipline, because positive discipline is reserved for people on a higher supervisory level

22. In order to maintain positive discipline of employees under his supervision, it is MOST important for a supervisor to
    A. assure each employee that he has nothing to worry about
    B. insist at the outset on complete cooperation from employees

C. be sure that each employee is well trained in his job
D. inform new employees of the penalties for not meeting standards

23. According to the above passage, a feature of negative discipline is that it   23.____

    A. may lower employee morale
    B. may restrain employees from disobeying the rules
    C. censures equal treatment of employees
    D. tends to create standards for quality of work

24. A REASONABLE conclusion based on the above passage is that positive discipline benefits a supervisor because   24.____

    A. he can turn over orientation and supervision of a new employee to one of his subordinates
    B. subordinates learn to cooperate with one another when working on an assignment
    C. it is easier to administer
    D. it cuts down, in the long run, on the amount of time the supervisor needs to spend on direct supervision

25. Based on the above passage, it is REASONABLE to assume, that an important difference between positive discipline and negative discipline is that positive discipline   25.____

    A. is concerned with the quality of work and negative discipline with the quantity of work
    B. leads to a more desirable basis for motivation of the employee
    C. is more likely to be concerned with agency rules and regulations
    D. uses fear while negative discipline uses penalties to prod employees to adequate performance

KEY (CORRECT ANSWERS)

1.	C	11.	B
2.	C	12.	C
3.	D	13.	A
4.	A	14.	A
5.	B	15.	C
6.	D	16.	B
7.	C	17.	C
8.	A	18.	B
9.	D	19.	A
10.	D	20.	B

21. A
22. C
23. B
24. D
25. B

TEST 2

Questions 1-6.

DIRECTIONS: Questions 1 through 6 are to be answered SOLELY on the basis of the following passage.

Inherent in all organized endeavors is the need to resolve the individual differences involved in conflict. Conflict may be either a positive or negative factor since it may lead to creativity, innovation and progress on the one hand, or it may result, on the other hand, in a deterioration or even destruction of the organization. Thus, some forms of conflict are desirable, whereas others are undesirable and ethically wrong.

There are three management strategies which deal with interpersonal conflict. In the *divide-and-rule strategy,* management attempts to maintain control by limiting the conflict to those directly involved and preventing their disagreement from spreading to the larger group. The *suppression-of-differences strategy* entails ignoring conflicts or pretending they are irrelevant. In the *working-through-differences strategy,* management actively attempts to solve or resolve intergroup or interpersonal conflicts. Of the three strategies, only the last directly attacks and has the potential for eliminating the causes of conflict. An essential part of this strategy, however, is its employment by a committed and relatively mature management team.

1. According to the above passage, the *divide-and-rule strategy tor* dealing with conflict is the attempt to

    A. involve other people in the conflict
    B. restrict the conflict to those participating in it
    C. divide the conflict into positive and negative factors
    D. divide the conflict into a number of smaller ones

2. The word *conflict* is used in relation to both positive and negative factors in this passage. Which one of the following words is MOST likely to describe the activity which the word *conflict,* in the sense of the passage, implies?

    A. Competition   B. Confusion
    C. Cooperation   D. Aggression

3. According to the above passage, which one of the following characteristics is shared by both the *suppression-of-differences strategy* and the *divide-and-rule strategy*?

    A. Pretending that conflicts are irrelevant
    B. Preventing conflicts from spreading to the group situation
    C. Failure to directly attack the causes of conflict
    D. Actively attempting to resolve interpersonal conflict

4. According to the above passage, the successful resolution of interpersonal conflict requires

    A. allowing the group to mediate conflicts between two individuals
    B. division of the conflict into positive and negative factors
    C. involvement of a committed, mature management team
    D. ignoring minor conflicts until they threaten the organization

5. Which can be MOST reasonably inferred from the above passage? Conflict between two individuals is LEAST likely to continue when management uses

   A. the *working-through differences strategy*
   B. the *suppression-of differences strategy*
   C. the *divide-and-rule strategy*
   D. a combination of all three strategies

5.____

6. According to the above passage, a DESIRABLE result of conflict in an organization is when conflict

   A. exposes production problems in the organization
   B. can be easily ignored by management
   C. results in advancement of more efficient managers
   D. leads to development of new methods

6.____

Questions 7-13.

DIRECTIONS: Questions 7 through 13 are to be answered SOLELY on the basis of the passage below.

Modern management places great emphasis on the concept of communication. The communication process consists of the steps through which an idea or concept passes from its inception by one person, the sender, until it is acted upon by another person, the receiver. Through an understanding of these steps and some of the possible barriers that may occur, more effective communication may be achieved. The first step in the communication process is ideation by the sender. This is the formation of the intended content of the message he wants to transmit. In the next step, encoding, the sender organizes his ideas into a series of symbols designed to communicate his message to his intended receiver. He selects suitable words or phrases that can be understood by the receiver, and he also selects the appropriate media to be used—for example, memorandum, conference, etc. The third step is transmission of the encoded message through selected channels in the organizational structure. In the fourth step, the receiver enters the process by tuning in to receive the message. If the receiver does not function, however, the message is lost. For example, if the message is oral, the receiver must be a good listener. The fifth step is decoding of the message by the receiver, as for example, by changing words into ideas. At this step, the decoded message may not be the same idea that the sender originally encoded because the sender and receiver have different perceptions regarding the meaning of certain words. Finally, the receiver acts or responds. He may file the information, ask for more information, or take other action. There can be no assurance, however, that communication has taken place unless there is some type of feedback to the sender in the form of an acknowledgement that the message was received.

7. According to the above passage, *ideation* is the process by which the

   A. sender develops the intended content of the message
   B. sender organizes his ideas into a series of symbols
   C. receiver tunes in to receive the message
   D. receiver decodes the message

7.____

8. In the last sentence of the passage, the word *feedback* refers to the process by which the sender is assured that the

    A. receiver filed the information
    B. receiver's perception is the same as his own
    C. message was received
    D. message was properly interpreted

9. Which one of the following BEST shows the order of the steps in the communication process as described in the passage?

    A. 1 - ideation   2 - encoding
       3 - decoding   4 - transmission
       5 - receiving   6 - action
       7 - feedback to the sender

    B. 1 - ideation   2 - encoding
       3 - transmission 4 - decoding
       5 - receiving   6 - action
       7 - feedback to the sender

    C. 1 - ideation   2 - decoding
       3 - transmission 4 - receiving
       5 - encoding   6 - action
       7 - feedback to the sender

    D. 1 - ideation   2 - encoding
       3 - transmission 4 - receiving
       5 - decoding   6 - action
       7 - feedback to the sender

10. Which one of the following BEST expresses the main theme of the passage?

    A. Different individuals have the same perceptions regarding the meaning of words.
    B. An understanding of the steps in the communication process may achieve better communication.
    C. Receivers play a passive role in the communication process.
    D. Senders should not communicate with receivers who transmit feedback.

11. The above passage implies that a receiver does NOT function properly when he

    A. transmits feedback   B. files the information
    C. is a poor listener   D. asks for more information

12. Which one of the following, according to the above passage, is included in the SECOND step of the communication process?

    A. Selecting the appropriate media to be used in transmission
    B. Formulation of the intended content of the message
    C. Using appropriate media to respond to the receiver's feedback
    D. Transmitting the message through selected channels in the organization

13. The above passage implies that the *decoding process* is MOST NEARLY the reverse of the _____ process.

    A. transmission   B. receiving
    C. feedback   D. encoding

Questions 14-19.

DIRECTIONS: Questions 14 through 19 are to be answered SOLELY on the basis of the following passage.

It is often said that no system will work if the people who carry it out do not want it to work. In too many cases, a departmental reorganization that seemed technically sound and economically practical has proved to be a failure because the planners neglected to take the human factor into account. The truth is that employees are likely to feel threatened when they learn that a major change is in the wind. It does not matter whether or not the change actually poses a threat to an employee; the fact that he believes it does or fears it might is enough to make him feel insecure. Among the dangers he fears, the foremost is the possibility that his job may cease to exist and that he may be laid off or shunted into a less skilled position at lower pay. Even if he knows that his own job category is secure, however, he is likely to fear losing some of the important intangible advantages of his present position—for instance, he may fear that he will be separated from his present companions and thrust in with a group of strangers, or that he will find himself in a lower position on the organizational ladder if a new position is created above his.

It is important that management recognize these natural fears and take them into account in planning any kind of major change. While there is no cut-and-dried formula for preventing employee resistance, there are several steps that can be taken to reduce employees' fears and gain their cooperation. First, unwarranted fears can be dispelled if employees are kept informed of the planning from the start and if they know exactly what to expect. Next, assurance on matters such as retraining, transfers, and placement help should be given as soon as it is clear what direction the reorganization will take. Finally, employees' participation in the planning should be actively sought. There is a great psychological difference between feeling that a change is being forced upon one from the outside, and feeling that one is an insider who is helping to bring about a change.

14. According to the above passage, employees who are not in real danger of losing their jobs because of a proposed reorganization

    A. will be eager to assist in the reorganization
    B. will pay little attention to the reorganization
    C. should not be taken into account in planning the reorganization
    D. are nonetheless likely to feel threatened by the reorganization

15. The passage mentions the *intangible advantages* of a position.
    Which of the following BEST describes the kind of advantages alluded to in the passage?

    A. Benefits such as paid holidays and vacations
    B. Satisfaction of human needs for things like friendship and status
    C. Qualities such as leadership and responsibility
    D. A work environment that meets satisfactory standards of health and safety

16. According to the passage, an employee's fear that a reorganization may separate him from his present companions is a (n)

    A. childish and immature reaction to change
    B. unrealistic feeling since this is not going to happen

C. possible reaction that the planners should be aware of
D. incentive to employees to participate in the planning

17. On the basis of the above passage, it would be DESIRABLE, when planning a departmental reorganization, to

    A. be governed by employee feelings and attitudes
    B. give some employees lower positions
    C. keep employees informed
    D. lay off those who are less skilled

17.____

18. What does the passage say can be done to help gain employees' cooperation in a reorganization?

    A. Making sure that the change is technically sound, that it is economically practical, and that the human factor is taken into account
    B. Keeping employees fully informed, offering help in fitting them into new positions, and seeking their participation in the planning
    C. Assuring employees that they will not be laid off, that they will not be reassigned to a group of strangers, and that no new positions will be created on the organization ladder
    D. Reducing employees' fears, arranging a retraining program, and providing for transfers

18.____

19. Which of the following suggested titles would be MOST appropriate for this passage?

    A. PLANNING A DEPARTMENTAL REORGANIZATION
    B. WHY EMPLOYEES ARE AFRAID
    C. LOOKING AHEAD TO THE FUTURE
    D. PLANNING FOR CHANGE: THE HUMAN FACTOR

19.____

Questions 20-22.

DIRECTIONS: Questions 20 through 22 are to be answered SOLELY on the basis of the following passage.

The achievement of good human relations is essential if a business office is to produce at top efficiency and is to be a pleasant place in which to work. All office workers plan an important role in handling problems in human relations. They should, therefore, strive to acquire the understanding, tactfulness, and awareness necessary to deal effectively with actual office situations involving co-workers on all levels. Only in this way can they truly become responsible, interested, cooperative, and helpful members of the staff.

20. The selection implies that the MOST important value of good human relations in an office is to develop

    A. efficiency   B. cooperativeness
    C. tact   D. pleasantness and efficiency

20.____

21. Office workers should acquire understanding in dealing with

    A. co-workers   B. subordinates
    C. superiors   D. all members of the staff

21.____

22. The selection indicates that a highly competent secretary who is also very argumentative is meeting office requirements 22._____

    A. wholly
    B. partly
    C. slightly
    D. not at all

Questions 23-25.

DIRECTIONS: Questions 23 through 25 are to be answered SOLELY on the basis of the following passage.

It is common knowledge that ability to do a particular job and performance on the job do not always go hand in hand. Persons with great potential abilities sometimes fall down on the job because of laziness or lack of interest in the job, while persons with mediocre talents have often achieved excellent results through their industry and their loyalty to the interests of their employers. It is clear; therefore, that in a balanced personnel program, measures of employee ability need to be supplemented by measures of employee performance, for the final test of any employee is his performance on the job.

23. The MOST accurate of the following statements, on the basis of the above paragraph, is that 23._____

    A. employees who lack ability are usually not industrious
    B. an employee's attitudes are more important than his abilities
    C. mediocre employees who are interested in their work are preferable to employees who possess great ability
    D. superior capacity for performance should be supplemented with proper attitudes

24. On the basis of the above paragraph, the employee of most value to his employer is NOT necessarily the one who 24._____

    A. best understands the significance of his duties
    B. achieves excellent results
    C. possesses the greatest talents
    D. produces the greatest amount of work

25. According to the above paragraph, an employee's efficiency is BEST determined by an 25._____

    A. appraisal of his interest in his work
    B. evaluation of the work performed by him
    C. appraisal of his loyalty to his employer
    D. evaluation of his potential ability to perform his work

KEY (CORRECT ANSWERS)

1.	B	11.	C
2.	A	12.	A
3.	C	13.	D
4.	C	14.	D
5.	A	15.	B
6.	D	16.	C
7.	A	17.	C
8.	C	18.	B
9.	D	19.	D
10.	B	20.	D

21. D
22. B
23. D
24. C
25. B

TEST 3

Questions 1-8.

DIRECTIONS: Questions 1 through 8 are to be answered SOLELY on the basis of the following information and directions.

Assume that you are a clerk in a city agency. Your supervisor has asked you to classify each of the accidents that happened to employees in the agency into the following five categories:

   A. An accident that occurred in the period from January through June, between 9 A.M. and 12 Noon, that was the result of carelessness on the part of the injured employee, that caused the employee to lose less than seven working hours, that happened to an employee who was 40 years of age or over, and who was employed in the agency for less than three years;

   B. An accident that occurred in the period from July through December, after 1 P.M., that was the result of unsafe conditions, that caused the injured employee to lose less than seven working hours, that happened to an employee who was 40 years of age or over, and who was employed in the agency for three years or more;

   C. An accident that occurred in the period from January through June, after 1 P.M., that was the result of carelessness on the part of the injured employee, that caused the injured employee to lose seven or more working hours, that happened to an employee who was less than 40 years old, and who was employed in the agency for three years or more;

   D. An accident that occurred in the period from July through December, between 9 A.M. and 12 Noon, that was the result of unsafe conditions, that caused the injured employee to lose seven or more working hours, that happened to an employee who was less than 40 years old, and who was employed in the agency for less than three years;

   E. Accidents that cannot be classified in any of the foregoing groups. NOTE: In classifying these accidents, an employee's age and length of service are computed as of the date of accident. In all cases, it is to be assumed that each employee has been employed continuously in city service, and that each employee works seven hours a day, from 9 A.M. to 5 P.M., with lunch from 12 Noon to 1 P.M. In each question, consider only the information which will assist you in classifying the accident. Any information which is of no assistance in classifying an accident should not be considered.

1. The unsafe condition of the stairs in the building caused Miss Perkins to have an accident on October 14, 2003 at 4 P.M. When she returned to work the following day at 1 P.M., Miss Perkins said that the accident was the first one that had occurred to her in her ten years of employment with the agency. She was born on April 27, 1962. 1.____

2. On the day after she completed her six-month probationary period of employment with the agency, Miss Green, who had been considered a careful worker by her supervisor, injured her left foot in an accident caused by her own carelessness. She went home immediately after the accident, which occurred at 10 A.M., March 19, 2004, but returned to work at the regular time on the following morning. Miss Green was born July 12, 1963 in New York City. 2.____

3. The unsafe condition of a duplicating machine caused Mr. Martin to injure himself in an accident on September 8, 2006 at 2 P.M. As a result of the accident, he was unable to work the remainder of the day, but returned to his office ready for work on the following morning. Mr. Martin, who has been working for the agency since April 1, 2003, was born in St. Louis on February 1, 1968.   3.___

4. Mr. Smith was hospitalized for two weeks because of a back injury resulted from an accident on the morning of November 16, 2006. Investigation of the accident revealed that it was caused by the unsafe condition of the floor on which Mr. Smith had been walking. Mr. Smith, who is an accountant, has been an employee of the agency since March 1, 2004, and was born in Ohio on June 10, 1968.   4.___

5. Mr. Allen cut his right hand because he was careless in operating a multilith machine. Mr. Allen, who was 33 years old when the accident took place, has been employed by the agency since August 17, 1992. The accident, which occurred on January 26, 2006, at 2 P.M., caused Mr. Allen to be absent from work for the rest of the day. He was able to return to work the next morning.   5.___

6. Mr. Rand, who is a college graduate, was born on December, 28, 1967, and has been working for the agency since January 7, 2002. On Monday, April 25, 2005, at 2 P.M., his carelessness in operating a duplicating machine caused him to have an accident and to be sent home from work immediately. Fortunately, he was able to return to work at his regular time on the following Wednesday.   6.___

7. Because he was careless in running down a flight of stairs, Mr. Brown fell, bruising his right hand. Although the accident occurred shortly after he arrived for work on the morning of May 22, 2006, he was unable to resume work until 3 P.M. that day. Mr. Brown was born on August 15, 1955, and began working for the agency on September 12, 2003, as a clerk, at a salary of $22,750 per annum.   7.___

8. On December 5, 2005, four weeks after he had begun working for the agency, the unsafe condition of an automatic stapling machine caused Mr. Thomas to injure himself in an accident. Mr. Thomas, who was born on May 19,1975, lost three working days because of the accident, which occurred at 11:45 A.M.   8.___

Questions 9-10.

DIRECTIONS: Questions 9 and 10 are to be answered SOLELY on the basis of the following paragraph.

An impending reorganization within an agency will mean loss by transfer of several professional staff members from the personnel division. The division chief is asked to designate the persons to be transferred. After reviewing the implications of this reduction of staff with his assistant, the division chief discusses the matter at a staff meeting. He adopts the recommendations of several staff members to have volunteers make up the required reduction.

9. The decision to permit personnel to volunteer for transfer is

9._____

   A. *poor;* it is not likely that the members of a division are of equal value to the division chief
   B. *good;* dissatisfied members will probably be more productive elsewhere
   C. *poor;* the division chief has abdicated his responsibility to carry out the order given to him
   D. *good;* morale among remaining staff is likely to improve in a more cohesive framework

10. Suppose that one of the volunteers is a recently appointed employee who has completed his probationary period acceptably, but whose attitude toward division operations and agency administration tends to be rather negative and sometimes even abrasive. Because of his lack of commitment to the division, his transfer is recommended. If the transfer is approved, the division chief should, prior to the transfer,

10._____

   A. discuss with the staff the importance of commitment to the work of the agency and its relationship with job satisfaction
   B. refrain from any discussion of attitude with the employee
   C. discuss with the employee his concern about the employee's attitude
   D. avoid mention of attitude in the evaluation appraisal prepared for the receiving division chief

Questions 11-16.

DIRECTIONS: Questions 11 through 16 are to be answered SOLELY on the basis of the following paragraph.

Methods of administration of office activities, much of which consists of providing information and *know-how* needed to coordinate both activities within that particular office and other offices, have been among the last to come under the spotlight of management analysis. Progress has been rapid during the past decade, however, and is now accelerating at such a pace that an *information revolution* in office management appears to be in the making. Although triggered by technological breakthroughs in electronic computers and other giant steps in mechanization, this information revolution must be attributed to underlying forces, such as the increased complexity of both governmental and private enterprise, and ever-keener competition. Size, diversification, specialization of function, and decentralization are among the forces which make coordination of activities both more imperative and more difficult. Increased competition, both domestic and international, leaves little margin for error in managerial decisions. Several developments during recent years indicate an evolving pattern. In 1960, the American Management Association expanded the scope of its activities and changed the name of its Office Management Division to Administrative Services Division. Also in 1960, the magazine *Office Management* merged with the magazine *American Business,* and this new publication was named *Administrative Management.*

11. A REASONABLE inference that can be made from the information in the above paragraph is that an important role of the office manager today is to

   A. work toward specialization of functions performed by his subordinates
   B. inform and train subordinates regarding any new developments in computer technology and mechanization
   C. assist the professional management analysts with the management analysis work in the organization
   D. supply information that can be used to help coordinate and manage the other activities of the organization

12. An IMPORTANT reason for the *information revolution* that has been taking place in office management is the

   A. advance made in management analysis in the past decade
   B. technological breakthrough in electronic computers and mechanization
   C. more competitive and complicated nature of private business and government
   D. increased efficiency of office management techniques in the past ten years

13. According to the above paragraph, specialization of function in an organization is MOST likely to result in

   A. the elimination of errors in managerial decisions
   B. greater need to coordinate activities
   C. more competition with other organizations, both domestic and international
   D. a need for office managers with greater flexibility

14. The word *evolving,* as used in the third from last sentence in the above paragraph, means MOST NEARLY

   A. developing by gradual changes
   B. passing on to others
   C. occurring periodically
   D. breaking up into separate, constituent parts

15. Of the following, the MOST reasonable implication of the changes in names mentioned in the last part of the above paragraph is that these groups are attempting to

   A. professionalize the field of office management and the title of Office Manager
   B. combine two publications into one because of the increased costs of labor and materials
   C. adjust to the fact that the field of office management is broadening
   D. appeal to the top managerial people rather than the office management people in business and government

16. According to the above paragraph, intense competition among domestic and international enterprises makes it MOST important for an organization's managerial staff to

   A. coordinate and administer office activities with other activities in the organization
   B. make as few errors in decision-making as possible
   C. concentrate on decentralization and reduction of size of the individual divisions of the organization
   D. restrict decision-making only to top management officials

Questions 17-21.

DIRECTIONS: Questions 17 through 21 are to be answered SOLELY on the basis of the following passage.

For some office workers, it is useful to be familiar with the four main classes of domestic mail; for others, it is essential. Each class has a different rate of postage, and some have requirements concerning wrapping, sealing, or special information to be placed on the package. First class mail, the class which may not be opened for postal inspection, includes letters, postcards, business reply cards, and other kinds of written matter. There are different rates for some of the kinds of cards which can be sent by first class mail. The maximum weight for an item sent by first class mail is 70 pounds. An item which is not letter size should be marked *First Class* on all sides. Although office workers most often come into contact with first class mail, they may find it helpful to know something about the other classes. Second class mail is generally used for mailing newspapers and magazines. Publishers of these articles must meet certain U.S. Postal Service requirements in order to obtain a permit to use second class mailing rates. Third class mail, which must weigh less than 1 pound, includes printed materials and merchandise parcels. There are two rate structures for this class - a single piece rate and a bulk rate. Fourth class mail, also known as parcel post, includes packages weighing from one to 40 pounds. For more information about these classes of mail and the actual mailing rates, contact your local post office.

17. According to this passage, first class mail is the *only* class which

    A. has a limit on the maximum weight of an item
    B. has different rates for items within the class
    C. may not be opened for postal inspection
    D. should be used by office workers

18. According to this passage, the one of the following items which may CORRECTLY be sent by fourth class mail is a

    A. magazine weighing one-half pound
    B. package weighing one-half pound
    C. package weighing two pounds
    D. postcard

19. According to this passage, there are different postage rates for

    A. a newspaper sent by second class mail and a magazine sent by second class mail
    B. each of the classes of mail
    C. each pound of fourth class mail
    D. printed material sent by third class mail and merchandise parcels sent by third class mail

20. In order to send a newspaper by second class mail, a publisher MUST

    A. have met certain postal requirements and obtained a permit
    B. indicate whether he wants to use the single piece or the bulk rate
    C. make certain that the newspaper weighs less than one pound
    D. mark the newspaper *Second Class* on the top and bottom of the wrapper

21. Of the following types of information, the one which is NOT mentioned in the passage is the

    A. class of mail to which parcel post belongs
    B. kinds of items which can be sent by each class of mail
    C. maximum weight for an item sent by fourth class mail
    D. postage rate for each of the four classes of mail

Questions 22-25.

DIRECTIONS: Questions 22 through 25 are to be answered SOLELY on the basis of the following paragraph.

A standard comprises characteristics attached to an aspect of a process or product by which it can be evaluated. Standardization is the development and adoption of standards. When they are formulated, standards are not usually the product of a single person, but represent the thoughts and ideas of a group, leavened with the knowledge and information which are currently available. Standards which do not meet certain basic requirements become a hindrance rather than an aid to progress. Standards must not only be correct, accurate, and precise in requiring no more and no less than what is needed for satisfactory results, but they must also be workable in the sense that their usefulness is not nullified by external conditions. Standards should also be acceptable to the people who use them. If they are not acceptable, they cannot be considered to be satisfactory, although they may possess all the other essential characteristics.

22. According to the above paragraph, a processing standard that requires the use of materials that cannot be procured is MOST likely to be

    A. incomplete   B. unworkable
    C. inaccurate   D. unacceptable

23. According to the above paragraph, the construction of standards to which the performance of job duties should conform is MOST often

    A. the work of the people responsible for seeing that the duties are properly performed
    B. accomplished by the person who is best informed about the functions involved
    C. the responsibility of the people who are to apply them
    D. attributable to the efforts of various informed persons

24. According to the above paragraph, when standards call for finer tolerances than those essential to the conduct of successful production operations, the effect of the standards on the improvement of production operations is

    A. negative   B. negligible
    C. nullified   D. beneficial

25. The one of the following which is the MOST suitable title for the above paragraph is

    A. THE EVALUATION OF FORMULATED STANDARDS
    B. THE ATTRIBUTES OF SATISFACTORY STANDARDS
    C. THE ADOPTION OF ACCEPTABLE STANDARDS
    D. THE USE OF PROCESS OR PRODUCT STANDARDS

KEY (CORRECT ANSWERS)

1. B
2. A
3. E
4. D
5. E

6. C
7. A
8. D
9. A
10. C

11. D
12. C
13. B
14. A
15. C

16. B
17. C
18. C
19. B
20. A

21. D
22. C
23. D
24. A
25. B

PREPARING WRITTEN MATERIAL
EXAMINATION SECTION
TEST 1

DIRECTIONS: Each question consists of a sentence which may or may not be an example of good English usage. Examine each sentence, considering grammar, punctuation, spelling, capitalization, and awkwardness. Then choose the correct statement about it from the four choices below it. If the English usage in the sentence given is better than any of the changes suggested in choices B, C, or D, pick choice A. (Do not pick a choice that will change the meaning of the sentence.) *PRINT THE LETTER OF THE CORRECT ANSWER IN THE SPACE AT THE RIGHT.*

1. We attended a staff conference on Wednesday the new safety and fire rules were discussed.
    A. This is an example of acceptable writing.
    B. The words "safety," "fire," and "rules" should begin with capital letters.
    C. There should be a comma after the word "Wednesday."
    D. There should be a period after the word "Wednesday" and the word "the" should begin with a capital letter.

1.____

2. Neither the dictionary or the telephone directory could be found in the office library.
    A. This is an example of acceptable writing.
    B. The word "or" should be changed to "nor."
    C. The word "library" should be spelled "libery."
    D. The word "neither" should be changed to "either."

2.____

3. The report would have been typed correctly if the typist could read the draft.
    A. This is an example of acceptable writing.
    B. The word "would" should be removed.
    C. The word "have" should be inserted after the word "could."
    D. The word "correctly" should be changed to "correct."

3.____

4. The supervisor brought the reports and forms to an employees desk.
    A. This is an example of acceptable writing.
    B. The word "brought" should be changed to "took."
    C. There should be a comma after the word "reports" and a comma after the word "forms."
    D. The word "employees" should be spelled "employee's."

4.____

5. It's important for all the office personnel to submit their vacation schedules on time.
    A. This is an example of acceptable writing.
    B. The word "It's" should be spelled "Its."
    C. The word "their" should be spelled "they're."
    D. The word "personnel" should be spelled "personal."

5.____

147

6. The report, along with the accompanying documents, were submitted for review.
   A. This is an example of acceptable writing.
   B. The words "were submitted" should be changed to "was submitted."
   C. The word "accompanying" should be spelled "accompaning."
   D. The comma after the word "report" should be taken out.

7. If others must use your files, be certain that they understand how the system works, but insist that you do all the filing and refiling.
   A. This is an example of acceptable writing.
   B. There should be a period after the word "works," and the word "but" should start a new sentence.
   C. The words "filing" and "refiling" should be spelled "fileing" and "refileing."
   D. There should be a comma after the word "but."

8. The appeal was not considered because of its late arrival.
   A. This is an example of acceptable writing.
   B. The word "its" should be changed to "it's."
   C. The word "its" should be changed to "the."
   D. The words "late arrival" should be changed to "arrival late."

9. The letter must be read carefuly to determine under which subject it should be filed.
   A. This is an example of acceptable writing.
   B. The word "under" should be changed to "at."
   C. The word "determine" should be spelled "determin."
   D. The word "carefuly" should be spelled "carefully."

10. He showed potential as an office manager, but he lacked skill in delegating work.
    A. This is an example of acceptable writing.
    B. The word "delegating" should be spelled "delagating."
    C. The word "potential" should be spelled "potencial."
    D. The words "he lacked" should be changed to "was lacking."

KEY (CORRECT ANSWERS)

1.	D	6.	B
2.	B	7.	A
3.	C	8.	A
4.	D	9.	D
5.	A	10.	A

TEST 2

DIRECTIONS: Each question consists of a sentence which may or may not be an example of good English usage. Examine each sentence, considering grammar, punctuation, spelling, capitalization, and awkwardness. Then choose the correct statement about it from the four choices below it. If the English usage in the sentence given is better than any of the changes suggested in choices B, C, or D, pick choice A. (Do not pick a choice that will change the meaning of the sentence.) *PRINT THE LETTER OF THE CORRECT ANSWER IN THE SPACE AT THE RIGHT.*

1. The supervisor wants that all staff members report to the office at 9:00 A.M.
   A. This is an example of acceptable writing.
   B. The word "that" should be removed and the word "to" should be inserted after the word "members."
   C. There should be a comma after the word "wants" and a comma after the word "office."
   D. The word "wants" should be changed to "want" and the word "shall" should be inserted after the word "members."

   1.____

2. Every morning the clerk opens the office mail and distributes it.
   A. This is an example of acceptable writing.
   B. The word "opens" should be changed to "open."
   C. The word "mail" should be changed to "letters."
   D. The word "it" should be changed to "them."

   2.____

3. The secretary typed more fast on a desktop computer than on a laptop computer.
   A. This is an example of acceptable writing.
   B. The words "more fast" should be changed to "faster."
   C. There should be a comma after the words "desktop computer."
   D. The word "than" should be changed to "then."

   3.____

4. The new stenographer needed a desk a computer, a chair and a blotter.
   A. This is an example of acceptable writing.
   B. The word "blotter" should be spelled "blodder."
   C. The word "stenographer" should begin with a capital letter.
   D. There should be a comma after the word "desk."

   4.____

5. The recruiting officer said, "There are many different goverment jobs available."
   A. This is an example of acceptable writing.
   B. The word "There" should not be capitalized.
   C. The word "government" should be spelled "government."
   D. The comma after the word "said" should be removed.

   5.____

6. He can recommend a mechanic whose work is reliable.
   A. This is an example of acceptable writing.
   B. The word "reliable" should be spelled "relyable."
   C. The word "whose" should be spelled "who's."
   D. The word "mechanic should be spelled "mecanic."

   6.____

149

7. She typed quickly; like someone who had not a moment to lose. 7._____
   A. This is an example of acceptable writing.
   B. The word "not" should be removed.
   C. The semicolon should be changed to a comma.
   D. The word "quickly" should be placed before instead of after the word "typed."

8. She insisted that she had to much work to do. 8._____
   A. This is an example of acceptable writing.
   B. The word "insisted" should be spelled "incisted."
   C. The word "to" used in front of "much" should be spelled "too."
   D. The word "do" should be changed to "be done."

9. He excepted praise from his supervisor for a job well done. 9._____
   A. This is an example of acceptable writing.
   B. The word "excepted" should be spelled "accepted."
   C. The order of the words "well done" should be changed to "done well."
   D. There should be a comma after the word "supervisor."

10. What appears to be intentional errors in grammar occur several times in the passage. 10._____
    A. This is an example of acceptable writing.
    B. The word "occur" should be spelled "occurr."
    C. The word "appears" should be changed to "appear."
    D. The phrase "several times" should be changed to "from time to time."

KEY (CORRECT ANSWERS)

1.	B	6.	A
2.	A	7.	C
3.	B	8.	C
4.	D	9.	B
5.	C	10.	C

TEST 3

DIRECTIONS: Each question consists of a sentence which may or may not be an example of good English usage. Examine each sentence, considering grammar, punctuation, spelling, capitalization, and awkwardness. Then choose the correct statement about it from the four choices below it. If the English usage in the sentence given is better than any of the changes suggested in choices B, C, or D, pick choice A. (Do not pick a choice that will change the meaning of the sentence.) *PRINT THE LETTER OF THE CORRECT ANSWER IN THE SPACE AT THE RIGHT.*

1. The clerk could have completed the assignment on time if he knows where these materials were located.
    A. This is an example of acceptable writing.
    B. The word "knows" should be replaced by "had known."
    C. The word "were" should be replaced by "had been."
    D. The words "where these materials were located" should be replaced by "the location of these materials."

2. All employees should be given safety training. Not just those who accidents.
    A. This is an example of acceptable writing.
    B. The period after the word "training" should be changed to a colon.
    C. The period after the word "training" should be changed to a semicolon, and the first letter of the word "Not" should be changed to a small "n."
    D. The period after the word "training" should be changed to a comma, and the first letter of the word "Not" should be changed to a small "n."

3. This proposal is designed to promote employee awareness of the suggestion program, to encourage employee participation in the program, and to increase the number of suggestions submitted.
    A. This is an example of acceptable writing.
    B. The word "proposal" should be spelled "proposal."
    C. The words "to increase the number of suggestions submitted" should be changed to "an increase in the number of suggestions is expected."
    D. The word "promote" should be changed to "enhance" and the word "increase" should be changed to "add to."

4. The introduction of inovative managerial techniques should be preceded by careful analysis of the specific circumstances and conditions in each department.
    A. This is an example of acceptable writing.
    B. The word "technique" should be spelled "techneques."
    C. The word "inovative" should be spelled "innovative."
    D. A comma should be placed after the word "circumstances" and after the word "conditions."

151

5. This occurrence indicates that such criticism embarrasses him. 5.____
   A. This is an example of acceptable writing.
   B. The word "occurrence" should be spelled "occurence."
   C. The word "criticism" should be spelled "critisism.
   D. The word "embarrasses" should be spelled "embarasses.

KEY (CORRECT ANSWERS)

1. B
2. D
3. A
4. C
5. A

PREPARING WRITTEN MATERIAL

PARAGRAPH REARRANGEMENT
COMMENTARY

The sentences that follow are in scrambled order. You are to rearrange them in proper order and indicate the letter choice containing the correct answer at the space at the right.

Each group of sentences in this section is actually a paragraph presented in scrambled order. Each sentence in the group has a place in that paragraph; no sentence is to be left out. You are to read each group of sentences and decide upon the best order in which to put the sentences so as to form a well-organized paragraph.

The questions in this section measure the ability to solve a problem when all the facts relevant to its solution are not given.

More specifically, certain positions of responsibility and authority require the employee to discover connection between events sometimes, apparently, unrelated. In order to do this, the employee will find it necessary to correctly infer that unspecified events have probably occurred or are likely to occur. This ability becomes especially important when action must be taken on incomplete information.

Accordingly, these questions require competitors to choose among several suggested alternatives, each of which presents a different sequential arrangement of the events. Competitors must choose the MOST logical of the suggested sequences.

In order to do so, they may be required to draw on general knowledge to infer missing concepts or events that are essential to sequencing the given events. Competitors should be careful to infer only what is essential to the sequence. The plausibility of the wrong alternatives will always require the inclusion of unlikely events or of additional chains of events which are NOT essential to sequencing the given events.

It's very important to remember that you are looking for the best of the four possible choices, and that the best choice of all may not even be one of the answers you're given to choose from.

There is no one right way to solve these problems. Many people have found it helpful to first write out the order of the sentences, as they would have arranged them, on their scrap paper before looking at the possible answers. If their optimum answer is there, this can save them some time. If it isn't, this method can still give insight into solving the problem. Others find it most helpful to just go through each of the possible choices, contrasting each as they go along. You should use whatever method feels comfortable and works for you.

While most of these types of questions are not that difficult, we've added a higher percentage of the difficult type, just to give you more practice. Usually there are only one or two questions on this section that contain such subtle distinctions that you're unable to answer confidently. And you then may find yourself stuck deciding between two possible choices, neither of which you're sure about.

EXAMINATION SECTION
TEST 1

DIRECTIONS: The following groups of sentences need to be arranged in an order that makes sense. Select the letter preceding the sequence that represents the BEST sentence order. *PRINT THE LETTER OF THE CORRECT ANSWER IN THE SPACE AT THE RIGHT.*

1. I. The keyboard was purposely designed to be a little awkward to slow typists down.
    II. The arrangement of letters on the keyboard of a typewriter was not designed for the convenience of the typist.
    III. Fortunately, no one is suggesting that a new keyboard be designed right away.
    IV. If one were, we would have to learn to type all over again.
    V. The reason was that the early machines were slower than the typists and would jam easily.
    The CORRECT answer is:
    A. I, III, IV, II, V
    B. II, V, I, IV, III
    C. V, I, II, III, IV
    D. II, I, V, III, IV

2. I. The majority of the new service jobs are part-time or low-paying.
    II. According to the U.S. Bureau of Labor Statistics, jobs in the service sector constitute 72% of all jobs in this country.
    III. If more and more workers receive less and less money, who will buy the goods and services needed to keep the economy going?
    IV. The service sector is by far the fastest growing part of the United States economy.
    V. Some economists look upon this trend with great concern.
    The CORRECT answer is:
    A. II, IV, I, V, III
    B. II, III, IV, I, V
    C. V, IV, II, III, I
    D. III, I, II, IV, V

3. I. They can also affect one's endurance.
    II. This can stabilize blood sugar levels, and ensure that the brain is receiving a steady, constant, supply of glucose, so that one is *hitting on all cylinders* while taking the test.
    III. By food, we mean real food, not junk food or unhealthy snacks.
    IV. For this reason, it is important not to skip a meal, and to bring food with you to the exam.
    V. One's blood sugar levels can affect how clearly one is able to think and concentrate during an exam.
    The CORRECT answer is:
    A. V, IV, II, III, I
    B. V, II, I, IV, III
    C. V, I, IV, III, II
    D. V, IV, I, III, II

4. I. Those who are the embodiment of desire are absorbed in material quests, and those who are the embodiment of feeling are warriors who value power more than possession.
    II. These qualities are in everyone, but in different degrees.
    III. But those who value understanding yearn not for goods or victory, but for knowledge.
    IV. According to Plato, human behavior flows from three main sources: desire, emotion, and knowledge.
    V. In the perfect state, the industrial forces would produce but not rule, the military would protect but not rule, and the forces of knowledge, the philosopher kings, would reign.
    The CORRECT answer is:
    A. IV, V, I, II, III
    B. V, I, II, III, IV
    C. IV, III, II, I, V
    D. IV, II, I, III, V

5. I. Of the more than 26,000 tons of garbage produced daily in New York City, 12,000 tons arrive daily at Fresh Kills.
    II. In a month, enough garbage accumulates there to fill the Empire State Building.
    III. In 1937, the Supreme Court halted the practice of dumping the trash of New York City into the sea.
    IV. Although the garbage is compacted, in a few years the mounds of garbage at Fresh Kills will be the highest points south of Maine's Mount Desert Island on the Eastern Seaboard.
    V. Instead, tugboats now pull barges of much of the trash to Staten Island and the largest landfill in the world, Fresh Kills.
    The CORRECT answer is:
    A. III, V, IV, I, II
    B. III, V, II, IV, I
    C. III, V, I, II, IV
    D. III, II, V, IV, I

6. I. Communists rank equality very high, but freedom very low.
    II. Unlike communists, conservatives place a high value on freedom and a very low value on equality.
    III. A recent study demonstrated that one way to classify people's political beliefs is to look at the importance placed on two words: freedom and equality.
    IV. Thus, by demonstrating how members of these groups feel about the two words, the study has proved to be useful for political analysts in several European countries.
    V. According to the study, socialists and liberals rank both freedom and equality very high, while fascists rate both very low.
    The CORRECT answer is:
    A. III, V, I, II, IV
    B. V, IV, III, I, II
    C. III, V, IV, II, I
    D. III, I, II, IV, V

7. I. "Can there be anything more amazing than this?"
    II. If the riddle is successfully answered, his dead brothers will be brought back to life.
    III. "Even though man sees those around him dying every day," says Dharmaraj, "he still believes and acts as if he were immortal."
    IV. "What is the cause of ceaseless wonder?" asks the Lord of the Lake.
    V. In the ancient epic, The Mahabharata, a riddle is asked of one of the Pandava brothers.
    The CORRECT answer is:
    A. V, II, I, IV, III
    B. V, IV, III, I, II
    C. V, II, IV, III, I
    D. V, II, IV, I, III

8. I. On the contrary, the two main theories—the cooperative (neoclassical) theory and the radical (labor theory)—clearly rest on very different assumptions, which have very different ethical overtones.
    II. The distribution of income is the primary factor in determining the relative levels of material well-being that different groups or individuals attain.
    III. Of all issues in economics, the distribution of income is one of the most controversial.
    IV. The neoclassical theory tends to support the existing income distribution (or minor changes), while the labor theory ends to support substantial changes in the way income is distributed.
    V. The intensity of the controversy reflects the fact that different economic theories are not purely neutral, *detached* theories with no ethical or moral implications.
    The CORRECT answer is:
    A. II, I, V, IV, III
    B. III, II, V, I, IV
    C. III, V, II, I, IV
    D. III, V, IV, I, II

9. I. The pool acts as a broker and ensures that the cheapest power gets used first.
    II. Every six seconds, the pool's computer monitors all of the generating stations in the state and decides which to ask for more power and which to cut back.
    III. The buying and selling of electrical power is handled by the New York Power Pool in Guilderland, New York.
    IV. This is to the advantage of both the buying and selling utilities.
    V. The pool began operation in 1970, and consists of the state's eight electric utilities.
    The CORRECT answer is:
    A. V, I, II, III, IV
    B. IV, II, I, III, V
    C. III, V, I, IV, II
    D. V, III, IV, II, I

10. I. Modern English is much simpler grammatically than Old English.
    II. Finnish grammar is very complicated; there are some fifteen cases, for example.
    III. Chinese, a very old language, may seem to be the exception, but it is the great number of characters/words that must be mastered that makes it so difficult to learn, not its grammar.
    IV. The newest literary language—that is, written as well as spoken—is Finish, whose literary roots go back only to about the middle of the nineteenth century.
    V. Contrary to popular belief, the longer a language is been in use the simpler its grammar—not the reverse.

    The CORRECT answer is:
    A. IV, I, II, III, V
    B. V, I, IV, II, III
    C. I, II, IV, III, V
    D. IV, II, III, I, V

10.____

KEY (CORRECT ANSWERS)

1.	D	6.	A
2.	A	7.	C
3.	C	8.	B
4.	D	9.	C
5.	C	10.	B

TEST 2

DIRECTIONS: This type of question tests your ability to recognize accurate paraphrasing, well-constructed paragraphs, and appropriate style and tone. It is important that the answer you select contains only the facts or concepts given in the original sentences. It is also important that you be aware of incomplete sentences, inappropriate transitions, unsupported opinions, incorrect usage, and illogical sentence order. Paragraphs that do not include all the necessary facts and concepts, that distort them, or that add new ones are not considered correct.

The format for this section may vary. Sometimes, long paragraphs are given, and emphasis is placed on style and organization. Our first five questions are of this type. Other times, the paragraphs are shorter, and there is less emphasis on style and more emphasis on accurate representation of information. Our second group of five questions are of this nature.

For each of Questions 1 through 10, select the paragraph that BEST expresses the ideas contained in the sentences above it. *PRINT THE LETTER OF THE CORRECT ANSWER IN THE SPACE AT THE RIGHT.*

1.
   I. Listening skills are very important for managers.
   II. Listening skills are not usually emphasized.
   III. Whenever managers are depicted in books, manuals or the media, they are always talking, never listening.
   IV. We'd like you to read the enclosed handout on listening skills and to try to consciously apply them this week.
   V. We guarantee they will improve the quality of your interactions.

   A. Unfortunately, listening skills are not usually emphasized for managers. Managers are always depicted as talking, never listening. We'd like you to read the enclosed handout on listening skills. Please try to apply these principles this week. If you do, we guarantee they will improve the quality of your interactions.
   B. The enclosed handout on listening skills will be important improving the quality of your interactions. We guarantee it. All you have to do is take sometime this week to read and to consciously try to apply the principles. Listening skills are very important for manages, but they are not usually emphasized. Whenever managers are depicted in books, manuals or the media, they are always talking, never listening.
   C. Listening well is one of the most important skills a manager can have, yet it's not usually given much attention. Think about any representation of managers in books, manuals, or in the media that you may have seen. They're always talking, never listening. We'd like you to read the enclosed handout on listening skills and consciously try to apply them the rest of the week. We guarantee you will see a difference in the quality of your interactions.

1.____

D. Effective listening, one very important tool in the effective manager's arsenal, is usually not emphasized enough. The usual depiction of managers in books, manuals or the media is one in which they are always talking, never listening. We'd like you to read the enclosed handout and consciously try to apply the information contained therein throughout the rest of the week. We feel sure that you will see a marked difference in the quality of your interactions.

2.   I. Chekhov wrote three dramatic masterpieces which share certain themes and formats: Uncle Vanya, The Cherry Orchard, and The Three Sisters.
   II. They are primarily concerned with the passage of time and how this erodes human aspirations.
   III. The plays are haunted by the ghosts of the wasted life.
   IV. The characters are concerned with life's lesser problems; however, such as the inability to make decisions, loyalty to the wrong cause, and the inability to be clear.
   V. This results in sweet, almost aching, type of a sadness referred to as Chekhovian.

2.____

   A. Chekhov wrote three dramatic masterpieces: Uncle Vanya, The Cherry Orchard, and The Three Sisters. These masterpieces share certain themes and formats: the passage of time, how time erodes human aspirations, and the ghosts of wasted life. Each masterpiece is characterized by a sweet, almost aching, type of sadness that has become known as Chekhovian. The sweetness of this sadness hinges on the fact that it is not the great tragedies of life which are destroying these characters, but their minor flaws: indecisiveness, misplaced loyalty, unclarity.
   B. The Cherry Orchard, Uncle Vanya, and The Three Sisters are three dramatic masterpieces written by Chekhov that use similar formats to explore a common theme. Each is primarily concerned with the way that passing time wears down human aspirations, and each is haunted by the ghosts of the wasted life. The characters are shown struggling futilely with the lesser problems of life: indecisiveness, loyalty to the wrong cause, and the inability to be clear. These struggles create a mood of sweet, almost aching, sadness that has become known as Chekhovian.
   C. Chekhov's dramatic masterpieces are, along with The Cherry Orchard, Uncle Vanya, and The Three Sisters. These plays share certain thematic and formal similarities. They are concerned most of all with the passage of time and the way in which time erodes human aspirations. Each play is haunted by the specter of the wasted life. Chekhov's characters are caught, however, by life's lesser snares: indecisiveness, loyalty to the wrong cause, and unclarity. The characteristic mood is a sweet, almost aching type of sadness that has come to be known as Chekhovian.
   D. A Chekhovian mood is characterized by sweet, almost aching, sadness. The term comes from three dramatic tragedies by Chekhov which revolve around the sadness of a wasted life. The three masterpieces (Uncle Vanya, The Three Sisters, and The Cherry Orchard) share the same

theme and format. The plays are concerned with how the passage of time erodes human aspirations. They are peopled with characters who are struggling with life's lesser problems. These are people who are indecisive, loyal to the wrong causes, or are unable to make themselves clear.

3.
I. Movie previews have often helped producers decide which parts of movies they should take out or leave in.
II. The first 1933 preview of King Kong was very helpful to the producers because many people ran screaming from the theater and would not return when four men first attacked by Kong were eaten by giant spiders.
III. The 1950 premiere of Sunset Boulevard resulted in the filming of an entirely new beginning, and a delay of six months in the film's release.
IV. In the original opening scene, William Holden was in a morgue talking with thirty-six other "corpses" about the ways some of them had died.
V. When he began to tell them of his life with Gloria Swanson, the audience found this hilarious, instead of taking the scene seriously.

3._____

A. Movie previews have often helped producers decide what parts of movies they should leave in or take out. For example, the first preview of King Kong in 1933 was very helpful. In one scene, four men were first attacked by Kong and then eaten by giant spiders. Many members of the audience ran screaming from the theater and would not return. The premiere of the 1950 film Sunset Boulevard was also very helpful. In the original opening scene, William Holden was in a morgue with thirty-six other "corpses," discussing the ways some of them had died. When he began to tell them of his life with Gloria Swanson, the audience found this hilarious. They were supposed to take the scene seriously. The result was a delay of six months in the release of the film while a new beginning was added.

B. Movie previews have often helped producers decide whether they should change various parts of a movie. After the 1933 preview of King Kong, a scene in which four men who had been attacked by Kong were eaten by giant spiders was taken out as many people ran screaming from the theater and would not return. The 1950 premiere of Sunset Boulevard also led to some changes. In the original opening scene, William Holden was in a morgue talking with thirty-six other "corpses" about the ways some of them had died. When he began to tell them of his life with Gloria Swanson, the audience found this hilarious, instead of taking the scene seriously.

C. What do Sunset Boulevard and King Kong have in common? Both show the value of using movie previews to test audience reaction. The first 1933 preview of King Kong showed that a scene showing four men being eaten by giant spiders after having been attacked by Kong was too frightening for many people. They ran screaming from the theater and couldn't be coaxed back. The 1950 premiere of Sunset Boulevard was also a scream, but not the kind the producers intended. The movie opens with William Holden lying in a morgue discussing the ways they had died with thirty-six other "corpses." When he began to tell them of his life with Gloria Swanson, the audience couldn't take him seriously. Their laughter caused a six-month delay while the beginning was rewritten.

D. Producers very often use movie previews to decide if changes are needed. The premiere of Sunset Boulevard in 1950 led to a new beginning and a six-month delay in film release. At the beginning, William Holden and thirty-six other "corpses" discuss the ways some of them died. Rather than taking this seriously, the audience thought it was hilarious when he began to tell them of his life with Gloria Swanson. The first 1933 preview of King Kong was very helpful for its producers because one scene so terrified the audience that many of them ran screaming from the theater and would not return. In this particular scene, four men who had first been attacked by Kong were eaten by giant spiders.

4. I. It is common for supervisors to view employees as "things" to be manipulated. 4.____
    II. This approach does not motivate employees, nor does the carrot-and-stick approach because employees often recognize these behaviors and resent them.
    III. Supervisors can change these behaviors by using self-inquiry and persistence.
    IV. The best managers genuinely respect those they work with, are supportive and helpful, and are interested in working as a team with those they supervise.
    V. They disagree with the Golden Rule that says "he or she who has the gold makes the rules."

    A. Some managers act as if they think the Golden Rule means "he or she who has the gold makes the rules." They show disrespect to employees by seeing them as "things" to be manipulated. Obviously, this approach does not motivate employees any more than the carrot-and-stick approach motivates them. The employees are smart enough to spot these behaviors and resent them. On the other hand, the managers genuinely respect those they work with, are supportive and helpful, and are interested in working as a team. Self-inquiry and persistence can change even the former type of supervisor into the latter.
    B. Many supervisors all into the trap of viewing employees as "things" to be manipulated, or try to motivate them by using a carrot-and-stick approach. These methods do not motivate employees, who often recognize the behaviors and resent them. Supervisors can change these behaviors, however, by using self-inquiry and persistence. The best managers are supportive and helpful, and have genuine respect for those with whom they work. They are interested in working as a team with those they supervise. To them, the Golden Rule is not "he or she who has the gold makes the rules."
    C. Some supervisors see employees as "things" to be used or manipulated using a carrot-and-stick technique. These methods don't work. Employees often see through them and resent them. A supervisor who

wants to change may do so. The techniques of self-inquiry and persistence can be used to turn him or her into the type of supervisor who doesn't think the Golden Rule is "he or she who has the gold makes the rules." They may become like the best managers who treat those with whom they work with respect and give them help and support. These are the manager who know how to build a team.

D. Unfortunately, many supervisors act as if their employees are objects whose movements they can position at will. This mistaken belief has the same result as another popular motivational technique—the carrot-and-stick approach. Both attitudes can lead to the same result—resentment from those employees who recognize the behaviors for what they are. Supervisors who recognize these behaviors can change through the use of persistence and the use of self-inquiry. It's important to remember that the best managers respect their employees. They readily give necessary help and support and are interested in working as a team with those they supervise. To these managers, the Golden Rule is not "he or she who has the gold makes the rules."

5.
I. The first half of the nineteenth century produced a group of pessimistic poets—Byron, De Musset, Heine, Pushkin, and Leopardi.
II. It also produced a group of pessimistic composers—Schubert, Chopin, Schumann, and even the later Beethoven.
III. Above all, in philosophy, there was the profoundly pessimistic philosopher, Schopenhauer.
IV. The Revolution was dead, the Bourbons were restored, the feudal barons were reclaiming their land, and progress everywhere was being suppressed, as the great age was over.
V. "I thank God," said Goethe, "that I am not young in so thoroughly finished a world."

A. "I thank God," said Goethe, "that I am not young in so thoroughly finished a world." The Revolution was dead, the Bourbons were restored, the feudal barons were reclaiming their land, and progress everywhere was being suppressed. The first half of the nineteenth century produced a group of pessimistic poets: Byron, De Musset, Heine, Pushkin, and Leopardi. It also produced pessimistic composers: Schubert, Chopin, Schumann. Although Beethoven came later, he fits into this group, too. Finally and above all, it also produced a profoundly pessimistic philosopher, Schopenhauer. The great age was over.

B. The first half of the nineteenth century produced a group of pessimistic poets: Byron, De Musset, Heine, Pushkin, and Leopardi. It produced a group of pessimistic composers: Schubert, Chopin, Schumann, and even the later Beethoven. Above all, it produced a profoundly pessimistic philosopher, Schopenhauer. For each of these men, the great age was over. The Revolution was dead, and the Bourbons were restored. The feudal barons were reclaiming their land, and progress everywhere was being suppressed.

C. The great age was over. The Revolution was dead—the Bourbons were restored, and the feudal barons were reclaiming their land. Progress everywhere was being suppressed. Out of this climate came a profound pessimism. Poets, like Byron, De Musset, Heine, Pushkin, and Leopardi; composers, like Schubert, Chopin, Schumann, and even the later Beethoven; and above all, a profoundly pessimistic philosopher, Schopenauer. This pessimism which arose in the first half of the nineteenth century is illustrated by these words of Goethe, "I thank God that I am not young in so thoroughly finished a world."

D. The first half of the nineteenth century produced a group of pessimistic poets, Byron, De Musset, Heine, Pushkin, and Leopardi—and a group of pessimistic composers, Schubert, Chopin, Schumann, and the later Beethoven. Above it all, it produced a profoundly pessimistic philosopher, Schopenhauer. The great age was over. The Revolution was dead, the Bourbons were restored, the feudal barons were reclaiming their land, and progress everywhere was being suppressed. "I thank God," said Goethe, "that I am not young in so thoroughly finished a world."

6. I. A new manager sometimes may feel insecure about his or her competence in the new position.
   II. The new manager may then exhibit defensive or arrogant behavior towards those one supervises, or the new manager may direct overly flattering behavior toward one's new supervisor.

   A. Sometimes, a new manager may feel insecure about his or her ability to perform well in this new position. The insecurity may lead him or her to treat others differently. He or she may display arrogant or defensive behavior towards those he or she supervises, or be overly flattering to his or her new supervisor.
   B. A new manager may sometimes feel insecure about his or her ability to perform well in the new position. He or she may then become arrogant, defensive, or overly flattering towards those he or she works with.
   C. There are times when a new manager may be insecure about how well he or she can perform in the new job. The new manager may also behave defensive or act in an arrogant way towards those he or she supervises, or overly flatter his or her boss.
   D. Sometimes a new manager may feel insecure about his or her ability to perform well in the new position. He or she may then display arrogant or defensive behavior towards those they supervise, or become overly flattering towards their supervisors.

7. I. It is possible to eliminate unwanted behavior by bringing it under stimulus control—tying the behavior to a cue, and then never, or rarely, giving the cue.
   II. One trainer successfully used this method to keep an energetic young porpoise from coming out of her tank whenever she felt like it, which was potentially dangerous.
   III. Her trainer taught her to do it for a reward, in response to a hand signal, and then rarely gave the signal.

A. Unwanted behavior can be eliminated by tying the behavior to a cue, and then never, or rarely, giving the cue. This is called stimulus control. One trainer was able to use this method to keep an energetic young porpoise from coming out of her tank by teaching her to come out for a reward in response to a hand signal, and then rarely giving the signal.
B. Stimulus control can be used to eliminate unwanted behavior. In this method, behavior is tied to a cue, and then the cue is rarely, if ever, given. One trainer was able to successfully use stimulus control to keep an energetic young porpoise from coming out of her tank whenever she felt like it—a potentially dangerous practice. She taught the porpoise to come out for a reward when she gave a hand signal, and then rarely gave the signal.
C. It is possible to eliminate behavior that is undesirable by bringing it under stimulus control by tying behavior to a signal, and then rarely giving the signal. One trainer successfully used this method to keep an energetic porpoise from coming out of her tank, a potentially dangerous situation. Her trainer taught the porpoise to do it for a reward, in response to a hand signal, and then would rarely give the signal.
D. By using stimulus control, it is possible to eliminate unwanted behavior by tying the behavior to a cue, and then rarely or never give the cue. One trainer was able to use this method to successfully stop a young porpoise from coming out of her tank whenever she felt like it. To curb this potentially dangerous practice, the porpoise was taught by the trainer to come out of the tank for a reward, in response to a hand signal, and then rarely given the signal.

8.
I. There is a great deal of concern over the safety of commercial trucks, caused by their greatly increased role in serious accidents since federal deregulation in 1981.
II. Recently, 60 percent of trucks in New York and Connecticut and 70 percent of trucks in Maryland randomly stopped by state troopers failed safety inspections.
III. Sixteen states in the United States require no training at all for truck drivers.

A. Since federal deregulation in 1981, there has been a great deal of concern over the safety of commercial trucks, and their greatly increased role in serious accidents. Recently, 60 percent of trucks in New York and Connecticut, and 70 percent of trucks in Maryland failed safety inspections. Sixteen states in the United States require no training at all for truck drivers.
B. There is a great deal of concern over the safety of commercial trucks since federal deregulation in 1981. Their role in serious accidents has greatly increased. Recently, 60 percent of trucks randomly stopped in Connecticut and New York and 70 percent in Maryland failed safety inspections conducted by state troopers. Sixteen states in the United States provide no training at all for truck drivers.
C. Commercial trucks have a greatly increased role in serious accidents since federal deregulation in 1981. This has led to a great deal of concern.

Recently, 70 percent of trucks in Maryland and 60 percent of trucks in New York and Connecticut failed inspection of those that were randomly stopped by state troopers. Sixteen states in the United States require no training for all truck drivers.

D. Since federal deregulation in 1981, the role that commercial trucks have played in serious accidents has greatly increased, and this has led to a great deal of concern. Recently, 60 percent of trucks in New York and Connecticut, and 70 percent of trucks in Maryland randomly stopped by state troopers failed safety inspections. Sixteen states in the U.S. don't require any training for truck drivers.

9.
I. No matter how much some people have, they still feel unsatisfied and want more, or want to keep what they have forever.
II. One recent television documentary showed several people flying from New York to Paris for a one-day shopping spree to buy platinum earrings, because they were bored.
III. In Brazil, some people were ordering coffins that cost a minimum of $45,000 and are equipping them with deluxe stereos, televisions, and other graveyard necessities.

A. Some people, despite having a great deal, still feel unsatisfied and want more, or think they can keep what they have forever. One recent documentary on television showed several people enroute from Paris to New York for a one day shopping spree to buy platinum earrings, because they were bored. Some people in Brazil are even ordering coffins equipped with such graveyard necessities as deluxe stereos and televisions. The price of the coffins start at $45,000.
B. No matter how much some people have, they may feel unsatisfied. This leads them to want more, or to want to keep what they have forever. Recently, a television documentary depicting several people flying from New York to Paris for a one day shopping spree to buy platinum earrings. They were bored. Some people in Brazil are ordering coffins that cost at least $45,000 and come equipped with deluxe televisions, stereos and other necessary graveyard items.
C. Some people will be dissatisfied no matter how much they have. They may want more, or they may want to keep what they have forever. One recent television documentary showed several people, motivated by boredom, jetting from New York to Paris for a one-day shopping spree to buy platinum earrings. In Brazil, some people are ordering coffins equipped with deluxe stereos, televisions and other graveyard necessities. The minimum price for these coffins—$45,000.
D. Some people are never satisfied. No matter how much they have they still want more, or think they can keep what they have forever. One television documentary recently showed several people flying from New York to Paris for the day to buy platinum earrings because they were bored. In Brazil, some people are ordering coffins that cost $45,000 and are equipped with deluxe stereos, televisions and other graveyard necessities.

10. I. A television signal or video signal has three parts.
    II. Its parts are the black-and-white portion, the color portion, and the synchronizing (sync) pulses, which keep the picture stable.
    III. Each video source, whether it's a camera or a video-cassette recorder contains its own generator of these synchronizing pulses to accompany the picture that it's sending in order to keep it steady and straight.
    IV. In order to produce a clean recording, a video-cassette recorder must "lock-up" to the sync pulses that are part of the video it is trying to record, and this effort may be very noticeable if the device does not have gunlock.

    A. There are three parts to a television or video signal: the black-and-white part, the color part, and the synchronizing (sync) pulses, which keep the picture stable. Whether it's a video-cassette recorder or a camera, each video source contains its own pulse that synchronizes and generates the picture it's sending in order to keep it straight and steady. A video-cassette recorder must "lock up" to the sync pulses that are part of the video it's trying to record. If the device doesn't have gunlock, this effort must be very noticeable.
    B. A video signal or television is comprised of three parts: the black-and-white portion, the color portion, and the sync (synchronizing) pulses, which keep the picture stable. Whether it's a camera or a video-cassette recorder, each video source contains its own generator of these synchronizing pulses. These accompany the picture that it's sending in order to keep it straight and steady. A video-cassette recorder must "lock up" to the sync pulses that are part of the video it is trying to record in order to produce a clean recording. This effort may be very noticeable if the device does not have gunlock.
    C. There are three parts to a television or video signal: the color portion, the black-and-white portion, and the sync (synchronizing pulses). These keep the picture stable. Each video source, whether it's a video-cassette recorder or a camera, generates these synchronizing pulses accompanying the picture it's sending in order to keep it straight and steady. If a clean recording is to be produced, a video-cassette recorder must store the sync pulses that are part of the video it is trying to record. This effort may not be noticeable if the device does not have gunlock.
    D. A television signal or video signal has three parts: the black-and-white portion, the color portion, and the synchronizing (sync) pulses. It's the sync pulses which keep the picture stable, which accompany it and keep it steady and straight. Whether it's a camera or a video-cassette recorder, each video source contains its own generator of these synchronizing pulses. To produce a clean recording, a video-cassette recorder must "lock up" to the sync pulses that are part of the video it is trying to record. If the device does not have gunlock, this effort may be very noticeable.

KEY (CORRECT ANSWERS)

1.	C	6.	A
2.	B	7.	B
3.	A	8.	D
4.	B	9.	C
5.	D	10.	D

ARITHMETICAL REASONING
EXAMINATION SECTION
TEST 1

DIRECTIONS: Each question or incomplete statement is followed by several suggested answers or completions. Select the one that BEST answers the question or completes the statement. *PRINT THE LETTER OF THE CORRECT ANSWER IN THE SPACE AT THE RIGHT.*

1. In 2015, a public agency spent $180 to buy pencils that cost three cents each. In 2017, the agency spent $420 to buy the same number of pencils that it had bought in 2015.
   The price per pencil that the agency paid in 2017 was _____ cents.
   A. 6⅓   B. ⅔   C. 7   D. 7¾

   1.____

2. A stenographer spent her 35 hour work week on taking dictation, transcribing the dictate material, and filing.
   If she spent 20% of the work week on taking dictation and ½ of the remaining time on transcribing the dictated material, the number of hours of the work week that she spent on filing was
   A. 7   B. 10.5   C. 14   D. 17.4

   2.____

3. A typist typed eight pages in two hours.
   If she typed an average of 50 lines per page and an average of 12 words per line, what was her typing speed, in words per minute?
   A. 40   B. 50   C. 60   D. 80

   3.____

4. The daily compensation to be paid to each consultant hired in a certain agency is computed by dividing his professional earnings in the previous year by 250. The maximum daily compensation they can receive is $200 each. Four consultants who were hired to work on a special project had the following professional earnings in the previous year: $37,500, $144,000, $46,500, and $61,100.
   What will be the TOTAL daily cost to the agency for these four consultants?
   A. $932   B. $824   C. $736   D. $712

   4.____

5. In a typing and stenographic pool consisting of 30 employees, 2/5 of them are typists, 1/3 of them are senior typists and senior stenographers, and the rest are stenographers.
   If there are 5 more stenographers than senior stenographers, how many senior stenographers are in the typing and stenographic pool?
   A. 3   B. 5   C. 8   D. 10

   5.____

6. There are 3,330 copies of a three-page report to be collated. One clerk starts collating at 9:00 A.M. and is joined 15 minutes later by two other clerks. It takes 15 minutes for each of these clerks to collate 90 copies of the report. At what time should the job be completed if all three clerks continue working at the same rate without breaks?
   A. 12:00 Noon   B. 12:15 P.M.   C. 1:00 P.M.   D. 1:15 P.M.

7. By the end of last year, membership in the blood credit program in a certain agency had increased from the year before by 500, bringing the total to 2,500. If the membership increased by the same percentage this year, the TOTAL number of members in the blood credit program for this agency by the end of this year should be
   A. 2,625   B. 3,000   C. 3,125   D. 3,250

8. During this year, an agency suggestion program put into practice suggestions from 24 employee, thereby saving the agency 40 times the amount of money it paid in awards.
   If $1/3$ of the employees were awarded $50 each, ½ of the employees were awarded $25 each, and the rest were awarded $10 each, how much money did the agency save by using the suggestions?
   A. $18,760   B. $29,600   C. $32,400   D. $46,740

9. A senior stenographer earned $20,100 a year and had 4.5% state tax withheld for the year.
   If she was paid every two weeks, the amount of state tax that was taken out of each of her paychecks, based on a 52-week year, was MOST NEARLY
   A. $31.38   B. $32.49   C. $34.77   D. $36.99

10. Two stenographers have been assigned to address 750 envelopes. One stenographer addresses twice as many envelopes per hour as the other stenographer.
    If it takes five hours for them to complete the job, the rate of the slower stenographer is _____ envelopes per hour.
    A. 35   B. 50   C. 75   D. 100

11. Suppose that the postage rate for mailing single copies of a magazine to persons not included on a subscription list is 18 cents for the first two ounces of the single copy and 3 cents for each additional ounce.
    Of 19 copies of a magazine, each of which weighs eleven ounces, are mailed to 19 different people, the TOTAL postage cost of these magazines is
    A. $3.42   B. $3.99   C. $6.18   D. $8.55

12. A senior stenographer spends about 40 hours a month taking dictation. Of that time, 44% is spent taking minutes of meetings, 38% if spent taking dictation of lengthy reports, and the rest of the time is spent taking dictation of letters and memoranda.
    How much more time is spent taking minutes of meetings than n taking dictation of letters and memoranda? 10 hours _____ minutes.
    A. 6   B. 16   C. 24   D. 40

3 (#1)

13. In one week, a stenographer typed 65 letter. Forty letters had 4 copies on colored paper. The rest had 3 copies on colored paper.
If the stenographer had 50 sheets of colored paper on hand at the beginning of the week when she started typing the letters, how many sheets of colored paper did she have left at the end of the week?
   A. 190   B. 235   C. 265   D. 305

13.____

14. An agency is planning to microfilm letters and other correspondence of the last five years. The number of letter-size documents that can be photographed on a 100-foot roll of microfilm is 2,995. The agency estimates that it will need 240 feet of microfilm to do all the pages of all of the letters.
How many pages of letter-size documents can be photographed on this microfilm?
   A. 5,990   B. 6,785   C. 7,188   D. 7,985

14.____

15. In an agency, $2/3$ of the total number of female stenographers and ½ of the total number of male stenographers attended a general staff meeting.
If there are a total of 56 stenographers in the agency and 25% of them are male, the number of female stenographers who attended the general staff meeting is
   A. 14   B. 28   C. 36   D. 42

15.____

16. A worker is currently earning $17,140 a year and pays $350 a month for rent. He expects to get a raise that will enable him to move into an apartment where his rent will be 25% of his new yearly salary.
If this new apartment is going to cost him $390 a month, what is the TOTAL amount of raise that he expects to get?
   A. $480   B. $980   C. $1,580   D. $1,840

16.____

17. The tops of five desks in an office are to be covered with a scratch-resistant material. Each desk top measures 60 inches by 36 inches.
How many square feet of material will be needed for the five desk tops?
   A. 15   B. 75   C. 96   D. 180

17.____

18. Three grades of bond paper are used in a central transcribing unit. The cost per ream of paper is $1.90 for Grade A, $1.70 for Grade B, and $1.60 for Grade C.
If the central transcribing unit used 6 reams of Grade A paper, 14 reams of Grade B paper, and 20 reams of Grade C paper, the AVERAGE cost, per ream, of the bond paper used by this unit is between
   A. $1.62 and $1.66   B. $1.66 and $1.70
   C. $1.70 and $1.74   D. $1.73 and $1.80

18.____

19. The Complaint Bureau of a city agency is composed of an investigation unit, a clerical unit, and a central transcribing unit. The sum of $264,000 has been appropriated for the operation of this bureau. Of this sum, $170,000 is to be allotted to the clerical unit.

19.____

Of this bureau's total appropriation, the percentage that is left for the central transcribing unit is MOST NEARLY _____ if 41,200 is allotted for investigations.
   A. 20%   B. 30%   C. 40%   D. 50%

20. Three typists were assigned to address a total of 2,655 postcards. Typist A addressed postcards at the rate of 170 per hour. Typist B addressed the postcards at the rate of 150 per hour. Typist C's rate is not known. After the three typists had addressed postcards for three and a half hours, Typist C was taken off this assignment. It was necessary for Typist A and Typist B to work two and a half hours more to complete this assignment. The rate per hour at which Typist C addressed the postcards was
   A. less than 150
   B. between 150 and 170
   C. more than 170 but less than 200
   D. more than 200

21. In 2015, a city agency bought 12,000 envelopes at $4.00 per hundred. In 2016, the price of envelopes purchased was 40 percent higher than the 2010 price, but only 60 percent as many envelopes were bought.
The total cost of the envelopes purchased in 2016 was MOST NEARLY
   A. $250   B. $320   C. $400   D. $480

22. A stenographer has been assigned to place entries on 500 forms. She places entries on 25 forms by the end of half an hour, when she is joined by another stenographer. The second stenographer places entries at the rate of 45 an hour.
Assuming both stenographers continue to work at their respective rates of speed, the TOTAL number of hours required to carry out the entire assignment is
   A. 5   B. 5½   C. 6½   D. 7

23. On Monday, a stenographer took dictation without interruption for 1½ hours and transcribed all the dictated material in 3½ hours. On Tuesday, she took dictation uninterruptedly for 1¾ hours and transcribed all the material in 3¾ hours. On Wednesday, she took dictation without interruption for 2¼ hours and transcribed all the material in 4½ hours.
If she took dictation at the average rate of 90 words per minute during these three days, then her average transcription rate, in words per minute, for the same three days was MOST NEARLY
   A. 36   B. 41   C. 54   D. 58

24. In a division of clerks and stenographers, 15 people are currently employed, 20% of whom are stenographers.
If management plans are to maintain the current number of stenographers, but to increase the clerical staff to the point where 12% of the total staff are stenographers, what is the MAXIMUM number of additional clerks that should be hired to meet these plans?
   A. 3   B. 8   C. 10   D. 12

25. In the first quarter of the year, a certain operator sent out 230 quarterly reports. 25.____
In the second quarter of that year, he sent out 310 quarterly reports.
The percent increase in the number of quarterly reports he sent out in the second quarter of the year compared to the first quarter of the year is MOST NEARLY
   A. 26%   B. 29%   C. 35%   D. 39%

KEY (CORRECT ANSWERS)

1.	C		11.	D
2.	C		12.	C
3.	A		13.	C
4.	C		14.	C
5.	A		15.	B
6.	B		16.	C
7.	C		17.	B
8.	B		18.	B
9.	C		19.	A
10.	B		20.	D

21. C
22. B
23. B
24. C
25. C

SOLUTIONS TO PROBLEMS

1. $180 ÷ .03 = 6000 pencils bought. In 2017, the price per pencil = $420/6000 = .07 = 7 cents

2. Number of hours on filing = 35 − (.20)(35) · (½)(28) = 14

3. Eight pages contain (8)(50)(12) = 4800 words. She thus typed 4800 words in 120 minutes = 40 words per minute

4. $37,500 ÷ 250 = $150; $144,000 ÷ 250 = $576; $46,500 ÷ 250 = $186; $61,100 ÷ 250 = $244.40. Since $200 = maximum compensation for any single consultant, total compensation = $150 + $200 + $186 + $200 = $736

5. Number of typists = (2/5)(30) = 12, number of senior typists and senior stenographers = (^{1}/$_3$)(30) = 10, number of stenographers = 30 − 12 − 10 = 8. Finally, number of senior stenographers = 8 − 5 = 3

6. At 9:15 A.M., 90 copies have been collated. The remaining 3,240 copies are being collated at the rate of (3)(90) = 270 every 15 minutes = 1080 per hour. Since 3240 ÷ 1080 = 3 hours, the clerks will finish at 9:15 A.M. + 3 hours = 12:15 P.M.

7. During the last year, the membership increased from 2000 to 2500, which represents a (500/2000)(100) = 25% increase. A 25% increase during this year means the membership = (2500)(1.25) = 3125

8. Total awards = (^{1}/$_3$)(24)($50) + (½)(24)($25) + (^{1}/$_6$)(24)($10) = $740. Thus, the savings = (40)($740) = $29,600

9. Her pay for 2 weeks = $20,100 ÷ 26 ≈ $773.08. Thus, her state tax for 2 weeks = ($773.08)(.045) ≈ $34.79. (Nearest correct answer is $34.77 in four selections.)

10. 750 ÷ 5 hours = 150 envelopes per hour for the 2 stenographers combined. Let x = number of envelopes addressed by the slower stenographer. Then, x + 2x = 150. Solving, = 50

11. Total cost = (19)[.18+(.03)(9)] = $8.55

12. (.44)(40) − (.18)(40) = 10.4 hours = 10 hrs. 24 min.

13. 500 − (40)(4) − (25)(3) = 265

14. 2995 ÷ 100 = 29.95 documents per foot of microfilm roll. Then, (29.95)(240 ft) = 7188 documents

15. There are (.75)(56) = 42 female stenographers. Then, (^{2}/$_3$)(42) = 28 of them attended the meeting

7 (#1)

16. ($390)(12) = $4679 new rent per year. Then, ($4680)(4) = $18,720 = his new yearly salary. His raise = $18,720 - $17,140 = $1580

17. Number of sq. ft. = (5)(60)(36) ÷ 144 = 75

18. Average cost per ream = [(1.90)(6) + ($1.70)(14) + ($1.60)(20)] /40 = $1.68, which is between $1.66 and $1.77

19. $264,000 - $170,000 - $41,200 = 52,800 = 20%

20. Let x = typist C's rate. Since Typists A and B each worked 6 hrs., while Typist C worked only 3.5 hours, we have (6)(170) + (6)(150) + 3.5x = 2655. Solving, x = 210, which is mre than 200

21. In 2016, the cost per hundred envelopes was ($4.00)(1.40) = $5.60 and (.60)(12,000) = 7200 envelopes were bought. Total cost in 2016 = (72)($5.60) = $403.20, or about $400

22. The first stenographer's rate is 50 forms per hour. After ½ hour, there are 500 – 25 = 475 forms to be done and the combined rate of the 2 stenographers is 95 forms per hr. Thus, total hours required = ½ + (475) ÷ (95) = 5½

23. Total time for dictation = 1¼ + 1¾ + 2¼ = 5¼ hrs. = 315 min. The number of words = (90)(315) = 28,350. The total transcription 3 time = 3¼ + 3¾ + 44 = 11½ hrs. = 690 min. Her average transcription rate = 28,350 ÷ 690 ≈ 41 words per min.

24. Currently, there are (.20)(15) = 3 stenographers, and thus 12 clerks. Let x = additional clerks. Then, $\frac{3}{3+12+x}$ = .12. This simplifies to 3 = (.12)(15+x). Solving, x = 10

25. Percent increase = $(\frac{80}{230})$(100) ≈ 35%

TEST 2

DIRECTIONS: Each question or incomplete statement is followed by several suggested answers or completions. Select the one that BEST answers the question or completes the statement. *PRINT THE LETTER OF THE CORRECT ANSWER IN THE SPACE AT THE RIGHT.*

1. A school has 112 homeroom classes. There were 15 school days in February. The aggregate register of the school for the month of February was 52,920; the aggregate attendance was 43,860.
   The average class size, to the NEAREST tenth, is
   A. 35.3   B. 31.5   C. 29.2   D. 26.9

   1.____

2. As the school secretary in charge of supplies, you are asked to order the following items on a supplementary requisition for general supplies:
   5 gross of red pencils at $8.90 per dozen
   5,000 manila envelopes at $2.35 per C
   36 rulers at $187.20 per gross
   6 boxes of manila paper at $307.20 per carton (24 boxes to a carton)
   180 reams of composition paper at $27.80 per carton (20 reams to a carton)
   The TOTAL amount of the order is
   A. $957.20   B. $1,025.30   C. $916.80   D. $991.30

   2.____

3. In the high school to which you have been assigned as a school secretary, the annual allotment for general supplies, textbooks, repairs, etc. for the school year 2015-16 was $37,500. A special allotment of $10,000 was granted for textbooks ordered from the State Textbook List. The original requisition for general and vocational supplies amounted to $12,514.75; for science supplies, $6,287.75; for textbooks, including the special funds, $13,785.00; monies spent for equipment repairs and science perishables through December 31, 2015, $1,389.68.
   The balance in your supply allotment account on January 1, 2016 will be
   A. $14,913.00   B. $13,523.32   C. $17,308.32   D. $3,523.32

   3.____

4. The teacher of one of the sixth term typing classes in the high school to which you are assigned as a school secretary has agreed to have her students type attendance cards for the incoming students for the new schoolyear, commencing in September, as a work project. There are 24 students in the class; each student can complete 8 cards during a typing period. There will be 4,032 new students in September.
   The number of typing periods required to complete the task is
   A. 31   B. 21   C. 28   D. 24

   4.____

5. As a school secretary assigned to payroll duties, you are required to prepare the extra-curricular payroll report for the coaches teams in your high school. The rate of pay for these activities was increased on November 1 from $148 per session to $174.50 per session. The pay period which you are reporting is for the months of October, November, and December. Mr. Jones, the football coach, conducted 15 practice sessions in October, 20 in November, and 30 in December.

   5.____

176

His TOTAL gross pay on the December extra-curricular payroll report is
A. $10,547.50   B. $10,415.00   C. $10,945.00   D. $11,342.50

6. The comparative results on a uniform examination given in your school for the last three years follow:

	2014	2015	2016
Number Taking Test	501	496	485
Number Passing Test	441	437	436

The percentage of passing, to the nearest tenth of a percent, for the year in which the HIGHEST percent of students passed is
A. 89.3%   B. 88%   C. 89.9%   D. 90.3%

7. During his first seven terms in high school, a student compiled the following averages:

Term	Numbers of Majors Completed	Average
1	4	81.25%
2	4	83.75%
3	5	86.2%
4	5	85.8%
5	5	87.0%
6	5	83.4%
7	5	82.6%

In his eighth term, the student had the following final marks in major subjects: 90%, 95%, 80%, 90%, 85%. The student's average for all eight terms of high school, correct to the nearest tenth of a percent, is
A. 84.8%   B. 84.7%   C. 84.9%   D. 85.8%

8. A secretary is asked by her employer to order an office machine which lists at a price of $360, less trade discounts of 20% and 10%, terms 2/10, n/30. There is a delivery charge of $8 and an installation charge of $12.
If the machine is paid for in 10 days, the TOTAL cost of the machine will be
A. $264.80   B. $258.40   C. $266.96   D. $274.02

9. The school to which you have been assigned as school secretary has an annual allowance of 5,120 hours for all teacher aides. The principal decides to employ 5 teacher aides from 8:00 A.M. to 12:00 Noon, and 5 other teacher aides from 12:00 Noon to 4:00 P.M. daily for as many days as his allowance permits.
If a teacher aide earns $17.00 an hour, and he is present every day, his TOTAL earnings for the school year will be more than
A. $7,000 but less than $8,000   B. $8,000 but less than $9,000
C. $9,000 but less than $10,000   D. $10,000

10. During examination week in a high school to which you have been assigned as school secretary, teachers are required to be in school at least 6 hours and 20 minutes daily although their arrival and departure times may vary each day. A teacher's time card that you have been asked to check shows the following entries for the week of June 17:

Date	Arrival	Departure
17	7:56 A.M.	2:18 P.M.
18	9:54 A.M.	4:22 P.M.
19	12:54 P.M.	7:03 P.M.
20	9:51 A.M.	4:15 P.M.
21	7:58 A.M.	2:11 P.M.

During the week of June 17 to June 21, the teacher was in school for AT LEAST the minimum required time on _____ days.
   A. 2 of the 5   B. 3 of the 5   C. 4 of the 5   D. all 5

10._____

11. As school secretary, you are asked to find the total of the following bill received in your school:
    750 yellow envelopes at $.22 per C
    2,400 white envelopes at $2.80 per M
    30 rulers at $5.04 per gross
The TOTAL of the bill is
   A. $69.90   B $24.27   C. $18.87   D. $9.42

11._____

12. A department in the school to which you have been assigned as school secretary has been given a textbook allowance of $5,50 for the school year. The department's textbook order is:
    75 books at $32.50 each
    45 books at $49.50 each
    25 books at $34.50 each
The TOTAL of the department's order is _____ the allowance.
   A. $27.50 over   B. $27.50 under
   C. $72.50 under   D. $57.50 over

12._____

13. The total receipts, including 5% city sales tax, for the G.O. store for the first week of school amounted to $489.09.
The receipts from the G.O. store for the first week of school, excluding the 5% city sales tax, amounted to
   A. $465.89   B. $364.64   C. $464.63   D. $513.54

13._____

14. Class sizes in the school to which you have been assigned as school secretary are as follows:

Number of Classes	Class Size
9	29
12	31
15	32
7	33
11	34

14._____

The average class size in this school, correct to the nearest tenth, is
A. 30.8   B. 31.9   C. 31.8   D. 30.9

15. In 2013, the social security tax was 4.2% for the first $6,600 earned a year. In 2014, the social security tax was 4.4% on the first $6,600 earned a year. For a teacher aide earning $19,200 in 2013 and $20,400 in 2014, the increase in social security tax deduction in 2014 over 2013 was
A. $132.00   B. $13.20   C. $19.20   D. $20.40

16. A teacher aide earning $23,900 a year will incur automatic deductions of 3.90% for social security and .50% for Medicare, based on the first $6,600 a year earnings.
The TOTAL deduction for these two items will be
A. $274   B. $290.40   C. $525.80   D. $300.40

17. The school store turns in receipts totaling $131.25 to the school treasurer, including 5% which has been collected for sales tax.
The amount of money which the treasurer MUST set aside for sales tax is
A. $6.56   B. $6.25   C. $5.00   D. $5.25

18. One of the custodial assistants can wash all the windows in the main office in 3 hours. A second assistant can wash the windows in the main office in 2 hours.
If the two men work together, they should complete the task in _____ hour(s) _____ minutes.
A. 1; 0   B. 1.5; 0   C. 1; 12   D. 1; 15

19. A school secretary is requested by the principal to order an office machine which lists at a price of $120, less discounts of 10% and 5%.
The net price of the machine to the school will be
A. $100.50   B. $102.00   C. $102.60   D. $103.00

20. Five students are employed at school under a work-study program through which they are paid $10.00 an hour for work in school offices, but no student may earn more than $450 a month. Three days before the end of the month, you note that the student payroll totals $2,062.50.
The number of hours which each of the students may work during the remainder of the month is _____ hour(s).
A. 4   B. 2   C. 1   D. 3

21. You are asked to summarize expenditures made by the school within the budget allocation for the school year. You determine that the following expenditures have been made: educational supplies, $2,600; postage, $650; emergency repairs, $225; textbooks, $5,100; instructional equipment, $1,200. Since $10,680 has been allocated to the school, the following sum still remains available for office supplies.
A. $905   B. $1,005   C. $800   D. $755

22. In preparing the percentage of attendance for the period report, you note that the aggregate attendance is 57,585 and the aggregate register is 62,000. The percentage of attendance, to the nearest tenth of a percent, is
    A. 91.9%   B. 93.0%   C. 92.8%   D. 92.9%

    22.____

23. You borrow $1,200 from your retirement fund which you must repay over a period of three years, with interest of $144, each payment to be divided equally among 36 total payments.
    The monthly deduction from your paycheck will be
    A. $37.33   B. $36.00   C. $33.00   D. $37.30

    23.____

24. Tickets for a school dance are printed, starting with number 401 and ending with number 1650. They are to be sold for $7.50 each. The tickets remaining unsold should start with number 1569.
    The amount of cash which should be collected for the sale of tickets is
    A. $876.75   B. $937.50   C. $876.00   D. $875.25

    24.____

25. Stage curtains are purchased by the school and delivered on October 3 under terms of 5/10, 2/30, net/60. The curtains are paid in full by a check for $522.50 on October 12.
    The invoice price was
    A. $533.16   B. $522.50   C. $540.00   D. $550.00

    25.____

KEY (CORRECT ANSWERS)

1.	B	11.	D
2.	B	12.	A
3.	B	13.	A
4.	B	14.	C
5.	C	15.	B
6.	C	16.	B
7.	C	17.	B
8.	D	18.	C
9.	B	19.	C
10.	B	20.	D

21. A
22. D
23. A
24. C
25. D

SOLUTIONS TO PROBLEMS

1. Average class size = 52,920 ÷ 15 ÷ 112 = 31.5

2. Total amount = (5)(12)($8.90) + (50)($2.35) + (36)($187.20) ÷ 144 + (6)($307.20) ÷ 24 + (9)($27.80) = $1,025.30

3. Balance = $37,500 + $10,000 - $12,514.75 - $6,287.25 - $13,785 - $1,389.68 = $13,523.32

4. (24)(8) = 192 cards completed in one period. Then, 4032 ÷ 192 = 21 typing periods required

5. Total pay = (15)($148.00) + (20)($174.50) + (30)($174.50) = $10,945.00

6. The passing rates for 2014, 2015, and 2016 were 88.0%, 88.1%, and 89.9%, respectively. So, 89.9% was the highest

7. His 8th term average was 88.0%. His overall average for all 8 terms = [(4)(81.25%) + (4)(83.75%) + (5)(86.2%) + (5)(85.8%) + (5)(87.0%) + (5)(83.4%) + (5)(82.6%) + (5)(88.0%)] ÷ 38 = 84.9%

8. Total cost = ($360)(.80)(.90)(.98) + $8 + $12 ≈ $274.02 (Exact amount = $274.016)

9. 5120 ÷ 4 = 1280 teacher-days. Then, 1280 ÷ 20 = 128 days per teacher. A teacher's earnings for these 128 days = ($17.00)(4)(128) = $8,704, which is more than $8,000 but less than $9,000

10. The number of hours present on each of the 5 days listed was 6 hrs. 22 min., 6 hrs. 29 min., 6 hrs. 9 min., 6 hrs. 24 min., and 6 hrs. 13 min. On 3 days, he met the minimum time.

11. Total cost = (7.5)(.22) + (2.4)($2.80) + (30/144)(5.04) = $9.42

12. Textbook order = (75)($32.50) + (45)($49.50) + (25)($34.50) = $5,527.5, which is $27.50 over the allowance

13. Receipts without the tax = $489.09 ÷ 1.05 = $465.80

14. Average class size = [(9)(29) + (12)(31) + (7)(33) + (15)(32)] ÷ 54 ≈ 31.8

15. ($6,600)(.044-.042) = $13.20

16. ($6,600)(.039+.005) = $290.40

17. $131.25 = 1.05x, x = 125, $131.25 − 125.00 = 6.25

7 (#2)

18. Let x = hours needed working together. Then, $(1/3)(x) + (1/2)(x) = 1$
Simplifying, 2x + 3x = 6. Solving, x = $1\frac{1}{5}$ hrs. = 1 hr. 12 min.

19. Net price = 120 – 10% (12) = 108; 108 – 5% (5.40) = 102.60

20. ($225)(5) - $1031.25 = $93.75 remaining in the month. Since the 5 students earn $25 per hour combined, $93.75 ÷ $25 = 3.75, which must be rounded down to 3 hours

21. $10,680 - $2,600 - $650 - $225 - $5,100 - $1,200 = $905 for office supplies

22. 57,585 ÷ 62,000 ≈ .9288 ≈ 92.9%

23. Monthly deduction = $1344 ÷ 36 = $37.33. (Technically, 35 payments of $37.33 and 1 payment of $37.45)

24. (1569-401) = $876.00

25. The invoice price (which reflects the 5% discount) is $522.50 ÷ .95 = $550.00

TEST 3

DIRECTIONS: Each question or incomplete statement is followed by several suggested answers or completions. Select the one that BEST answers the question or completes the statement. *PRINT THE LETTER OF THE CORRECT ANSWER IN THE SPACE AT THE RIGHT.*

1. If an inch on an office layout drawing equals 4 feet of actual floor dimension, then a room which actually measures 9 feet by 14 feet is represented on the drawing by measurements equaling _____ inches × _____ inches.   1._____
  A. 2¼; 3½   B. 2½; 3½   C. 2¼; 3¼   D. 2½; 3¼

2. A cooperative education intern works from 1:30 P.M. to 5 P.M. on Mondays, Wednesdays, and Fridays, and from 10 A.M. to 2:30 P.M. with no lunch hour on Tuesdays and Thursdays. He earns $13.50 an hour on this job. In addition, he has a Saturday job paying $16.00 an hour at which he works from 9 A.M. to 3 P.M. with a half hour off for lunch.   2._____
  The gross amount that the student earns each week is MOST NEARLY
  A. $321.90   B. $355.62   C. $364.02   D. $396.30

3. Thirty-five percent of the College Discovery students who entered community college earned an associate degree. Of these students, 89% entered senior college, of which 67% went on to earn baccalaureate degrees.   3._____
  If there were 529 College Discovery students who entered community college, then the number of those who went on to finally receive a baccalaureate degree is MOST NEARLY
  A. 354   B. 315   C. 124   D. 110

4. It takes 5 office assistants two days to type 125 letters. Each of the assistants works at an equal rate of speed.   4._____
  How many days will it take 10 office assistants to type 200 letters?
  A. 1   B. 1³/₅   C. 2   D. 2¹/₅

5. The following are the grades and credits earned by Student X during the first two years in college.   5._____

Grade	Credits	Weight	Quality Points
A	10 ½	×4	
B	24	×3	
C	12	×2	
D	4 ½	×1	
F, FW	5	×0	

   To compute an index number:
   I. Multiply the number of credits of each grade by the weight to get the number of quality points
   II. Add the credits
   III. Add the quality points
   IV. Divide the total quality point by the total credits and carry the division to two decimal places

On the basis of the given information, the index number for Student X is
A. 2.55   B. 2.59   C. 2.63   D. 2.68

6. Typist X can type 20 forms per hour, and Typist Y can type 30 forms per hour. If there are 30 forms to be typed and both typists are put to work on the job, how son should they be expected to finish the work?
_____ minutes.
A. 32   B. 34   C. 36   D. 38

7. Assume that there were 18 working days in February and that the six clerks in your unit had the following number of absences:

Clerk	Absences
F	3
G	2
H	8
I	1
J	0
K	5

The average percentage attendance for the six clerks in your unit in February was MOST NEARLY
A. 80%   B. 82%   C. 84%   D. 86%

8. A certain employee is paid at the rate of $7.50 per hour, with time and a half for overtime. Hours in excess of 40 hours a week count as overtime. During the past week, the employee put in 48 working hours.
The employee's gross wages for the week are MOST NEARLY
A. $330   B. $350   C. $370   D. $390

9. You are making a report on the number of inside and outside calls handled by a particular switchboard. Over a 15-day period, the total number of all inside and outside calls handled by the switchboard was 5,760. The average number of inside calls per day was 234. You cannot find one day's tally of outside calls, but the total number of outside calls for the other fourteen days was 2,065.
From this information, how many outside calls must have been reported on the missing tally?
A. 175   B. 185   C. 195   D. 205

10. A floor plan has been prepared for a new building, drawn to a scale of ¾ inch = 1 foot. A certain area is drawn 1 and ½ feet long and 6 inches wide on the floor plan.
What are the ACTUAL dimensions of this area in the new building?
_____ feet long and _____ feet wide
A. 21; 8   B. 24; 8   C. 27; 9   D. 30; 9

11. You are preparing a package of six books to mail to a professor who is on sabbatical. They weigh, respectively, 1 pound 11 ounces, 1 pound 6 ounces, 2 pounds 1 ounce, 2 pounds 2 ounces, 1 pound 7 ounces, and 1 pound 8 ounces. The packaging material weighs 6 ounces.
    The TOTAL weight of the package will be _____ pounds _____ ounces.
    A. 10; 3   B. 10; 9   C. 11; 5   D. 12; 5

11._____

12. Part-time students are charged $70 per credit for courses at a particular college. In addition, they musts pay a $24.00 student activity fee if they take six credits or more and $14.00 lab fee for each laboratory course.
    If a person takes one 3-credit course and one 4-credit course and his 4-credit course is a laboratory course, the TOTAL cost to him will be
    A. $504   B. $528   C. $542   D. $552

12._____

13. The graduating course of a certain community college consisted of 378 majors in secretarial science, 265 majors in engineering science, 57 majors in nursing, 513 majors in accounting, and 865 majors in liberal arts.
    The percent of students who major in liberal arts at this college was MOST NEARLY
    A. 24.0%   B. 41.6%   C. 52.3%   D. 71.6%

13._____

14. Donald Smith earns $12.80 an hour for forty hours a week, with time and a half for all hours over forty. Last week, his total earnings amounted to $627.20.
    He worked _____ hours.
    A. 46   B. 47   C. 48   D. 49

14._____

15. Mr. Jones desires to sell an article costing $28 at a gross profit of 30% of the selling price, and to allow a trade discount of 20% of the list price.
    The list price of the article should be
    A. $43.68   B. $45.50   C. $48.00   D. $50.00

15._____

16. The gauge of an oil storage tank in an elementary school indicates 1/5 full. After a truck delivers 945 gallons of oil, the gauge indicates 4/5 full.
    The capacity of the tank is _____ gallons.
    A. 1,260   B. 1,575   C. 1,625   D. 1,890

16._____

17. An invoice dated April 3, terms 3/10, 2/30, net/60, was paid in full with a check for $787.92 on May 1.
    The amount of the invoice was
    A. $772.16   B. $787.92   C. $804.00   D. $812.29

17._____

18. Two pipes supply the water for the swimming pool at Blenheim High School. One pipe can fill the pool in 9 hours. The second pipe can fill the pool in 6 hours.
    If both pipes were opened simultaneously, the pool could be filled in _____ hours _____ minutes.
    A. 3; 36   B. 4; 30   C. 5; 15   D. 7; 30

18._____

4 (#3)

19. John's father spent $24,000, which was one-fourth of his savings. He bought a car with three-eighths of the remainder of his savings.
His bank balance now amounts to
A. $30,000   B. $32,000   C. $45,000   D. $50,000

19.____

20. A clock that loses 4 minutes every 24 hours was set at 6 A.M. on October 1 What time was indicated by the clock when the CORRECT time was 12:00 Noon on October 6th?
A. 11:36   B. 11:38   C. $11:39   D. 11:40

20.____

21. Unit S's production fluctuated substantially from one year to another. In 2009, Unit s's production was 100% greater than in 2008. In 2010, production decreased by 25% from 2009. In 2011, Unit S's production was 10% greater than in 2010.
On the basis of this information, it is CORRECT to conclude that Unit S's production in 2011 exceeded Unit S's production in 2008 by
A. 65%   B. 85%   C. 95%   D. 135%

21.____

22. Agency X is moving into a new building. It has 1,500 employees presently on its staff and does not contemplate much variance from this level. The new building contains 100 available offices, each with a maximum capacity of 30 employees. It has been decided that only 2/3 of the maximum capacity of each office will be utilized.
The TOTAL number of office that will be occupied by Agency X is
A. 30   B. 65   C. 75   D. 90

22.____

23. One typist completes a form letter every 5 minutes and another typist completes one every 6 minutes.
If the two typists start together, how many minutes later will they again start typing new letters simultaneously and how many letters will they have completed by that time?
A. 11; 30   B. 12; 24   C. 24; 12   D. 30; 1

23.____

24. During one week, a machine operator produces 10 fewer pages per hour of work than he usually does.
If it ordinarily takes him six hours to produce a 300-page report, how many hour LONGER will that same 300-page report take him during the week when he produces more slowly?
A. 1½   B. 1²/₃   C. 2   D. 2¾

24.____

25. A study reveals that Miss Brown files N cards in M hours, and Miss Smith files the same number of cards in T hours.
If the two employees work together, the number of hours it will take them to file N cards is
A. $\dfrac{N}{\frac{N}{M}+\frac{N}{N}}$ B. $\dfrac{N}{T+M} + \dfrac{2N}{MT}$ C. $N(\dfrac{M}{N} + \dfrac{N}{T})$ D. $\dfrac{N}{NT+MN}$

25.____

KEY (CORRECT ANSWERS)

1.	A	11.	B
2.	B	12.	B
3.	D	13.	B
4.	B	14.	A
5.	A	15.	D
6.	C	16.	B
7.	B	17.	C
8.	D	18.	A
9.	B	19.	C
10.	B	20.	C

21. A
22. C
23. D
24. A
25. A

SOLUTIONS TO PROBLEMS

1. $9/4 = 2¼"$ and $14/4 = 3½"$

2. Gross amount = $(3)(\$6.75)(3.5) + (2)(\$6.75)(4.5) + (\$8.00)(5.5) = \$174.624$, which is closest to selection B ($177.81)

3. $(529)(.35)(.89)(.67) \approx 110$

4. 10 worker-days are needed to type 125 letters, so $(200)(10) \div 125 = 16$ worker-days are needed to type 200 letters. Finally, $16 \div 10$ workers = 1 3/5 days

5. Index number = $[(14)(10½) + (3)(24) + (2)(12) + (1)(4½) + (0)(5)] \div 56 \approx 2.54$

6. Typist X could do 30 forms in $30/20 = 1½$ hours. Let x = number of hour needed when working together with Typist Y.
   Then, $(\frac{1}{1\frac{1}{2}})(x) + (\frac{1}{1})x = 1$. Simplifying, $2x + 3x = 3$, so $x = \frac{3}{5}$ hr. = 36 min.

7. $(3+2+8+1+0+5) \div 6 = 3.1\overline{6}$. Then, $18 - 3.\overline{6} = 14.8\overline{3}$.

   Finally, $14.8\overline{3} \div 18 \approx 82\%$

8. Wages = $(\$7.50)(40) + (\$11.25)(8) = \$390$

9. $(234)(15) = 3510$ inside calls. Then, $5760 - 3510 = 2259$ outside calls. Finally, $2250 - 2065 = 185$ outside calls on the missing day.

10. $18 \div ¾ - 24$ feet long and $6 \div ¾ = 8$ feet wide

11. Total weight = 1 lb. 11 oz. + 1 lb. 6 oz. + 2 lbs. 1 oz. + 2 lbs. 2 oz. + 1 lb. 7 oz. + 1 lb. 8 oz. + 6 oz = 8 lbs. 41 oz. 10 lbs. 9 oz.

12. Total cost = $(\$70)(7) + \$24 + \$14 = \$528$

13. $865 \div 2078 \approx 41.6\%$ liberal arts majors

14. $(\$12.80)(40) = \$512$, so he made $\$627.20 - \$512 = \$115.20$ in overtime. His overtime rate = $(\$12.80)(1.5) = \$19.20$ per hour. Thus, he worked $\$115.20 \div \$19.20 = 6$ overtime hours. Total hours worked = 46

15. Let x = list price. Selling price = .80x. Then, $.80x - (.30)(.80x) = \$28$. Simplifying, $.56x = \$28$. Solving, $x = \$50.00$

7 (#3)

16. 945 gallons represents $\frac{4}{5} \cdot \frac{1}{5} = \frac{3}{5}$ of the tank's capacity.

    Then, the capacity = $945 \div \frac{3}{5}$ = 1575 gallons

17. $787.92 ÷ .98 = $804.00

18. Let x = number of required hours. Then, (1/9)(x) + (1/6)(x) = 1
    Simplifying, 2x + 3x = 18. Solving, x = 3.6 hours = 3 hours 36 minutes

19. Bank balance = $96,000 - $24,000 – (3/8)($72,000) = $45,000

20. From Oct. 1, 6 A.M. to Oct. 6, Noon = 5½ days. The clock would show a loss of (4 min.)(5½) = 21 min. Thus, the clock's time would incorrectly) show 12:00 Noon – 21 min. = 11:39 A.M.

21. 2008 = x, 2009 = 200x, 2010 = 150x, 2011 = 165x
    65% more

22. (2/3)(30) = 20 employees in each office. Then, 1500 ÷ 20 = 75 offices

23. After 30 minutes, the typists will have finished a total of 6 + 5 = 11 letters

24. When he works more slowly, he will only produce 300 – (6)(10) = 240 pages in 6 hrs. His new slower rate is 40 pages per hour, so he will need 60/40 = 1½ more hours to do the remaining 60 pages.

25. Let x = required hours. Then $(\frac{1}{M})(x) + (\frac{1}{10})(x) = 1$.

    Simplifying, x(T+M) = MT. Solving, x = MT/(T+M)

    Note: The N value is immaterial. Also, choice A reduces to MT/(T+M)

PHILOSOPHY, PRINCIPLES, PRACTICES, AND TECHNICS
OF
SUPERVISION, ADMINISTRATION, MANAGEMENT, AND ORGANIZATION

TABLE OF CONTENTS

	Page
MEANING OF SUPERVISION	1
THE OLD AND THE NEW SUPERVISION	1
THE EIGHT (8) BASIC PRINCIPLES OF THE NEW SUPERVISION	1
I. Principle of Responsibility	1
II. Principle of Authority	2
III. Principle of Self-Growth	2
IV. Principle of Individual Worth	2
V. Principle of Creative Leadership	2
VI. Principle of Success and Failure	2
VII. Principle of Science	3
VIII. Principle of Cooperation	3
WHAT IS ADMINISTRATION?	3
I. Practices Commonly Classed as "Supervisory"	3
II. Practices Commonly Classed as "Administrative"	3
III. Practices Commonly Classed as Both "Supervisory" and "Administrative"	4
RESPONSIBILITIES OF THE SUPERVISOR	4
COMPETENCIES OF THE SUPERVISOR	4
THE PROFESSIONAL SUPERVISOR-EMPLOYEE RELATIONSHIP	4
MINI-TEXT IN SUPERVISION, ADMINISTRATION, MANAGEMENT, AND ORGANIZATION	5
I. Brief Highlights	5
A. Levels of Management	6
B. What the Supervisor Must Learn	6
C. A Definition of Supervision	6
D. Elements of the Team Concept	6
E. Principles of Organization	6
F. The Four Important Parts of Every Job	7
G. Principles of Delegation	7
H. Principles of Effective Communications	7
I. Principles of Work Improvement	7
J. Areas of Job Improvement	7
K. Seven Key Points in Making Improvements	8

L.	Corrective Techniques for Job Improvement	8
M.	A Planning Checklist	8
N.	Five Characteristics of Good Directions	9
O.	Types of Directions	9
P.	Controls	9
Q.	Orienting the New Employee	9
R.	Checklist for Orienting New Employees	9
S.	Principles of Learning	10
T.	Causes of Poor Performance	10
U.	Four Major Steps in On-the-Job Instructions	10
V.	Employees Want Five Things	10
W.	Some Don'ts in Regard to Praise	11
X.	How to Gain Your Workers' Confidence	11
Y.	Sources of Employee Problems	11
Z.	The Supervisor's Key to Discipline	11
AA.	Five Important Processes of Management	12
BB.	When the Supervisor Fails to Plan	12
CC.	Fourteen General Principles of Management	12
DD.	Change	12

II. Brief Topical Summaries — 13

   A. Who/What is the Supervisor? — 13
   B. The Sociology of Work — 13
   C. Principles and Practices of Supervision — 14
   D. Dynamic Leadership — 14
   E. Processes for Solving Problems — 15
   F. Training for Results — 15
   G. Health, Safety, and Accident Prevention — 16
   H. Equal Employment Opportunity — 16
   I. Improving Communications — 16
   J. Self-Development — 17
   K. Teaching and Training — 17
      1. The Teaching Process — 17
         a. Preparation — 17
         b. Presentation — 18
         c. Summary — 18
         d. Application — 18
         e. Evaluation — 18
      2. Teaching Methods — 18
         a. Lecture — 18
         b. Discussion — 18
         c. Demonstration — 19
         d. Performance — 19
         e. Which Method to Use — 19

PHILOSOPHY, PRINCIPLES, PRACTICES, AND TECHNICS
OF
SUPERVISION, ADMINISTRATION, MANAGEMENT, AND ORGANIZATION

MEANING OF SUPERVISION

The extension of the democratic philosophy has been accompanied by an extension in the scope of supervision. Modern leaders and supervisors no longer think of supervision in the narrow sense of being confined chiefly to visiting employees, supplying materials, or rating the staff. They regard supervision as being intimately related to all the concerned agencies of society, they speak of the supervisor's function in terms of "growth," rather than the "improvement" of employees.

This modern concept of supervision may be defined as follows: Supervision is leadership and the development of leadership within groups which are cooperatively engaged in inspection, research, training, guidance, and evaluation.

THE OLD AND THE NEW SUPERVISION

TRADITIONAL
1. Inspection
2. Focused on the employee
3. Visitation
4. Random and haphazard
5. Imposed and authoritarian
6. One person usually

MODERN
1. Study and analysis
2. Focused on aims, materials, methods, supervisors, employees, environment
3. Demonstrations, intervisitation, workshops, directed reading, bulletins, etc.
4. Definitely organized and planned (scientific)
5. Cooperative and democratic
6. Many persons involved (creative)

THE EIGHT (8) BASIC PRINCIPLES OF THE NEW SUPERVISION

I. Principle of Responsibility
   Authority to act and responsibility for acting must be joined.
   A. If you give responsibility, give authority.
   B. Define employee duties clearly.
   C. Protect employees from criticism by others.
   D. Recognize the rights as well as obligations of employees.
   E. Achieve the aims of a democratic society insofar as it is possible within the area of your work.
   F. Establish a situation favorable to training and learning.
   G. Accept ultimate responsibility for everything done in your section, unit, office, division, department.
   H. Good administration and good supervision are inseparable.

II. Principle of Authority
The success of the supervisor is measured by the extent to which the power of authority is not used.
   A. Exercise simplicity and informality in supervision
   B. Use the simplest machinery of supervision
   C. If it is good for the organization as a whole, it is probably justified.
   D. Seldom be arbitrary or authoritative.
   E. Do not base your work on the power of position or of personality.
   F. Permit and encourage the free expression of opinions.

III. Principle of Self-Growth
The success of the supervisor is measured by the extent to which, and the speed with which, he is no longer needed.
   A. Base criticism on principles, not on specifics.
   B. Point out higher activities to employees.
   C. Train for self-thinking by employees to meet new situations.
   D. Stimulate initiative, self-reliance, and individual responsibility
   E. Concentrate on stimulating the growth of employees rather than on removing defects.

IV. Principle of Individual Worth
Respect for the individual is a paramount consideration in supervision.
   A. Be human and sympathetic in dealing with employees.
   B. Don't nag about things to be done.
   C. Recognize the individual differences among employees and seek opportunities to permit best expression of each personality.

V. Principle of Creative Leadership
The best supervision is that which is not apparent to the employee.
   A. Stimulate, don't drive employees to creative action.
   B. Emphasize doing good things.
   C. Encourage employees to do what they do best.
   D. Do not be too greatly concerned with details of subject or method.
   E. Do not be concerned exclusively with immediate problems and activities.
   F. Reveal higher activities and make them both desired and maximally possible.
   G. Determine procedures in the light of each situation but see that these are derived from a sound basic philosophy.
   H. Aid, inspire, and lead so as to liberate the creative spirit latent in all good employees.

VI. Principle of Success and Failure
There are no unsuccessful employees, only unsuccessful supervisors who have failed to give proper leadership.
   A. Adapt suggestions to the capacities, attitudes, and prejudices of employees.
   B. Be gradual, be progressive, be persistent.
   C. Help the employee find the general principle; have the employee apply his own problem to the general principle.
   D. Give adequate appreciation for good work and honest effort.
   E. Anticipate employee difficulties and help to prevent them.
   F. Encourage employees to do the desirable things they will do anyway.
   G. Judge your supervision by the results it secures.

VII. Principle of Science
Successful supervision is scientific, objective, and experimental. It is based on facts, not on prejudices.
   A. Be cumulative in results.
   B. Never divorce your suggestions from the goals of training.
   C. Don't be impatient of results.
   D. Keep all matters on a professional, not a personal, level.
   E. Do not be concerned exclusively with immediate problems and activities.
   F. Use objective means of determining achievement and rating where possible.

VIII. Principle of Cooperation
Supervision is a cooperative enterprise between supervisor and employee.
   A. Begin with conditions as they are.
   B. Ask opinions of all involved when formulating policies.
   C. Organization is as good as its weakest link.
   D. Let employees help to determine policies and department programs.
   E. Be approachable and accessible—physically and mentally.
   F. Develop pleasant social relationships.

WHAT IS ADMINISTRATION

Administration is concerned with providing the environment, the material facilities, and the operational procedures that will promote the maximum growth and development of supervisors and employees. (Organization is an aspect and a concomitant of administration.)

There is no sharp line of demarcation between supervision and administration; these functions are intimately interrelated and, often, overlapping. They are complementary activities.

I. Practices Commonly Classed as "Supervisory"
   A. Conducting employees' conferences
   B. Visiting sections, units, offices, divisions, departments
   C. Arranging for demonstrations
   D. Examining plans
   E. Suggesting professional reading
   F. Interpreting bulletins
   G. Recommending in-service training courses
   H. Encouraging experimentation
   I. Appraising employee morale
   J. Providing for intervisitation

II. Practices Commonly Classified as "Administrative"
   A. Management of the office
   B. Arrangement of schedules for extra duties
   C. Assignment of rooms or areas
   D. Distribution of supplies
   E. Keeping records and reports
   F. Care of audio-visual materials
   G. Keeping inventory records
   H. Checking record cards and books

      I. Programming special activities
      J. Checking on the attendance and punctuality of employees

III. Practices Commonly Classified as Both "Supervisory" and "Administrative"
    A. Program construction
    B. Testing or evaluating outcomes
    C. Personnel accounting
    D. Ordering instructional materials

RESPONSIBILITIES OF THE SUPERVISOR

A person employed in a supervisory capacity must constantly be able to improve his own efficiency and ability. He represent the employer to the employees and only continuous self-examination can make him a capable supervisor.

Leadership and training are the supervisor's responsibility. An efficient working unit is one in which the employees work with the supervisor. It is his job to bring out the best in his employees. He must always be relaxed, courteous, and calm in his association with his employees. Their feelings are important, and a harsh attitude does not develop the most efficient employees.

COMPETENCES OF THE SUPERVISOR

I. Complete knowledge of the duties and responsibilities of his position.
II. To be able to organize a job, plan ahead, and carry through.
III. To have self-confidence and initiative.
IV. To be able to handle the unexpected situation and make quick decisions.
V. To be able to properly train subordinates in the positions they are best suited for.
VI. To be able to keep good human relations among his subordinates.
VII. To be able to keep good human relations between his subordinates and himself and to earn their respect and trust.

THE PROFESSIONAL SUPERVISOR-EMPLOYEE RELATIONSHIP

There are two kinds of efficiency: one kind is only apparent and is produced in organizations through the exercise of mere discipline; this is but a simulation of the second, or true, efficiency which springs from spontaneous cooperation. If you are a manager, no matter how great or small your responsibility, it is your job, in the final analysis, to create and develop this involuntary cooperation among the people whom you supervise. For, no matter how powerful a combination of money, machines, and materials a company may have, this is a dead and sterile thing without a team of willing, thinking, and articulate people to guide it.

The following 21 points are presented as indicative of the exemplary basic relationship that should exist between supervisor and employee:

1. Each person wants to be liked and respected by his fellow employee and wants to be treated with consideration and respect by his superior.
2. The most competent employee will make an error. However, in a unit where good relations exist between the supervisor and his employees, tenseness and fear do not exist. Thus, errors are not hidden or covered up, and the efficiency of a unit is not impaired.

3. Subordinates resent rules, regulations, or orders that are unreasonable or unexplained.
4. Subordinates are quick to resent unfairness, harshness, injustices, and favoritism.
5. An employee will accept responsibility if he knows that he will be complimented for a job well done, and not too harshly chastised for failure; that his supervisor will check the cause of the failure, and, if it was the supervisor's fault, he will assume the blame therefore. If it was the employee's fault, his supervisor will explain the correct method or means of handling the responsibility.
6. An employee wants to receive credit for a suggestion he has made, that is used. If a suggestion cannot be used, the employee is entitled to an explanation. The supervisor should not say "no" and close the subject.
7. Fear and worry slow up a worker's ability. Poor working environment can impair his physical and mental health. A good supervisor avoids forceful methods, threats, and arguments to get a job done.
8. A forceful supervisor is able to train his employees individually and as a team, and is able to motivate them in the proper channels.
9. A mature supervisor is able to properly evaluate his subordinates and to keep them happy and satisfied.
10. A sensitive supervisor will never patronize his subordinates.
11. A worthy supervisor will respect his employees' confidences.
12. Definite and clear-cut responsibilities should be assigned to each executive.
13. Responsibility should always be coupled with corresponding authority.
14. No change should be made in the scope or responsibilities of a position without a definite understanding to that effect on the part of all persons concerned.
15. No executive or employee, occupying a single position in the organization, should be subject to definite orders from more than one source.
16. Orders should never be given to subordinates over the head of a responsible executive. Rather than do this, the officer in question should be supplanted.
17. Criticisms of subordinates should, whoever possible, be made privately, and in no case should a subordinate be criticized in the presence of executives or employees of equal or lower rank.
18. No dispute or difference between executives or employees as to authority or responsibilities should be considered too trivial for prompt and careful adjudication.
19. Promotions, wage changes, and disciplinary action should always be approved by the executive immediately superior to the one directly responsible.
20. No executive or employee should ever be required, or expected, to be at the same time an assistant to, and critic of, another.
21. Any executive whose work is subject to regular inspection should, wherever practicable, be given the assistance and facilities necessary to enable him to maintain an independent check of the quality of his work.

MINI-TEXT IN SUPERVISION, ADMINISTRATION, MANAGEMENT, AND ORGANIZATION

I. Brief Highlights

Listed concisely and sequentially are major headings and important data in the field for quick recall and review.

A. Levels of Management
Any organization of some size has several levels of management. In terms of a ladder, the levels are:

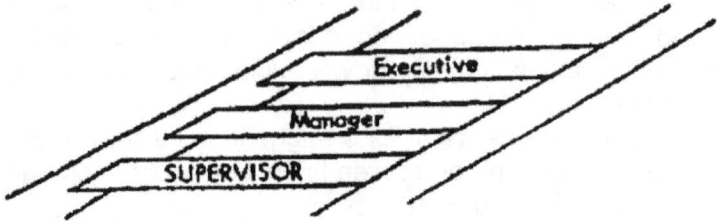

The first level is very important because it is the beginning point of management leadership.

B. What the Supervisor Must Learn
A supervisor must learn to:
1. Deal with people and their differences
2. Get the job done through people
3. Recognize the problems when they exist
4. Overcome obstacles to good performance
5. Evaluate the performance of people
6. Check his own performance in terms of accomplishment

C. A Definition of Supervisor
The term supervisor means any individual having authority, in the interests of the employer, to hire, transfer, suspend, lay-off, recall, promote, discharge, assign, reward, or discipline other employees or responsibility to direct them, or to adjust their grievances, or effectively to recommend such action, if, in connection with the foregoing, exercise of such authority is not of a merely routine or clerical nature but requires the use of independent judgment.

D. Elements of the Team Concept
What is involved in teamwork? The component parts are:
1. Members
2. A leader
3. Goals
4. Plans
5. Cooperation
6. Spirit

E. Principles of Organization
1. A team member must know what his job is.
2. Be sure that the nature and scope of a job are understood.
3. Authority and responsibility should be carefully spelled out.
4. A supervisor should be permitted to make the maximum number of decisions affecting his employees.
5. Employees should report to only one supervisor.
6. A supervisor should direct only as many employees as he can handle effectively.
7. An organization plan should be flexible.

8. Inspection and performance of work should be separate.
9. Organizational problems should receive immediate attention.
10. Assign work in line with ability and experience.

F. The Four Important Parts of Every Job
1. Inherent in every job is the *accountability* for results.
2. A second set of factors in every job is *responsibilities*.
3. Along with duties and responsibilities one must have the *authority* to act within certain limits without obtaining permission to proceed.
4. No job exists in a vacuum. The supervisor is surrounded by key *relationships*.

G. Principles of Delegation
Where work is delegated for the first time, the supervisor should think in terms of these questions:
1. Who is best qualified to do this?
2. Can an employee improve his abilities by doing this?
3. How long should an employee spend on this?
4. Are there any special problems for which he will need guidance?
5. How broad a delegation can I make?

H. Principles of Effective Communications
1. Determine the media.
2. To whom directed?
3. Identification and source authority.
4. Is communication understood?

I. Principles of Work Improvement
1. Most people usually do only the work which is assigned to them.
2. Workers are likely to fit assigned work into the time available to perform it.
3. A good workload usually stimulates output.
4. People usually do their best work when they know that results will be reviewed or inspected.
5. Employees usually feel that someone else is responsible for conditions of work, workplace layout, job methods, type of tools/equipment, and other such factors.
6. Employees are usually defensive about their job security.
7. Employees have natural resistance to change.
8. Employees can support or destroy a supervisor.
9. A supervisor usually earns the respect of his people through his personal example of diligence and efficiency.

J. Areas of Job Improvement
The areas of job improvement are quite numerous, but the most common ones which a supervisor can identify and utilize are:
1. Departmental layout
2. Flow of work
3. Workplace layout
4. Utilization of manpower
5. Work methods
6. Materials handling

7. Utilization
8. Motion economy

K. Seven Key Points in Making Improvements
1. Select the job to be improved
2. Study how it is being done now
3. Question the present method
4. Determine actions to be taken
5. Chart proposed method
6. Get approval and apply
7. Solicit worker participation

I. Corrective Techniques of Job Improvement
Specific Problems
1. Size of workload
2. Inability to meet schedules
3. Strain and fatigue
4. Improper use of men and skills
5. Waste, poor quality, unsafe conditions
6. Bottleneck conditions that hinder output
7. Poor utilization of equipment and machine
8. Efficiency and productivity of labor

General Improvement
1. Departmental layout
2. Flow of work
3. Work plan layout
4. Utilization of manpower
5. Work methods
6. Materials handling
7. Utilization of equipment
8. Motion economy

Corrective Techniques
1. Study with scale model
2. Flow chart study
3. Motion analysis
4. Comparison of units produced to standard allowance
5. Methods analysis
6. Flow chart and equipment study
7. Down time vs. running time
8. Motion analysis

M. A Planning Checklist
1. Objectives
2. Controls
3. Delegations
4. Communications
5. Resources
6. Manpower

7. Equipment
8. Supplies and materials
9. Utilization of time
10. Safety
11. Money
12. Work
13. Timing of improvements

N. Five Characteristics of Good Directions
In order to get results, directions must be:
1. Possible of accomplishment
2. Agreeable with worker interests
3. Related to mission
4. Planned and complete
5. Unmistakably clear

O. Types of Directions
1. Demands or direct orders
2. Requests
3. Suggestion or implication
4. volunteering

P. Controls
A typical listing of the overall areas in which the supervisor should establish controls might be:
1. Manpower
2. Materials
3. Quality of work
4. Quantity of work
5. Time
6. Space
7. Money
8. Methods

Q. Orienting the New Employee
1. Prepare for him
2. Welcome the new employee
3. Orientation for the job
4. Follow-up

R. Checklist for Orienting New Employees   Yes   No
1. Do you appreciate the feelings of new employees
   when they first report for work?   ___   ___
2. Are you aware of the fact that the new employee must
   make a big adjustment to his job?   ___   ___
3. Have you given him good reasons for liking the job and
   the organization?   ___   ___
4. Have you prepared for his first day on the job?   ___   ___
5. Did you welcome him cordially and make him feel needed?   ___   ___

	Yes	No

6. Did you establish rapport with him so that he feels free to talk and discuss matters with you? ___ ___
7. Did you explain his job to him and his relationship to you? ___ ___
8. Does he know that his work will be evaluated periodically on a basis that is fair and objective? ___ ___
9. Did you introduce him to his fellow workers in such a way that they are likely to accept him? ___ ___
10. Does he know what employee benefits he will receive? ___ ___
11. Does he understand the importance of being on the job and what to do if he must leave his duty station? ___ ___
12. Has he been impressed with the importance of accident prevention and safe practice? ___ ___
13. Does he generally know his way around the department? ___ ___
14. Is he under the guidance of a sponsor who will teach the right way of doing things? ___ ___
15. Do you plan to follow-up so that he will continue to adjust successfully to his job? ___ ___

S. Principles of Learning
   1. Motivation
   2. Demonstration or explanation
   3. Practice

T. Causes of Poor Performance
   1. Improper training for job
   2. Wrong tools
   3. Inadequate directions
   4. Lack of supervisory follow-up
   5. Poor communications
   6. Lack of standards of performance
   7. Wrong work habits
   8. Low morale
   9. Other

U. Four Major Steps in On-The-Job Instruction
   1. Prepare the worker
   2. Present the operation
   3. Tryout performance
   4. Follow-up

V. Employees Want Five Things
   1. Security
   2. Opportunity
   3. Recognition
   4. Inclusion
   5. Expression

W. Some Don'ts in Regard to Praise
1. Don't praise a person for something he hasn't done.
2. Don't praise a person unless you can be sincere.
3. Don't be sparing in praise just because your superior withholds it from you.
4. Don't let too much time elapse between good performance and recognition of it

X. How to Gain Your Workers' Confidence
Methods of developing confidence include such things as:
1. Knowing the interests, habits, hobbies of employees
2. Admitting your own inadequacies
3. Sharing and telling of confidence in others
4. Supporting people when they are in trouble
5. Delegating matters that can be well handled
6. Being frank and straightforward about problems and working conditions
7. Encouraging others to bring their problems to you
8. Taking action on problems which impede worker progress

Y. Sources of Employee Problems
On-the-job causes might be such things as:
1. A feeling that favoritism is exercised in assignments
2. Assignment of overtime
3. An undue amount of supervision
4. Changing methods or systems
5. Stealing of ideas or trade secrets
6. Lack of interest in job
7. Threat of reduction in force
8. Ignorance or lack of communications
9. Poor equipment
10. Lack of knowing how supervisor feels toward employee
11. Shift assignments

Off-the-job problems might have to do with:
1. Health
2. Finances
3. Housing
4. Family

Z. The Supervisor's Key to Discipline
There are several key points about discipline which the supervisor should keep in mind:
1. Job discipline is one of the disciplines of life and is directed by the supervisor.
2. It is more important to correct an employee fault than to fix blame for it.
3. Employee performance is affected by problems both on the job and off.
4. Sudden or abrupt changes in behavior can be indications of important employee problems.
5. Problems should be dealt with as soon as possible after they are identified.
6. The attitude of the supervisor may have more to do with solving problems than the techniques of problem solving.
7. Correction of employee behavior should be resorted to only after the supervisor is sure that training or counseling will not be helpful.

8. Be sure to document your disciplinary actions.
9. Make sure that you are disciplining on the basis of facts rather than personal feelings.
10. Take each disciplinary step in order, being careful not to make snap judgments, or decisions based on impatience.

AA. Five Important Processes of Management
1. Planning
2. Organizing
3. Scheduling
4. Controlling
5. Motivating

BB. When the Supervisor Fails to Plan
1. Supervisor creates impression of not knowing his job
2. May lead to excessive overtime
3. Job runs itself—supervisor lacks control
4. Deadlines and appointments missed
5. Parts of the work go undone
6. Work interrupted by emergencies
7. Sets a bad example
8. Uneven workload creates peaks and valleys
9. Too much time on minor details at expense of more important tasks

CC. Fourteen General Principles of Management
1. Division of work
2. Authority and responsibility
3. Discipline
4. Unity of command
5. Unity of direction
6. Subordination of individual interest to general interest
7. Remuneration of personnel
8. Centralization
9. Scalar chain
10. Order
11. Equity
12. Stability of tenure of personnel
13. Initiative
14. Esprit de corps

DD. Change

Bringing about change is perhaps attempted more often, and yet less well understood, than anything else the supervisor does. How do people generally react to change? (People tend to resist change that is imposed upon them by other individuals or circumstances.

Change is characteristic of every situation. It is a part of every real endeavor where the efforts of people are concerned.

1. Why do people resist change?
   People may resist change because of:
   a. Fear of the unknown
   b. Implied criticism
   c. Unpleasant experiences in the past
   d. Fear of loss of status
   e. Threat to the ego
   f. Fear of loss of economic stability

2. How can we best overcome the resistance to change?
   In initiating change, take these steps:
   a. Get ready to sell
   b. Identify sources of help
   c. Anticipate objections
   d. Sell benefits
   e. Listen in depth
   f. Follow up

II. Brief Topical Summaries

   A. Who/What is the Supervisor?
      1. The supervisor is often called the "highest level employee and the lowest level manager."
      2. A supervisor is a member of both management and the work group. He acts as a bridge between the two.
      3. Most problems in supervision are in the area of human relations, or people problems.
      4. Employees expect: Respect, opportunity to learn and to advance, and a sense of belonging, and so forth.
      5. Supervisors are responsible for directing people and organizing work. Planning is of paramount importance.
      6. A position description is a set of duties and responsibilities inherent to a given position.
      7. It is important to keep the position description up-to-date and to provide each employee with his own copy.

   B. The Sociology of Work
      1. People are alike in many ways; however, each individual is unique.
      2. The supervisor is challenged in getting to know employee differences. Acquiring skills in evaluating individuals is an asset.
      3. Maintaining meaningful working relationships in the organization is of great importance.
      4. The supervisor has an obligation to help individuals to develop to their fullest potential.
      5. Job rotation on a planned basis helps to build versatility and to maintain interest and enthusiasm in work groups.
      6. Cross training (job rotation) provides backup skills.

7. The supervisor can help reduce tension by maintaining a sense of humor, providing guidance to employees, and by making reasonable and timely decisions. Employees respond favorably to working under reasonably predictable circumstances.
8. Change is characteristic of all managerial behavior. The supervisor must adjust to changes in procedures, new methods, technological changes, and to a number of new and sometimes challenging situations.
9. To overcome the natural tendency for people to resist change, the supervisor should become more skillful in initiating change.

C. Principles and Practices of Supervision
1. Employees should be required to answer to only one superior.
2. A supervisor can effectively direct only a limited number of employees, depending upon the complexity, variety, and proximity of the jobs involved.
3. The organizational chart presents the organization in graphic form. It reflects lines of authority and responsibility as well as interrelationships of units within the organization.
4. Distribution of work can be improved through an analysis using the "Work Distribution Chart."
5. The "Work Distribution Chart" reflects the division of work within a unit in understandable form.
6. When related tasks are given to an employee, he has a better chance of increasing his skills through training.
7. The individual who is given the responsibility for tasks must also be given the appropriate authority to insure adequate results.
8. The supervisor should delegate repetitive, routine work. Preparation of recurring reports, maintaining leave and attendance records are some examples.
9. Good discipline is essential to good task performance. Discipline is reflected in the actions of employees on the job in the absence of supervision.
10. Disciplinary action may have to be taken when the positive aspects of discipline have failed. Reprimand, warning, and suspension are examples of disciplinary action.
11. If a situation calls for a reprimand, be sure it is deserved and remember it is to be done in private.

D. Dynamic Leadership
1. A style is a personal method or manner of exerting influence.
2. Authoritarian leaders often see themselves as the source of power and authority.
3. The democratic leader often perceives the group as the source of authority and power.
4. Supervisors tend to do better when using the pattern of leadership that is most natural for them.
5. Social scientists suggest that the effective supervisor use the leadership style that best fits the problem or circumstances involved.
6. All four styles—telling, selling, consulting, joining—have their place. Using one does not preclude using the other at another time.

7. The theory X point of view assumes that the average person dislikes work, will avoid it whenever possible, and must be coerced to achieve organizational objectives.
8. The theory Y point of view assumes that the average person considers work to be a natural as play, and, when the individual is committed, he requires little supervision or direction to accomplish desired objectives.
9. The leader's basic assumptions concerning human behavior and human nature affect his actions, decisions, and other managerial practices.
10. Dissatisfaction among employees is often present, but difficult to isolate. The supervisor should seek to weaken dissatisfaction by keeping promises, being sincere and considerate, keeping employees informed, and so forth.
11. Constructive suggestions should be encouraged during the natural progress of the work.

E. Processes for Solving Problems
1. People find their daily tasks more meaningful and satisfying when they can improve them.
2. The causes of problems, or the key factors, are often hidden in the background. Ability to solve problems often involves the ability to isolate them from their backgrounds. There is some substance to the cliché that some persons "can't see the forest for the trees."
3. New procedures are often developed from old ones. Problems should be broken down into manageable parts. New ideas can be adapted from old one.
4. People think differently in problem-solving situations. Using a logical, patterned approach is often useful. One approach found to be useful includes these steps:
   a. Define the problem
   b. Establish objectives
   c. Get the facts
   d. Weigh and decide
   e. Take action
   f. Evaluate action

F. Training for Results
1. Participants respond best when they feel training is important to them.
2. The supervisor has responsibility for the training and development of those who report to him.
3. When training is delegated to others, great care must be exercised to insure the trainer has knowledge, aptitude, and interest for his work as a trainer.
4. Training (learning) of some type goes on continually. The most successful supervisor makes certain the learning contributes in a productive manner to operational goals.
5. New employees are particularly susceptible to training. Older employees facing new job situations require specific training, as well as having need for development and growth opportunities.
6. Training needs require continuous monitoring.
7. The training officer of an agency is a professional with a responsibility to assist supervisors in solving training problems.

8. Many of the self-development steps important to the supervisor's own growth are equally important to the development of peers and subordinates. Knowledge of these is important when the supervisor consults with others on development and growth opportunities.

G. Health, Safety, and Accident Prevention
1. Management-minded supervisors take appropriate measures to assist employees in maintaining health and in assuring safe practices in the work environment.
2. Effective safety training and practices help to avoid injury and accidents.
3. Safety should be a management goal. All infractions of safety which are observed should be corrected without exception.
4. Employees' safety attitude, training and instruction, provision of safe tools and equipment, supervision, and leadership are considered highly important factors which contribute to safety and which can be influenced directly by supervisors.
5. When accidents do occur, they should be investigated promptly for very important reasons, including the fact that information which is gained can be used to prevent accidents in the future.

H. Equal Employment Opportunity
1. The supervisor should endeavor to treat all employees fairly, without regard to religion, race, sex, or national origin.
2. Groups tend to reflect the attitude of the leader. Prejudice can be detected even in very subtle form. Supervisors must strive to create a feeling of mutual respect and confidence in every employee.
3. Complete utilization of all human resources is a national goal. Equitable consideration should be accorded women in the work force, minority-group members, the physically and mentally handicapped, and the older employee. The important question is: "Who can do the job?"
4. Training opportunities, recognition for performance, overtime assignments, promotional opportunities, and all other personnel actions are to be handled on an equitable basis.

I. Improving Communications
1. Communications is achieving understanding between the sender and the receiver of a message. It also means sharing information—the creation of understanding.
2. Communication is basic to all human activity. Words are means of conveying meanings; however, real meanings are in people.
3. There are very practical differences in the effectiveness of one-way, impersonal, and two-way communications. Words spoken face-to-face are better understood. Telephone conversations are effective, but lack the rapport of person-to-person exchanges. The whole person communicates.
4. Cooperation and communication in an organization go hand in hand. When there is a mutual respect between people, spelling out rules and procedures for communicating is unnecessary.
5. There are several barriers to effective communications. These include failure to listen with respect and understanding, lack of skill in feedback, and misinterpreting the meanings of words used by the speaker. It is also common

practice to listen to what we want to hear, and tune out things we do not want to hear.
   6. Communication is management's chief problem. The supervisor should accept the challenge to communicate more effectively and to improve interagency and intra-agency communications.
   7. The supervisor may often plan for and conduct meetings. The planning phase is critical and may determine the success or the failure of a meeting.
   8. Speaking before groups usually requires extra effort. Stage fright may never disappear completely, but it can be controlled.

J. Self-Development
   1. Every employee is responsible for his own self-development.
   2. Toastmaster and toastmistress clubs offer opportunities to improve skills in oral communications.
   3. Planning for one's own self-development is of vital importance. Supervisors know their own strengths and limitations better than anyone else.
   4. Many opportunities are open to aid the supervisor in his developmental efforts, including job assignments; training opportunities, both governmental and non-governmental—to include universities and professional conferences and seminars.
   5. Programmed instruction offers a means of studying at one's own rate.
   6. Where difficulties may arise from a supervisor's being away from his work for training, he may participate in televised home study or correspondence courses to meet his self-development needs.

K. Teaching and Training
   1. The Teaching Process
   Teaching is encouraging and guiding the learning activities of students toward established goals. In most cases this process consists of five steps: preparation, presentation, summarization, evaluation, and application.

   a. Preparation
   Preparation is two-fold in nature; that of the supervisor and the employee. Preparation by the supervisor is absolutely essential to success. He must know what, when, where, how, and whom he will teach. Some of the factors that should be considered are:
   1) The objectives
   2) The materials needed
   3) The methods to be used
   4) Employee participation
   5) Employee interest
   6) Training aids
   7) Evaluation
   8) Summarization

   Employee preparation consists in preparing the employee to receive the material. Probably the most important single factor in the preparation of the employee is arousing and maintaining his interest. He must know the objectives of the training, why he is there, how the material can be used, and its importance to him.

b. Presentation
   In presentation, have a carefully designed plan and follow it. The plan should be accurate and complete, yet flexible enough to meet situations as they arise. The method of presentation will be determined by the particular situation and objectives.

c. Summary
   A summary should be made at the end of every training unit and program. In addition, there may be internal summaries depending on the nature of the material being taught. The important thing is that the trainee must always be able to understand how each part of the new material relates to the whole.

d. Application
   The supervisor must arrange work so the employee will be given a chance to apply new knowledge or skills while the material is still clear in his mind and interest is high. The trainee does not really know whether he has learned the material until he has been given a chance to apply it. If the material is not applied, it loses most of its value.

e. Evaluation
   The purpose of all training is to promote learning. To determine whether the training has been a success or failure, the supervisor must evaluate this learning.
   In the broadest sense, evaluation includes all the devices, methods, skills, and techniques used by the supervisor to keep himself and the employees informed as to their progress toward the objectives they are pursuing. The extent to which the employee has mastered the knowledge, skills, and abilities, or changed his attitudes, as determined by the program objectives, is the extent to which instruction has succeeded or failed.
   Evaluation should not be confined to the end of the lesson, day, or program but should be used continuously. We shall note later the way this relates to the rest of the teaching process.

2. Teaching Methods
   A teaching method is a pattern of identifiable student and instructor activity used in presenting training material.
   All supervisors are faced with the problem of deciding which method should be used at a given time.

   a. Lecture
      The lecture is direct oral presentation of material by the supervisor. The present trend is to place less emphasis on the trainer's activity and more on that of the trainee.

   b. Discussion
      Teaching by discussion or conference involves using questions and other techniques to arouse interest and focus attention upon certain areas, and by doing so creating a learning situation. This can be one of the most

valuable methods because it gives the employees an opportunity to express their ideas and pool their knowledge.

    c. Demonstration
The demonstration is used to teach how something works or how to do something. It can be used to show a principle or what the results of a series of actions will be. A well-staged demonstration is particularly effective because it shows proper methods of performance in a realistic manner.

    d. Performance
Performance is one of the most fundamental of all learning techniques or teaching methods. The trainee may be able to tell how a specific operation should be performed but he cannot be sure he knows how to perform the operation until he has done so.
As with all methods, there are certain advantages and disadvantages to each method.

    e. Which Method to Use
Moreover, there are other methods and techniques of teaching. It is difficult to use any method without other methods entering into it. In any learning situation, a combination of methods is usually more effective than any one method alone.

Finally, evaluation must be integrated into the other aspects of the teaching-learning process.

It must be used in the motivation of the trainees; it must be used to assist in developing understanding during the training; and it must be related to employee application of the results of training.

This is distinctly the role of the supervisor.

www.ingramcontent.com/pod-product-compliance
Lightning Source LLC
Chambersburg PA
CBHW082035300426
44117CB00015B/2497